VIDA
His Own Story

VIDA
His Own Story

·

by
Bill Libby
and
Vida Blue

·

PRENTICE-HALL, INC., Englewood Cliffs, New Jersey

Library of Congress Cataloging in Publication Data
Blue, Vida, 1949–
    Vida: his own story.
    I. Libby, Bill, joint author. II. Title.
GV865.B57A3   796.357'092'4 [B]   72-3635
ISBN 0-13-941773-7

ACKNOWLEDGMENTS

This book would not have been possible without the complete cooperation of Vida Blue and his attorney and manager, Bob Gerst, of Los Angeles, to whom the author is deeply indebted.

He wishes also to thank especially Nick D'Incecco and Bob Howland of Prentice-Hall, Glenn Schwarz of the San Francisco *Examiner*, Ron Bergman of the *Oakland Tribune*, Sam Skinner of *Skinner's News Service*, San Francisco, and Michael Haggerty and Mary Brubaker, formerly of the Oakland A's, for their invaluable contributions.

And, finally, he is grateful to Charles O. Finley, Dick Williams, Tom Corwin, Monte Moore and Bill Posedel of the Oakland A's official family, players Tommy Davis, Jim Grant and Reggie Jackson, photographer Ron Reisterer of the Oakland *Tribune*, the photographers of *Sports Illustrated* and Time-Life, Inc. and other journalists and all others who have contributed in one way or another to this book.

DEDICATION

For Linda and Howard Leight,
who were always there when
Sharon and I needed them.

LIB.

CHAPTER ONE

He was recognized wherever he went. It had been that way for a couple of months and he was just getting used to it. Now he was even spotted as he drove the streets of Oakland. At stoplights, men in other cars would pull alongside, see who he was and say, "Hey, man . . . Vida Blue . . . How ya doin'? . . . You gonna win twenty? . . . You gonna win thirty?" And he'd say, "I'm doin' jus' fine, thank you. . . I'm gonna' win all I can." And they'd exchange smiles. Girls would smile at him and his smile would widen in response. "Hey," he'd call to them, laughing at himself, enjoying his fame, "you know who Vida Blue is?" And to himself he'd say, "Vida Blue is a bachelor. Hey, hey, hey!" Kids would chase the car until it was out of sight, yelling, "Hey, it's Vida Blue! Hey, Vida Blue! Vi-Da Bluuuuuue!" And he'd smile and wave at them.

Softly, he sang, "Smiling faces . . . they don't mean what they say."

He had been the cover stories not only of *The Sporting News* and *Sport* magazine and *Sports Illustrated,* but of *Time* magazine. He had been featured in *Life* and *Look* and *Newsweek* and even the *New Yorker,* where more often those of arts and letters are discussed. He had just turned twenty-two years of age and he was barely halfway through his first full season in baseball's major leagues and suddenly he was famous. Needing someone, the sports world had swiftly seized him. "It's nice . . . you know . . . but it's not all that nice," he said.

It had all started when he was called up from the minors to the majors late the season before and pitched a one-hitter and then a no-hitter, and then, after losing the opening game of the 1971 season, had won ten straight before losing another game and now was near to winning his twentieth near midseason, in July, which is more than most pitchers ever win in a full season, any season, all their careers. He threw so hard he was hard to hit. He had a colorful style and a colorful name. He was pitching his team to a pennant. He was new and he was pumping new life into an old game.

But now the phone never stopped ringing and all the sportswriters and broadcasters wanted interviews and he had found he had friends he never knew he had before and girls asked him for dates before he could ask them and he couldn't even eat in a restaurant without someone staring at him to see if he got gravy on his shirt, and he was beginning to bend from it a bit and wondering if he would break, and his skull was beginning to feel as though it was going to cave in from the pressure.

It was an incredible year for an incredible yearling!

When it all started he said, "It's easy, man. I just take the ball and throw. Hard! It's a Godgiven talent. No one can teach it to you. They either hit it or they don't. They haven't been hitting it, that's all. No sweat." And he grinned, glad to be who he was.

But now he said, "They think it's easy. They think all I do is throw and rack up the wins. Well, it's not easy. It's hard. It's hard work. I'm sweating out there. I'm busting my back out there. I don't know how to pitch yet. I'm just learning my trade. They're gonna hit me, I've found that out. They got their jobs to do, too, you know. And they know how. And they're gonna beat me some." And he sighed, sad with wondering why others couldn't see the way it was.

When it all started he said, "I'm having the time of my life. Big stadiums full of people cheering me. Meeting nice people. Big, nice hotels full of nice people. Traveling first-class. Living first-class. Reading about myself. Getting famous. I'm not rich yet, but I will be. It looks like maybe I'll be everything I ever dreamed of being."

Later he said, "All I am is Vida Blue from a small town in

Louisiana and I'm not used to all this fuss and I'm beginning to think I could live without a lot of it." And still later he said, "I just wish people could leave me alone sometimes. Just sometimes. Not all the time. Is that asking too much?"

But he had come too far for that now, and, young as he was, he knew it. He had come to know enough to know that. It had happened quickly, but it had happened and he was here now, not there, where he used to be. And as he drove through his new hometown, he said, "I want to win twenty games because I want to win my next game and my next win will be my twentieth, but I try not to even think of thirty. Before the season started, I would have said I'd like to win fifty if I could, but now I know if I win fifty, they'll ask me if I'm gonna win 55. I want to win the pennant because this is a team game and that's why we play this game, but I try not to think about it because if we win the pennant I'll have to pitch in the playoffs and prove myself all over again."

He made a funny face, an expression of wistful wonder wandering across his features, sighed and said, "I try to give the public what it wants, but I'm beginning to wonder if anything I ever give will ever be enough. No matter how many autographs I sign, there's always someone else waiting at the end of the line. I haven't found the end of the line yet. I don't think the line ever ends. I try to give the writers what they want, but they always want something new and I just haven't lived long enough to have done enough different things to please them all. They want to know how I've been able to do what I've been doing but I can't tell 'em because I don't know, myself.

"I just don't know, myself," he repeated softly, his voice drifting off as some kids spotted him and began to yell, "Hey, it's Vida Blue."

He is an extraordinarily handsome person. His skin is the color of sweet chocolate, his features are round and good, his teeth are white and even, his eyes are clear and bright and when he smiles his face dimples up and his eyes sparkle and a compelling personality envelops you. He is young and trim and graceful. He is six feet tall and weighs 190 pounds and he has wide shoulders and narrow hips and no belly at all. When he showed up to do a

television show, a Hollywood type came away as though overwhelmed, saying, "Migawd, he's beautiful, he's the most beautiful
thing I ever saw." The Hollywood type had dollar-signs where
his eyeballs should have been. He knew, as everyone knew, this
was really a rookie, bending his back for slave wages but bound
for the big money. Vida had told them himself in a television
commercial, "I'm gonna make a whole lot of money."

But the Hollywood type wouldn't get his hands on any of it.
Blue had found himself a tough and conservative manager, Bob
Gerst in Los Angeles, a lawyer who was determined to steer him
to the best things. Vida was still very young, though growing up
fast, still playful, wanting only to have some fun. He was often hiding from the world, once in a while missing an appointment. The
money wasn't that important to him. Not yet. How could it be?
He'd never had any. He didn't know what it was. He was playing
a game, like Monopoly. Win twenty games and you can buy the
boardwalk. Win thirty and the world is yours. But it's play money
and a pretend world. Nothing seemed real to him anymore. "I'm
real," he said. "I don't know about the rest."

It was hard for him to take himself as seriously as others were
doing. He was trying to look at his suddenly-altered life with
humor, to shrug off pressure, to see things in perspective.

He wanted to do the right things. He was trying. Right now he
was doing a right thing, on his way to pick up a social worker
who would direct him to the home of a boy suffering from sickle-
cell anemia, who worshiped Vida Blue, who had never dreamed
he might be visited by Vida Blue. It was part of the price Vida
Blue had to pay for success. Vida Blue sang a song written about
Vida Blue as he drove.

The social worker said just this one thing, this visit, was all she
would ask of him, but would Vida Blue mind picking up her
sister first. Her sister was just dying to meet Vida Blue. No, Vida
Blue wouldn't mind, he said, smiling at the social worker, but, yes
he would mind, said the face he made. But then when he saw
the sister, he didn't mind at all, his giggling eyes suggested to the
writer, for the social worker was one thing, an older lady, and the
sister was something else, a younger lady, and stunning, but
then, after a while, he began to mind again, because she put on

airs. Vida who? Oh, the baseball player. It is baseball, isn't it? Well, I might just as well go along, not that it is any big thing to me, you understand. I have so many things to do. An appointment at the beauty parlor for a big date tonight, for one thing. And Vida Blue began to mind a great deal.

As directed, he steered his car into an alley of a ghetto and got out and was instantly surrounded by youngsters who had been told he was coming. Signing autographs for them, he seemed to relax with them. Clearly, he was a man who liked kids.

On the second floor of an old wood-frame house with peeling paint, he was welcomed by a black family. In the center of the living room, the sick youngster sat, surrounded by other children. He was a thin youngster with a fine face, and from the moment he set eyes on Vida Blue he seemed all eyes, his face radiated joy, he literally beamed, giving off bright lights as though someone had polished his skin to a high shine. His name was Woodrow and he was smaller than some of his younger brothers and sisters, perhaps because of his illness. He was shy, but Vida Blue sat down right next to him and took his hand and began to talk to him and kid him until his shyness disappeared.

"I hear all the Oakland A's games on radio," Woodrow said. "I hear you strike out all those batters. I root for the A's and I root for you. Could I feel your muscle?" And Vida Blue said, "Why, of course, my good man, you may feel my muscle." And he made a muscle in his right arm, but the boy said, "No, your left arm, your pitching arm." So Vida Blue said all right, and he made a muscle in his left arm and the boy felt it and his eyes got wider and his face beamed brighter. "And now," asked Vida Blue, "can I feel your muscle?" And the boy asked, "My muscle, you want to feel my muscle?" And Vida Blue said, "Yes, I let you feel my muscle, now I want to feel your muscle." So the little boy made a little muscle and Vida felt it and marveled at it. "My, oh, my, that is some kind of muscle for a boy your age, you'll have to hurry up and get well so you can pitch, too, because with a muscle like that I'm sure you can throw mighty hard."

"Can we get you some coffee," the mother asked Vida Blue and the social worker and her sister and the writer, and they said yes, but he said no, thanks, he had to run back down to the car to get this fine young man a baseball, and off he went through the door and out of sight. The moment he was gone, the boy's face fell and darkened. "He'll be right back," someone said. And the boy nodded. And then he got up and began to hobble toward the balcony. And his mother said, "Where are you going, Woodrow, you know you're not allowed out there." He hung his head and turned back, but then someone said, "He just wants to watch Vida go to the car to get his baseball." And the mother said, "Oh, oh well, that's all right then," and the boy brightened immediately and went right on to the balcony, where he watched Vida get the baseball from his car and start back to the house because he did not want to lose sight of him for a second if he could help it.

When Vida returned to sit next to Woodrow and gave him the baseball, Woodrow asked him to autograph it, which Vida did, "to Woodrow," and Woodrow squeezed the ball so hard after that it is a wonder the stuffing did not come out of it, and he probably still is carrying it with him wherever he goes, if he is going anywhere now. Woodrow said, "My father says the Giants are better than the A's, but I said the A's are better and you're going to beat them in the World Series. Aren't you going to beat them in the World Series?" And Vida Blue said, "Of course we're going to beat them in the World Series." And Woodrow said, "My father's favorite player is Willie Mays, but you're my favorite player." And a brother, who felt neglected sitting off to the side, said, "Willie Mays is my favorite player."

An older brother had gone out to get some film for a Polaroid camera and now returned and began to take pictures and everyone wanted a picture taken with Vida Blue, who hugged the girls and teased the boys, but never left the side of Woodrow and never stopped talking to him. Woodrow said, "The A's even have the best shoes. They be white. Kang-ah-roo shoes and white." And his brother, who right then even envied Woodrow his illness because it gave him the seat next to Vida Blue, said, "The Oakland Raiders are my favorite team." And Vida laughed, understanding, and he said, "Well, they're my favorite team, too, next to the A's, and I like football, too."

They were a fine family, warm and friendly and pleased that

Vida Blue had come to visit Woodrow, whose eyes never left Vida Blue. Vida talked to him with such ease Woodrow had every right to think Vida really truly cared—until it came time to go, which was a terrible time, but then, even friends can't be together all the time. Vida said he'd get the family some tickets for a coming game, and when he said good-bye to Woodrow he put his left hand on the boy's cheek and tears glistened in the lad's eyes. And as he walked down the stairs, Vida said, softly, "Oh, my God." This had been something he hadn't expected, almost too much for him to handle.

But, out by the car, when the children convened around him again, this was something else again, this was something he could handle, and he was easy with it. The social worker asked Woodrow's brother if he would take one last picture, of her sister with Vida, and he said he would, and Vida said it would be all right, and the sister, who seemed to feel she had been neglected, said oh, all right, and so Vida hugged her and smiled for the camera, and she took the picture and put it in her purse, and Vida avoided looking up at the balcony, from where Woodrow watched until they had driven away.

As Vida drove them home, the social worker spoke of how much she could use his help in combating the drug problem in the area and Vida said he would try to give her some time and the sister said maybe she wouldn't mind going to a baseball game sometime although she really wasn't crazy about baseball and Vida said well, that would be fine, and when he dropped them off he took the sister's phone number on a slip of paper, but after he drove off he crumpled it up and threw it away and shook his head.

In the East Oakland apartment he shares with the owner, "Spider" Hodges, a former merchant seaman and a friend of the famous, and with teammates Tommy Davis and "Mudcat" Grant, Vida put some Supremes records on the hi-fi and stretched out on a couch. From behind closed eyelids he said, "I was with this girl the other night. We ate in this fabulous hamburger place in San Francisco. This guy said, 'Aren't you Vida Blue?' I said, 'OK, I'll be Vida Blue, but don't you tell no one.' And would you believe it, he didn't tell no one. No one else noticed me. Lights low.

Fine food. A fine lady. Just fine. Then home. Lights low. Music low. Just sitting around. Just fine. Just quiet. Just a quiet night. Like it was a miracle. Man, it was a miracle."

He was quiet a long time. Then he said, "I get on a plane, I'm Mr. Quiet. I take off my shoes and put on slippers. I hide behind shades. I try to fall asleep. I hear people say, 'Where's Vida Blue?' I don't say nothing. I pretend to be asleep. There's no place to go. No place to hide. One day flying out of Boston a stewardess waved this pad under my face. She wanted an autograph for her brother or her nephew. I pretended to be asleep. She shook me. Son of a gun, if she didn't shake me. I pretended she couldn't wake me. She finally gave up. Man, I want to tell you I spend a lot of time behind closed eyelids," he said.

The phone rang, and kept ringing. Finally, he got up to get it, running for it in that peculiar high-kicking gait of his, saying, "Duty calls, duty calls." Answering it, he said, "Vida Blue? No, Vida Blue ain't here. He's off getting a trophy for being the greatest player in the history of baseball. Who's this? Oh, this is no one. This is Tommy Davis, Vida's butler. Will I give Vida a message? I surely will. Who's that you say? Yes, I got it. An old friend, you say. Yes, I'll give him the message." He hung up, but before he could get back to the couch the phone rang again. "Oh, mercy, mercy, mercy," he said.

On the way to the ballpark he picked up Angel Mangual and they stopped at a coffee shop for a hamburger. No one recognized them. After a while, wanting to have some fun, Vida called over the waitress. Pointing to his teammate he said, "You know who this is, this is Vida Blue, the greatest pitcher in baseball today."

"That's very nice," she said.

"Would you like his autograph?" he asked.

"That would be very nice."

"Give her your autograph," he directed Mangual. Mangual signed "Sandy Koufax." She didn't even look at it.

"Do you want mine, too?" Vida asked.

"Are you a ballplayer, too?" she asked.

"Sort of," he said.

"OK," she said.

He signed "Joe Namath."

He was wearing an old Joe Namath football jersey and jeans. On the back of the jersey was the name "Namath."

"I'm supposed to be the black Sandy Koufax. Namath is the white Vida Blue," Vida said.

In the dressing room at the ballpark, he undressed, jump-shooting and hook-shooting his clothes into his locker.

"You must be the first bad black basketball player," a teammate said.

"Football's my game," Vida said.

On the field, a red sign hung from the lower stands behind third base, "Vida Blue, We Love You." The message board said, "Today's A's Colors—Kelly Green, California Gold, Wedding Gown White and Vida Blue." The organist played "Rhapsody in Blue." Vida took batting practice.

A busty gal in hot pants and a tight T-shirt came down the stands behind the dugout and asked Vida if he could autograph her shirt. He smiled and said, "I could, but I better not." He autographed her program instead. As he signed other autographs, sweat streamed down his cheeks. He called to teammates for a towel. They ignored him. An outsider threw him a towel and he mopped up.

A teammate said, "Got to keep him in his place."

"Is he getting out of his place?"

"No, he's all right. He's under a lot of pressure. People expect a lot of him. The press asks a lot of him. He comes out and does his job. He kids around a lot. He says, 'Boy, get me this,' and 'Boy, get me that,' and he's smiling so you know he's kidding, but you don't get it for him just in case he isn't kidding."

"How good is he?"

"He could be the greatest. But he's not that yet. Whatever he does this year, it's still only one year. He put us in first place, but others helped, too. He gets most of the credit. He doesn't ask for it. We know that. But he gets it. It's hard not to be jealous of him. He's a very nice man, but a professional ballplayer learns to wait awhile before passing final judgments."

He rode up and down the A's private elevator for a while, teasing the elevator girl to ease the pressure. It was beginning to crowd him now. He had tried twice for his twentieth victory. The victories were coming harder now than they had earlier in the season. This was early August and the thirty that seemed probable in early July now seemed barely possible. As time to warm up for the game drew near, he went off to be by himself, hiding in the trainer's room, lying on the rubbing table, but he was not able to sleep as he had a month or two before. His eyes were closed, but he was awake behind his eyelids, and his hands moved restlessly by his side on the table. He began to feel sick to his stomach. This feeling was something new to him now.

There were more than 27,000 persons in the Oakland-Alameda Coliseum, the cold concrete saucer that serves as home to the gaudily clad club belonging to that controversial character, Charles O. Finley, the insurance tycoon with a passion for publicity. The fans *oohhed* and *aahhed* as Blue warmed up, his fast ball cracking into the catcher's mitt. They cheered and applauded him as he trotted to the mound to face the visiting Chicago White Sox.

He stands splay-footed, one white shoe pointing to one dugout, the other pointing to the other. Going into his motion, he dips deeply, rears far back, cocks his right knee shoulder-high, brings the ball held in his left hand behind him almost ground low, then unfurls in a whipping motion that is not quite completely over-arm and the ball streaks to the plate in a blur. Few throw as hard or as accurately. He throws his curve hard, too, and while it is not as accurate, it keeps the hitters off stride. He seldom throws a slow change-of-pace.

He was wild at first. With one out he hit a batter, then grooved a pitch on which the next batter doubled. He then walked a batter to load the bases with two out, but he got a hitter on a popup for the third out. He ran off the mound, kicking so high his heels almost reached his rear end. He got through the second inning all right. He hit another batter in the third, but erased him with a double-play. With one out in the fourth, he gave up two-straight singles, but then got two-straight outs, on a ground ball and a fly ball. As the game went on he got better: the White Sox were swinging and missing.

The A's got a run in the fifth and that was all Blue needed.

This was one of his days. It was a bright Sunday afternoon and under the hot sun, working fast, Vida kept turning his foes away inning after inning, protecting his 1–0 lead. When he got the last out in the ninth inning to win his twentieth, his teammates ran to him to congratulate him and he ran off, grinning broadly with relief.

In the dressing room he sat half-stripped in his soggy underwear, sweat staining his skin, his left arm soaking in a tub of ice water to help heal the damage each pitching turn does to it, and he said, "I felt sick before the game and I didn't feel right warming up and I was sure I'd be bombed and then I had to take something to settle my stomach during the game, but somehow I got by."

The reporters crowded around him scribbling on their pads and broadcasters stuck microphones in his face and it was somehow as though it was cornered. He tried to answer all their questions. He said, "I'm tired. I'm not as strong as I was early in the season. I can't throw as hard. My fast ball isn't as fast. I'm just glad it's over. It's just another victory but twenty is like a milestone and maybe now that it's out of the way the pressure won't be so bad for a while."

Someone asked him if he thought he could win thirty and he reacted to it instantly, slamming his free fist on a table. "There's that pressure again," he said. "How do I know if I can win thirty? I don't even want to think about thirty. I just want to think about this one for a while. Then, after a while, about the next one. I'll take 'em one at a time. I'll win every one I can." This was his eighth shutout. Someone pointed out that the record for a left-hander was nine, held by Babe Ruth, and asked Vida if he thought he could get it. Blue shook his head and pounded his fist on the table and said, "Of course, and I'll hit sixty home runs, too."

Someone asked him how the White Sox got their five hits off him. He said, "They swung their bats. I threw the ball and they swung their bats and some of them hit the ball."

Off to a side, Reggie Jackson said, "I know what he is going through. I went through it a couple of years ago when I made a run at the home-run record and they kept asking me when I was going to hit my next home run and how many home runs I was going to hit and if I could break the record. There is no way any man can know any such thing. You do your best, that's all. That was my best year and it got my face on the covers of the magazines and my name in headlines and it made me famous and it made me some money and I'm not sure it was worth it. You don't get a moment's peace. Everything begins to crowd you until you don't know which way to turn and you start looking for ways out to escape."

He sighed and said, "You escape when you slip back. The only escape is a bad year. They turn on you, then, all the glad-handers and back-pounders, the smiling faces, they turn their backs on you when you go bad. I found that out and Vida will, too. I've told him. He knows. He's not stupid. He knows this is unreal. He knows it can't last."

He shook his head in disgust and said, "All I ever want to do anymore is hit about .280 and drive in a hundred runs with around thirty home runs. I don't want to hit .400 or drive in 200 runs or hit sixty home runs. I don't want to break any records. From now on, I just want to have good years, not great years, and get a little raise every year, and be left to live my life in peace."

We told this to Vida Blue when he returned from his shower. The other writers had gone by then, as had most of the other players. The room was quiet now. Vida said, "Reggie's right. I'm sure he's right. All I want to do right now is run, escape to some desert island to be left alone for a while."

But why, we asked, why isn't it what it should be? "I don't know," he said. "Maybe if we take it apart piece by piece, we can figure it out. Maybe it can't be figured out. All I know is I waited all my young life for this and now that it's here I wish it would just go away."

He was dressing now in fancy flares. He seemed to have everything, and what he didn't have seemed at his fingertips. "Still, it has to be something, being a superstar," we said.

He fixed us with a hard look and said, "You said I was a superstar, all you writers; I didn't."

And then he walked outside, where a hundred people waited

for him, kids and adults, men and women, yelling, "Hey, Vida Blue. Vida Blue. Hey, Twenty-Game Winner. Hey, here comes thirty. Hey, Vida, Finley'll have to pay ya a hundred grand now. Hey, Vida, sign here, please . . . please, Vida . . ."   And he stood there among them smiling and signing his autograph with his right hand. He uses his left hand only for pitching.

CHAPTER TWO

Mansfield, Louisiana, is a small town of some 6,300 persons forty miles south of Shreveport. It is hot and humid in the summer and your clothes stick to you with sweat, and it is cold and gray in the winter and you must wear a coat to keep warm.

This is a mill and farming community in the rolling hills of northern Louisiana. Vida Blue says, "A lot of people think when you're from Louisiana you live in the bayous, but it isn't like that. There are some tall buildings and all that good stuff in Louisiana, too. Though not much in Mansfield."

There is a small downtown and the usual shops, but most of the town's men work in the local mills, the pants factory or the trailer plant. Some commute to Shreveport, where many work at the Western Electric plant, stamping out telephones.

There are more blacks than whites in Mansfield. In this time of integration, there is still some segregation in this town, which is a typical Deep South town. There is "a black part of town" and "a white part of town." Most of the blacks are lower on the income scale. Even when Vida was going to high school in the middle 1960's, there was a "black school" and a "white school." Vida is black and went to the black school, DeSoto High, which at that time did not have a single white student.

The Blues live in an eight-room wood-frame house at the end of Mary Street in the black section. This part of the street is not paved, but most, though not all, of the houses around them are well-kept and the lawns are green. Patches of corn, stringbeans and strawberries grow in some of the yards, flowers flourish in others. Some of the houses are modern. The Blues' house is older.

Vida Rochelle Meshach Abednego Blue moved from Troy, Alabama, to Mansfield, Louisiana, where he met Sallie Henderson in 1946 and married her in 1947. He had gone to work where her father worked in the Hendrix Manufacturing Company plant, an iron foundry, where he helped to make buckets and other crane equipment, and he worked there twenty-three years until he got sick and then died.

They named their first child Vida Rochelle Blue, Jr., without giving him all of the father's Biblical name. The first name is pronounced to rhyme with "Ida," but it is Spanish and means "life." And "Junior," as he was called in the early part of his life, inherited it when he was born on July 28, 1949.

After him came twins Cheryl and Jean, born May 2, 1951; Annette, born January 20, 1958; Michael, born February 24, 1961, and Sandra, born December 2, 1964. Vida and his four sisters and younger brother were reared in the whitewashed three-bedroom home where the family still resides. Mrs. Blue's brother and his family lived next door and her mother and grandmother lived two blocks away, and they still do.

Vida says, "My father left home when he was seventeen and he never went back. He came from a large family of ten and he all but lost track of them after he left. He did locate one of his brothers years later, but they were all older, up in age and had drifted apart and gone off in their own directions. My mother came from a family of seven children and it was her family that I grew up around. I played a lot with my cousins Freddie and Clee Henderson, who lived next door. Freddie was a few years older, but Clee was my age. And I had other friends in my schools and in my neighborhood, too, of course, including Elijah Williams, who lived across the street.

"I was just another nap-headed kid with no understanding of life. Your ten-year-old kids in the northern ghettoes today understand racial problems, but they don't really understand, they just learn to hate because their daddies couldn't do this or that or go here or there even though they can now. The South is the South and Mansfield is just another southern town and growing up in it I just accepted my limitations without thinking about them. By the time I was growing up there weren't any more 'colored only' signs on washrooms and we didn't have to ride in the back of the bus. But the black kids played baseball in T-shirts and blue-jeans while the white kids had uniforms. I didn't notice. Now I notice the least little thing, even some things that aren't there."

With raises, Vida's father was earning $75 a week in his last years. He also did part-time work as a gardener for extra money and the family got by without the mother having to work until the elder Blue got sick in 1966. "We were about average for that place," Vida says. "We always had enough to eat. I had a few clothes. I couldn't change every day of the week, but I always had clean clothes to wear to church on Sundays. We had a car. We didn't get a new one ever. Everyone had a TV. We had a TV. We didn't have a color TV. For a while there I wanted a bicycle but I didn't get one. I got turned down once or twice by Santa Claus. We couldn't just get what we wanted.

"My father was a hardworking man. He was what you'd call a common laborer. He'd get up and go to work at 7:30 A.M. and get home about 4:30 P.M. and go to work in people's gardens after his regular job. He went without things so we could have everything we needed even if we couldn't have everything we wanted. I respect that, but I don't want to have to do that. I don't care about being filthy rich, but I also don't ever want to be dirt poor. I don't guess now I ever will have to be poor, but I'd be satisfied to be in the middle. I mean I want to get paid for what I can produce, but if I had to go to work at an ordinary job tomorrow, I don't think it would kill me.

"It's funny, but I never saw my daddy at work, I never even saw the inside of his place: big, huge building, tall smokestacks. Some day I want to go inside. It scares me some to think of goin' to work in a place like that every day of my life and punchin' a time clock, but I guess I could do it if I had to do it. Bein' able to pay your bills is a very important thing. My father always paid his bills. He was a very honest man. He worked hard and he always paid his bills.

"My folks were hardworking, church-going people. My father worked hard to bring in the money and my mother worked hard to keep our home and us in order. They had strong ideas of right and wrong. We had to be respectful of them. I wouldn't say they were real, real strict, but our home was a place where you had to do right or pay the dues. Mama was the disciplinarian. If she believed something was wrong she could make a believer out of you. She had a pretty good wallop and she's the reason I'm not spoiled today. And my kids won't be spoiled, either, because I won't spare the rod.

"Not that I ever was in any real trouble. Our neighborhood was no big-city ghetto. We didn't have any traffic in narcotics or vice. We didn't have any real crime. We didn't have any gangs. I never was arrested for anything. But she watched out for the small things. Like getting bad grades in school or stealing cookies or harassing my sisters. I was the oldest child, Mr. Big Shot, and I wasn't too quiet, I was a little wild, I had my ups and downs. Mama could put me down pretty good.

"I didn't mind. Mama's a warm woman. All mothers are warm, aren't they? They want to see their children have the best and grow up to be big and strong and healthy with good ideas about right and wrong. I always felt closer to my mama than to my papa. Mama was always there for us. She was easy to talk to. She understood. My father always seemed to be busy, working and all. You know something—he never even saw me play a game of high school football. I hate it that he didn't," Vida sighs.

His mother says, "I guess Junior was something of a mama's boy. No sissy or anything like that. A little rough and wild, for a fact. But he always seemed to like hangin' around Mama and talkin' to Mama. I used to worry about cuttin' him loose from my apron-strings when the time came, but I had nothing to worry about, when the time came, he just turned loose and went. But we were still close and he still likes to call me up to talk and he still likes to sit around talkin' when he's home.

"His daddy and me, we tried to raise our children right, emphasizin' religion and school and family and things like that. His father meant well for him. He meant well for all of them. He just didn't have time for them.

"Ever since Vida was two or three years old, all he wanted to do was play ball—baseball or basketball or football. I feared for football, afraid he'd get hurt, but there was no stoppin' him. I liked him playin' baseball better. My father told me, 'Some day that boy's goin' to be a great baseball player. If you're smart, you'll keep him in baseballs. Every time he wants a ball, you go out to the store and get him one.' So that's what I did. And I never asked him to get a job.

"For a long time, we kept him in rubber balls. We didn't dare give him a hard ball because he threw so hard even when he was young and he was so wild he'd break all our windowpanes. But later on he got baseballs. And even footballs. In school, he was just a fair student. He always had his mind on ball. He was always in some kind of game. It was his life. I shoulda seen it would be his whole life."

Vida was raised in rural surroundings. He knows what woods are. But he never swam in the local creek. He says, "I never learned how to swim. While I was growing up, some kids drowned in the creek and it scared me off. Death frightened me." Nor did he hunt or fish much, as the other kids did. He says, "All the time I was growing up, I was always across the street in a vacant lot, playing ball. Just being around home in the summertime, being black and not having anything to do, you'd get up and eat and go play ball and then come back and eat and then go back and play ball some more. That's how it was with me. By the time I entered high school, I was almost a fully developed athlete.

"I started with tennis balls and broomsticks. Later on, we'd get baseballs and bats and use 'em till we had to hold 'em together with bicycle tape. We'd get gloves and use them till they were all torn up. I got to throwin' hard, I used to smoke my scuffed-up baseball into Elijah Williams' tattered glove 'til his hand couldn't take it no more. I found out early I had this Godgiven talent to throw hard. No one ever taught me how to throw hard. Later on, managers and coaches and pitchers and catchers taught me tricks, but no one ever taught me how to throw hard, and that's my main thing.

"My father never taught me anything about playing any sport. He was a fair-sized man, tall and all, and strong, but he was never an athlete and never interested. He said he'd never played.

My mother had some athletes on her side of the family, my uncles. A couple of her brothers were good high-school athletes and one, Lee, was a good football and basketball player in college at Grambling. They encouraged me. And bein' an athlete was about all I ever wanted to be as far back as I can remember. Some kids want to grow up to be some things, other kids other things, and lots of 'em change along the way, but all I ever thought to be was an athlete, though a football player more than a baseball player.

"Of course, a kid plays all sports and he never really believes he's going to be a professional athlete, he just dreams about it, but he knows it's a dream that can come true. Some black men become doctors and lawyers and big businessmen, but they have to overcome a lot to do it, it's not so easy for a black boy, especially in the South. Becoming a jazz musician or an athlete or something like that, well, that seems practical. Some blacks from Mansfield got to go to college to play ball and some from Louisiana became pros, so I could see that was possible. I didn't know it was going to happen to me, mind you, but I knew it could and I dreamed about it and went after it. I didn't want to hunt or fish like some kids, I just wanted to play ball."

In these situations, the church not only is a place of religion, but a place of recreation and a social meeting ground. The Blues attended Wesley Methodist Church regularly and Vida used to go right from church to the ballfield to play ball, sometimes messing up his good clothes, much to the distress of his mother, and he got his start in organized sports in community and church softball leagues and later baseball and basketball leagues, some sponsored by the schools or by the recreation departments.

Vida says, "We called the early leagues T-shirt leagues. We all got T-shirts and blue-jeans and just played happily. We didn't worry about who had the highest batting average or whose socks stretched the highest. We didn't get much coaching at first. Later on we got coaching from clinics and programs put on by the school department. W. F. Jones was one of the first coaches who ever worked with me, I remember that. I always played football, but I never got any coaching in football until I got into high school."

Freddie Henderson remembers, "Vida didn't need much coaching. He was a natural from the start. When he was younger he was playing with us older kids and he was always the quarterback in football and the pitcher in baseball because he was the best and he just naturally took it on himself. If we talked about maybe making the big time, we didn't believe it. These were only pipe dreams and inside us we knew that's all they were. Maybe they turned out to be more than that for Vida, but that's all they turned out to be for the rest of us."

Vida says, "I started pitching in our T-shirt league. Originally, I played the outfield and first base. I was a pretty good hitter, too. Then I was. We needed someone else to pitch one day and I could throw hard so I went in and I pitched. I could throw hard all right. Hard and wild. I had no idea where the ball was going. I hit a lot of people. But my teammates seemed to like it. And so did I. So I kept on with it. Even though when I wasn't pitching in high school, I played center field and batted cleanup and was a .300 hitter."

Clyde Washington was the DeSoto High School baseball coach and he says, "Vida could hit because he was a good athlete, but from the time I saw him playing on the sandlots when he was only in the fifth or sixth grade I knew he was a pitcher because he had such a tremendous fast ball." The school didn't even have a team at the time, but when principal Lee Jacobs saw Vida smoking them in on the sandlots, he decided to organize a team "to exploit the potential of Blue." A diamond was laid out in a corner of the football field. There were no fences. There were light-poles in the outfield. But it was good enough to give Blue a base.

Once coach Washington reprimanded an outfielder for leaning against a light pole and told him to straighten up. "Why? The ball's not coming out here," the player pointed out. "After all, Vida Blue was pitching and he was overpowering," notes Washington. Once Vida pitched two no-hitters in a row. Another time he pitched a no-hitter and struck out 21 men in a seven-inning game, and lost. He walked ten men in that game. Washington explains, "Vida's problem was somebody to catch him. There were a lot of passed balls and missed third strikes. We bought

our catcher, Elijah Williams, the best catcher's mitts and gave
him sponges to stick inside them and still his hand would swell
up and he couldn't catch again for three days after a day of
catching Vida." Williams remembers, "I wore a glove inside my
glove and my hand still swole up after every game."

Vida says, "I was part of the problem, too. I could throw hard,
all right, but I was also wild. I never knew where the ball was
going. It was as apt to wind up in the stands as in the catcher's
glove. And I had a better curve ball in those days than I do now.
I don't know where it went. I threw straight overarm then and
later I was changed to a little more sidearm and it changed my
curve, but the curve I threw in those days really broke and it
was hard to handle. When they write, like they do, that I had
this many no-hitters or that many no-hitters in high school they're
making it up because no one really knows. We didn't have any
real official scorers there and there were men on base and runs
scored off me from walks and hit batters and wild pitches and
passed balls, so it was hard to keep track of the no-hitters."

Coach Washington kept track of the losses, however, and reports, "There only were two in his entire high school career. He
pitched us to two district titles and might have pitched us to a
third if he had not gotten injured late in his sophomore season
when we were leading our league." Blue recalls, "I was standing
in a driveway when my cousin Fred was backing his car in. The
door was open and before either of us realized what was happening I got trapped between the wall and the car. The door hit
my leg and spun me around. The leg wasn't broken and I didn't
need an operation, but it was so badly banged up and cut I was
out the rest of the season and we lost some games and lost the
title."

He came back healthy and better than ever for his junior and
senior seasons, however, and coach Washington began to have
trouble keeping track of the scouts who were interested in his
star pitcher: "They began to show up in my small town from all
over asking me questions about him and watching him and asking
me to keep in touch with them and at one time there was no
room in my wallet for anything but their cards. Scouts were
calling me at three in the morning to find out when he was going

to pitch next. I felt like telling them it wasn't at four in the morning, but it was sort of thrilling."

It is not every coach who gets to coach a Vida Blue, of course, to help to develop him, to have a share in his flight to fame, and for this one, it was a wonder, which shows in his speech.

For Blue, the showing-up of the scouts bolstered his interest in baseball. He says, "It really gave me incentive. It meant they saw something in me. It helped me believe in me."

The basketball coach missed by the margin of nonsense indulged in by Blue in the eighth grade when he placed some thumbtacks on a chair and was dismissed from the team. He played intramural basketball after that, climaxing in a career of hook-shots of clothing into a locker or a hamper, or pickup games with other athletes or stray youngsters in playgrounds and school-yards. He has the moves, the touch, the look of a basketball player on court, however, and believes he would have been a good one, but then he believes he would have been good at any game, and perhaps he is right.

"I might have been great at football," he says, and perhaps he is right there, too, for he was great, as far as he went. Which was to a black high school which had no prejudice against black quarterbacks.

The football coach did not miss. Blue remembers that it was an assistant, Tony Rhodes, who steered him into football, and another assistant, Willie Robinson, who helped to develop him, but it was the head coach, Clarence Baldwin, who truly recognized the gem he had. Blue believes he was always put at quarterback because those who saw how well he threw a baseball figured he had to be able to toss a football pretty well, too, but Baldwin says it went deeper than that. Baldwin says, "First of all, he was a natural leader, a winner. Second, the way he could throw a football was different than the way he could throw a baseball. He had the arm, of course. It was nothing for him to throw fifty or sixty yards. Third, he could really run. He was the most complete player I ever saw.

"Mrs. Blue was a Henderson and her brother was a noted left-handed passer at Grambling. When Vida first came along and I saw how he could throw left-handed and I heard he was a Hen-

derson, too, I went out on the campus looking for somebody who
could catch the ball. I found Jesse Hudson, who is now a pitcher
owned by the Mets. Jesse said he wasn't going to tackle anybody
and he wasn't going to carry any football, but he could catch any
pass Vida could throw within six feet of him. He could, too.

"Vida threw bullets, not arching passes. On short passes, he'd
knock the receivers right down. I heard boys ask him not to
throw so hard. There would be defenders on both sides of a man
and Vida would still put the ball right in the receiver's belly. In
a pinch, like when he was rolling out to his right and was pressed,
he would adjust by passing with his right hand. He couldn't
throw as far with his right hand, but he could throw as accurately. In his senior year, he threw 35 touchdown passes and
Hudson caught seventeen.

"Vida could run as well as he could throw. As soon as I saw
him do both I knew I had a run-and-shoot quarterback and I
changed my whole offense to fit him. He was my offense. Blue
was one of those quarterbacks who live dangerously. I remember
when we played Booker T. Washington High in Shreveport and
it started raining cats and dogs at the half. So Vida ran the ball
the whole second half, every play we had the ball he ran. He
wouldn't throw it or hand it off. He could take a beating. They'd
get up saying, 'We know we killed Blue,' but he'd get back up
and run again. We won, 13–0. In his senior year, he averaged
more than ten yards a carry, and ran for around fifteen touchdowns.

"He played defense, too, and he was our punter, also. He was
our inspiration. He could control himself. You'd drop a pass on
him and he'd say, 'Go ahead, get it next time.' He didn't get dis-
couraged. He had faith. We had faith in him. And he rewarded
our faith. We were 9–2–1 his junior year and 10–1–1 his senior
year. He ran for some 1,600 yards, passed for some 3,400 yards
and totaled some 5,000 yards on offense his senior year. He was
as good a football player as he was a baseball player, and that is
very good, indeed."

How good? Vida himself says, "I think I could have made any
college team in the country. When I first started, I couldn't stand
the hitting. When I'd played awhile, I began to get up smiling.

After a while, I started to tell the tacklers, 'I thought you guys could hit.' I hardly ever saw a touchdown pass completed. To stop us, they had to get me. They knocked me down on every play, often long after I'd thrown the ball. I didn't mind. I came to like the contact. I miss it now. I actually do. I really do.

"I loved running the ball. I ran for a lot of touchdowns. I didn't just throw for them. I ran a lot of different ways, too. I remember a play where there was a fumble and I picked it up and I ran it eighty yards for a touchdown. I remember returning an intercepted pass for a touchdown. I never ran a kickoff back for a touchdown, however, and I always wanted to do that. I wanted to do everything in football. I could throw the ball pretty damn good. It's a science, you know, not just being able to throw, but being able to throw long and short, hard and soft, leading a receiver just right. It's a feel you have to have, a touch, and I felt I had it.

"Maybe I'm kidding myself. It's fun to dream, though. When I was a kid, my idol wasn't Sandy Koufax of the Los Angeles Dodgers, it was Johnny Unitas of the Baltimore Colts. I used to root for the Colts. I used to dream about someday succeeding Unitas as quarterback of the Colts, of being the first big black quarterback in pro football. I still dream about it. In my dreams I'm also Joe Namath and Archie Manning and Jim Plunkett and Greg Landry and Scott Hunter. I dream about wearing white shoes like Namath and Manning and rolling out like Landry and throwing the ball right between the defenders to a receiver for the winning touchdown. It's like throwing a 3-and-0 fastball past Harmon Killebrew. You do it or you don't. In my dreams," he grins, "I do it."

Wistful with wonder, he shakes his head. He says, "For me, it's a more scientific game than baseball and I'm more a student at it. You scout your foes and study film and figure out tendencies and you plot your offense and your defense, your game plan, and you make your moves, and when you're all through with the science it becomes real physical, blocking and tackling, breaking tackles and hitting your receivers, accepting the contact and going on, coming from behind. It's more exciting than baseball. Fans cheer and stomp. 'Go, mighty Tigers!' They used to really rock, rattle and roll our little old wooden bleachers, which seated 1,300. Now they got a new steel structure, pressbox and all. The house that Blue built. We drew well. Every Friday night the people came out to see Vida Blue do his thing.

"I was really wrapped up in it. It got so I'd call practice a half-hour early on my own, get the team together and work out some things. If I'd stayed another year, I'd have been coaching, too. I was even dating the football queen. The sweetheart of the team, Samantha Brown. The first year, they voted her in. The second year, I appointed her. I darn near married her. A darn nice girl, too. But I was married to football.

"One of the few times I ever cried in my life was when we lost a football game. I was only thirteen or fourteen years old. It was only a game. And in time you learn not to cry. But I loved the game. And I hated losing. My senior year we lost in the semi-finals of the state playoffs to Carroll High of Monroe. I hated losing that as much as I ever have hated losing any game, but I had no idea my football career was over. I thought I might have a lot of victories ahead of me."

He hangs his head for a moment, distressed by it. He says, "There was no reason there couldn't be a great black quarterback. There is no reason. There's just a reason it couldn't be me."

Just before Vida's senior year in high school, his father got sick. "He had the black dust in his lungs. He also had a weak heart. He went into the hospital. He had a successful operation. He went home. He never went back to work again. A couple of months later he went to sleep and he never woke up. I was the only one in the room when he died. It just happened that way. I was only seventeen years old and I'll never forget it. I went over to him and I saw that he was gone. I just stood there a long time. Then I cried. Then I went to get Mom.

"I knew I had to get over it, but I haven't got over it yet. He was a young man, around forty. He was my father. But I think I'd have felt the same for a mother or a sister or a brother or an aunt or an uncle or a first cousin or a third cousin. Everyone born has to die, but no one wants to die and I don't want anyone to die and I don't want to be there when anyone dies, especially not anyone close to me. You just don't believe it when it happens.

One minute he's there, a person, and the next minute, he's not there anymore."

Vida Blue looks away and says, "I was raised to be religious. I was brought up being brought to church. I'm not religious, but I'm religious-minded. I don't go to church as much as I should, but I believe in God. I just don't know what to believe about death."

The last year, while his father was failing, his mother had to go to work. She found work as a cleaning woman in a shirt factory four hours a day for $1.25 an hour and part-time work as a substitute in an elementary school cafeteria. That brought in a few extra dollars a week. After her husband died, on September 30, 1966, she had $155 a month from his retirement pension and G.I. widows' benefits to support her five children and to help out her 70-year-old mother and 83-year-old grandmother, who lived nearby. "It wasn't easy," she sighs.

When her husband died, she said to Vida, "Junior, now you're the man of the house." She says, "He just seemed to grow right up." He says, "I didn't sit around and moan about Dad's death. I tried to get it out of my system. I tried to accept it and accept the responsibilities it meant for me. I was seventeen years old, but I *was* the man of the house. We had always had a happy, decent family life, but suddenly there we were with unhappiness in the house and with no real, solid means of support. I knew it would be a frightening thing and an unsettling thing for my sisters and my brother and I felt I had to do things that would show them I could be a leader, but I didn't know what to do."

"The day he died, that night, I went out and played a football game, the Booker T. Washington game in Shreveport. At first I didn't want to. I thought I shouldn't. But Mama said I should. She said I couldn't do anything for him by staying home. She said I had this obligation to my team. And she was right. Maybe it looked wrong, but if it was right, it was right. It's been said, it's been written he died while I was playing a game. That's not true. He died before the game, but I played in the game and I played good. I didn't dedicate it to him or anything like that. He never even saw me play in a game. I just played. And for a while, I thought I could go on playing, in college, maybe."

He was sought by twenty to thirty major colleges, including Notre Dame, Purdue, Arizona, Arizona State and the University of California at Berkeley. Even such southern schools as Houston and Wake Forest wanted him. Houston had been having Elvin Hayes as a black basketball star, and now wanted Blue for football. Coach Bill Yeomans enthused, "This young fellow is going to be the first big-name Negro quarterback. He's going to be the best left-handed passer of all time, better than Frankie Albert. There's nothing he can't do. And his name alone will sell tickets." Carroll Schoalts courted him and was pleased by him personally. "He didn't try to take me for a lot of steaks. He ordered seven or eight extra hamburgers, but they were for his brothers or sisters or girlfriends." Later, after having wooed and lost him and Vida had found fame in baseball, he met him and marveled, "He seems still to be as real and as pure as when I knew him then."

Flown to Houston to visit the campus, Blue was escorted on a tour of the university's home football field, the awesome Astrodome. On a whim, he went to the mound and threw an imaginary pitch. "I don't know why I did it," he says now. It would seem, though, that he was torn between football and baseball. With the graduation of his high school class, Blue would be eligible for major-league baseball's free-agent draft and open to bonus offers to turn pro immediately. A college football career would put off play-for-pay for four years. And his family needed money.

He admits he came closer to signing a letter of intent to enroll at Houston than at any other school. But another problem presented itself. He was one credit short of being able to graduate with his class. He could not have enrolled at Houston. Cal wanted him to make up the credit and then prep at Laney Junior College on the West Coast, but he did not want to wait.

The black colleges presented an alternative. Grambling, Southern University, Texas Southern, Prairie View, Alcorn A&M and others pursued him passionately. He hadn't wanted to settle for one of them. It would not make him special to be the black quarterback of a black team. But they persisted and were willing to work out his scholastic problem. He succumbed to a pitch by Alcorn to settle him in summer school at Temple High in Vicksboro, Mississippi, where he made up his missing credit, and it was here, not at home, that he graduated from high school in 1967. But Alcorn lost him, too.

The A's drafted him, scout Ray Swallow romanced him and Charles O. Finley telephoned a fat bonus offer. Blue bargained with them. Their bid topped at $25,000—$12,500 a year for two years. It has been reported at more and it has been reported at less, but it was just that, no more and no less, except for a limited offer to help toward college and extra monies for advancing up the baseball ladder which brought him $7,500. It has been reported Finley visited Vida personally, but he did not, speaking with him only on the phone and seeing him for the first time only much later. It has been reported Finley threw in a box of baseballs with which Vida wanted to practice, that they were ordered from a local store that would not issue Finley credit, and so had to be sent to Blue from the team, but that came two years later.

Vida discussed the situation with his mother. There were many considerations. The family needed money right then. Mrs. Blue did not want to deprive Vida of the sport he preferred, but this was a risky sport and she had feared it from the first. His right arm had been stepped on playing football and he still has the scars. His back had been wrenched and he had to have help getting dressed for a week. He says he knew as well as anyone that an injured knee could ruin his football future. Of course, he could get a sore arm that would destroy his baseball future, but by then he would have banked $25,000 and been guaranteed the cash for college. Then there was the prevailing prejudice against black quarterbacks that might destroy his dream in the end in any event. His mother urged him to take the bonus and enter baseball. Reluctantly, he agreed it was the wisest thing he could do. Years later, watching a football game on television, with friends, he would wave at the screen and say, "If it wasn't for a certain woman, that could be me up there."

He says it with wistful good humor, however. He says, "I miss football. I'd rather have been a football hero than a baseball star. There are times when I shut my eyes and I see myself standing behind the offensive line, calling signals for the Baltimore Colts, audibilizing to beat a blitz, shooting one of those fine spirals downfield, but that just isn't the way life has worked out for me.

If I'd gone into football, I might have been injured and finished before I began. Or maybe they'd have turned me into a defensive back, like they do with most blacks. At best, I'd still be trying to prove myself in football, while here I am, established in baseball, the big bonus in the bank and the big dough beginning to roll in."

Blue's high-school coach, Baldwin, says, "We've had a lot of good athletes who didn't get the chance or didn't take the chance. Blue got it and took it and made the most of it and he deserves a lot of credit for it." Blue says, "Half the athletes on my high-school teams deserved a chance. Some should be all-star or all-pro today. Some may make it yet, like Jesse Hudson. Some made it as far as college ball and no further. I played with three players who played at Grambling. I played with a player, Willie Houston, who was the greatest high-school fullback I ever saw, and he went into the navy. Vietnam got some. Bad grades got others. Bad breaks got still others. It's not just having talent, you see. I can see that. I had talent. Maybe I had more talent for football than baseball. Or maybe I'm a fool for thinking so. But I'd be a fool if I didn't know that there are guys with my kind of talent who come along who never get the chance or never take it and I'd sure be some kind of a fool for cursing success in any sport."

CHAPTER THREE

Although Vida Blue was brilliant enough to pitch a no-hitter his first year in the minors, to pitch in the majors his second year out of high school, to pitch a no-hitter in the majors by the third year and to be a superstar by the fourth year, when he would have been just a college senior had he followed football, baseball scouts were not brilliant enough to predict anything like this for him. Each of the twenty teams in the majors at that time, including the A's, passed him up on the first round of the draft of graduating schoolboys and other free-agents in 1967, and he was, in fact, only the twenty-seventh player taken, although, for a fact, if every player in the country today, if every proven superstar and promising prospect were made available to an open draft, Vida Blue no doubt would be the first player taken.

Professionals in sports will tell you that it is more difficult to determine a baseball player's ability to make the majors, much less become a star, than it is a football player's ability or a basketball player's ability. The ability to throw a ball past a big-league batter or hit a big-league pitcher's ball seems to be more subtle than the ability to pass a football or run with one or shoot a basketball or rebound one or pass one, and the players usually are signed younger before they have been exposed to more demanding competition. The pros make many mistakes in picking players from college football and basketball ranks, but not as many as they do choosing youngsters from high school or college baseball ranks. Most pros felt sure Lew Alcindor would become a dominant figure in pro basketball, which he has as Kareem Abdul-Jabbar, or that Jim Plunkett, if given the chance, would become an outstanding pro-football quarterback, which he has, but Vida Blue was just one of many boys rated highly in baseball in 1967.

The Los Angeles Dodgers have one of the most extensive scouting staffs and minor-league systems in baseball and they get their share of outstanding new stars from year to year, but Al Campanis, their director of player personnel, says, "There is no sure way to make the wisest selections from the young talent available to you each year. It's not just a question of their physical skills. You're talking about seventeen- and eighteen-year-olds and you don't know what's in their heads and their hearts. And these things—their desire, their determination, their willingness to learn, their courage, their intelligence—will determine their future as much as their raw ability."

Lefty Phillips, the former manager of the California Angels, who has signed as many stars as almost any scout, says, "It comes down to a matter of personal judgment. You take everything you've learned in the game and make an educated guess. The problem is, your job is always at stake. The teams sometimes spend a lot of money on players you tout. You hesitate to low-rate a kid for fear he'll make it big with someone else, and you hesitate to go overboard on a kid for fear he'll flop. It takes a lot of guts for scouts not to steer a middle course."

The New York Mets haven't done bad. They came from ridiculed expansionists to the world championship in 1969, mainly with some outstanding young pitchers. Mets' official Joe McDonald says, "We knew about Blue. Red Murff gave us a good scouting report on him. We thought enough of him to invite him to a tryout camp at Rockdale, Texas. Before the camp we had him rated behind his teammate, Jesse Hudson. After the camp we upgraded him ahead of Hudson. We had him thirty-sixth on our list of 249 players going into the draft. We consider that pretty high when you think of all the ballplayers who are eligible each year. Maybe it wasn't high enough, but we weren't the only ones who made that mistake."

Murff's report read, "Strong and a fine athlete, but he can't throw as hard as Jesse Hudson and Jerry Ray" (also Blue's teammates). The Mets took Jon Matlack, but wound up with Hudson, too, though neither has made it yet. The Mets took Gary Gentry that year, too, and he wound up in the majors as a winner just three years later, though not the kind of winner Vida Blue turned out to be.

Cincinnati's Reds have done pretty well. They wound up in the World Series in 1970. One big reason was Wayne Simpson, whom they selected when they could have chosen Blue. He helped pitch them to a pennant with a 14–3 mark before he began to struggle with a sore arm. Baltimore's Orioles have done pretty well. They wound up winning the world championship in 1970. Instead of Blue they went for Bobby Grich, an infielder did not make their team until 1972, but is one of the most highly regarded prospects in baseball. However, they would trade Grich and twenty other prospects for Blue tomorrow.

The Pittsburgh Pirates have done pretty well. They beat out Baltimore for the world championship in 1971. Rex Bowens, who was with Pittsburgh in 1967 and is now with Cincinnati, insists, "We knew all about Blue. We thought he was the best prospect in America." But they didn't take him. These are sound organizations staffed with shrewd personnel, but they proceed under pressures in a multimillion-dollar profession and they make mistakes.

The New York Yankees didn't even have Blue on their list. They had first choice, too, in the draft at the Americana Hotel in New York on the sixth of June, 1967, and they selected Ron Blomberg, who hit .322 for them in a third of a season as a rookie in 1971. He is the Jewish prospect they have been seeking since long before their Bronx neighborhood stopped being a Jewish area and became a black ghetto, and they passed up the black Blue for him. The Cardinals took Ted Simmons, who has become an excellent young catcher.

Most of the youngsters selected have not yet come to anything and most never will. The Indians took Jack Heidemann, the Cubs Terry Hughes, the Astros John Mayberry, the Giants David Roby, the White Sox Bill Haynes, the Twins Steve Brye, the Tigers Jim Foor and so forth and so on. Some teams even had a second

choice and made a second selection without taking Blue while
he still was available. One of the most astonishing things about
this situation is that the A's did not even take him first, nor was
he even their second choice, though they selected him second.

Their first choice was Pete Broberg, the hard-throwing youngster who was resisting major-league bonus offers until he could
complete a college career. Each time a player is selected, but not
signed, he goes back into the grab-bag for the next draw. A's
owner Charles O. Finley did not want to waste a pick on Broberg
if he could not sign him. He offered him $75,000 for the assurance
he could sign him, then twice that, finally $175,000, but still Bro-
berg held back, and, finally, Finley gave up. The A's took instead
a youngster from El Cajon, California, Brien Bickerton, who remains a mystery at this time. Broberg finally signed in 1971, with
the Washington Senators (now the Texas Rangers), was rushed
right to the majors, started eighteen games, finished seven, won
five, lost nine, had one two-hit shutout and did show some promise, though not Blue's brilliance. It is not impossible he will sur-
pass Vida, but one would not want to wager a lot on it.

In 1967 the A's were located in Kansas City and Connie Ryan,
a former major-league infielder, was their scout in the Louisiana
territory. Now coaching for Atlanta, Ryan recalls, "I was scouting
a game in Ruston, Louisiana, when I heard there was a night
game that night about thirty or forty miles away in a little town
called Mansfield. I had nothing to do that night except sit around
my hotel room, so I decided to drive over and see the game. It
was a chance to see two teams I had not scouted before." So, on
an impulse, because he had nothing better to do, because he was
not afraid of a little extra work if it would help him do his job
better, Ryan drove to Mansfield and was the right man in the
right place at the right time.

Circumstances were right because Blue and not teammates
Hudson or Ray were pitching that night and because Blue was
at his best that night. Ryan reports, "I liked what I saw. It would
be hard not to like him. Anybody who saw him that night would
have had to have liked him. And I found that others were interested in him. But he wasn't facing the best of foes and I figured
the poor arclights might have made his fastball seem faster, so I

wanted to return for a second look. I found out when he was going to pitch again and the next week I returned to see him pitch in daylight and I liked him even better than I had before. Before long, everyone in the business was turning up to see him pitch and most of them liked him. How much they liked him, I can't say. Scouts talk to one another, but they don't say anything. You can't trust their comments. They're not in a position to give away trade secrets," Ryan says.

"I called my office and told them about this kid left-hander. I told them he was the best left-handed pitcher I had seen in nine years of scouting. Then I filed a report on him. You have to put it down on paper. I'll admit I went out on a limb for him. And I was told to set up some talks with him. I went to his home and met him and his mother and told him and her of our interest in him and the fact that we might like to draft him and wanted some of our people to talk to him about what it would take to sign him. After that it was out of my hands. The decisions on who to draft and who not to draft aren't made by the scouts, they're made higher up. Other scouts are sent to submit their opinions on the player prospects most highly regarded by an organization. In the A's organization, Mr. Finley probably pretty much has the final say. He is the organization. He runs the show. Maybe he's not an experienced baseball man, but he's been in baseball awhile, he's a businessman, and it's his money and his team.

"Shortly afterwards, I left the A's organization and accepted the job with the Braves. I haven't seen Vida since we had that meeting at his house. But I feel I had a hand in signing him. Any scout who signs a boy dreams of his becoming a Vida Blue. That's your job. Most scouts weren't superstars or they'd be doing something else. Scouting is hard, lonely work, a lot of traveling for little money. It's a way to stay close to the game. You live through the players you sign. If they make it big, it's almost like you made it big. I had a hand in signing Rusty Staub, too. It's a great thrill to see your boys doing well. But all the players I signed haven't done well. As much as I liked Vida, I never dreamed he'd do this well. I'm not ridiculing other scouts. Some of them may not have seen Blue on a very good day. I did. That doesn't make me smarter than any other scout. I was just lucky I saw him on a good night."

Finley says, "Ryan said Blue couldn't miss. He strongly recommended we draft him first. I went after Broberg instead. Others felt Broberg couldn't miss. And maybe he won't. Others were high on the other boy. Ryan wasn't our only scout who saw Blue and recommended him as the best, but you have other scouts seeing other boys and recommending them, and you can't see them all yourself, and in the end you figure it out as best you can. Jack Sanford saw Blue in two games and the former fine major-league pitcher called me after the second game and reported Blue was a natural and couldn't miss and we should go after him. And we did go after him. We wanted him, obviously more than others wanted him. If he wasn't first on our list, he was very high. And we were fortunate he was still available when our turn came up on the second round."

The Atlanta Braves took Ralph Garr, "The Roadrunner," who was a sensation in 1971, second in batting in the National League with a .344 average, an outfielder who had 219 hits and was so swift he stole thirty bases. Ralph Garr is from Monroe, Louisiana, and he went to Grambling in Louisiana, and maybe he will turn out to be a more prized product of the Bayou state than Vida Blue.

Twenty teams picked players on the first round and six teams picked players on the second round before the Kansas City Athletics picked Vida Blue as the No. 27 choice of the 1967 free-agent draft and Charles O. Finley sent Ray Swallow to bargain with the boy and his newly widowed mother and enforced the bidding with "two or three" phone calls as he bought him away from football and Alcorn A&M or Houston or Notre Dame or maybe even the Baltimore Colts. And if Minnesota's Twins had taken him they would have taken the 1971 pennant instead of Oakland's A's, or if any one of the other teams had taken him it would have been taking in his victories and the money from the ten to twenty thousand extra fans who turned out every day and night he pitched in 1971.

Blue accepted the $25,000 offer and took the $12,500 first installment and banked it. "My money in Mansfield is in my mother's name and in mine," he explains. "They have written I bought her a new house, but that isn't so. She didn't want a new house. She wanted the old house fixed up, so the old house was fixed up. She got a car. She can have anything she wants. She has her own account and I make deposits in it. She has not had to work since the day I signed my contract and if I can help it she will never have to work another day of her life. She has kids to raise at home, my brother and sister. My twin sisters are nice, quiet girls and good students in college at Grambling and I am helping them through college.

"I don't deserve any medals. I am not doing anything anyone else in my position wouldn't do. My daddy's dead and I'm the man of my family. I haven't done that much. Since the bonus until now I haven't made that much that I could do that much. I could do some of the things I wanted to do, but I didn't want to do that much. I'm the same ol' easygoin' Vida Blue. I buy things I want, but I don't buy $500 suits. My first year I was only making $500 a month. My next year I was making $850 a month. You don't make much money in the minors and if that bonus had been it for me in baseball I'd have made a bad deal going into baseball. You can blow 25 grand in a hurry. I didn't. That's not my way. And now I'm going to make much more. But, I didn't know that then. I wasn't sure. Who could be? I thought I was good, but I didn't know how good. And thinkin' and doin' are two different things. As it turns out, it came fast, but it seemed slow, and there was some strugglin' to it, too."

CHAPTER FOUR

Charles O. Finley is a flamboyant and fascinating fellow. He followed his grandfather and his father into the Gary, Indiana, steel mills, where he worked for five years for 47¢ an hour while playing semipro baseball on the side. While putting in a full shift for less than $4 a day, he also was working on an engineering degree at the Gary campus of Indiana University. He served as a machine-shop apprentice and worked his way up to foreman in the maintenance department. Following this he worked five years for a defense plant in LaPorte, Indiana, starting as a supervisor and rising to superintendent's status while selling insurance and studying the insurance business at night.

Going to work for the Travelers' Company, he broke sales records. His prodigious pace was slowed when he was stricken with pneumonic tuberculosis. During twenty-seven months in a sanitorium, his weight dropped from more than 200 pounds to less than 100 pounds. His wife, Shirley, worked to support herself, her two children and his medical bills. Meanwhile, discovering doctors did not have a satisfactory group-insurance program to cover their own medical bills, he dreamed up a plan while lying on his back. Recovering his weight, his strength and his health, he emerged on a dead run, carrying his proposal to company after company until he found one that would underwrite his plan. After he found one and after the American College of Surgeons and the American Medical Association bought his plan, he was on his way. Now a wealthy man, he has offices in Chicago and a home for his wife, five sons and two daughters on a 1,280-acre farm in LaPorte.

He bought the Kansas City Athletics baseball team in 1960, which he shifted to Oakland in 1968, and the Oakland Seals hockey team in 1970, which he renamed the California Golden Seals, outfitting both in gaudy green and gold uniforms. He added white kangaroo shoes to the baseball team's attire.

The staid establishment in baseball resisted his colorful and revolutionary ways and at first rejected many reforms he proposed, some of which it later introduced, such as night All-Star and World Series games. Finley flails away until he gets what he wants. Dissatisfied with attendance in Kansas City, he threatened the town with his team's departure, then pressured his powerful partners until big-league baseball let him go, setting up a new expansion team in the vacated Kansas City territory. Advised by the firm he had hired to select Seattle he went instead to Oakland. By 1971 he was dissatisfied with attendance in Oakland and there were rumors that he'd move to Washington. Commented one observer, "Finley runs the fattest floating crap game in the country."

His balding head fringed by white hair, always dressed with conservative class, the fast-talking Finley is a character of contrasts. He swears by a philosophy of life, "Sweat Plus Sacrifice Equals Success," yet is given to gimmicks such as turning loose a mule named after himself, "Charlie O.," to graze in an outfield enclosure in Kansas City, and moved the mule with his team to Oakland. On the surface he would seem a soul who aspires to personal publicity, yet he often is unavailable to the press and is the only owner in sports who limits the free food served writers at his stadiums, which is no way to the writers' hearts.

He speaks freely of large sums spent to buy bonus babies for his A's, yet later is so reluctant to grant raises to these same players they turn on him in outrage. A remarkable young slugger, Reggie Jackson, raged when he did not get the sort of money he deemed he deserved in 1969 and 1970 and demanded to be traded, but while many teams made offers for him, Finley refused to raise or trade him until Jackson reluctantly surrendered. Out of this case grew the inevitable speculation that Vida Blue would have trouble getting the sort of raise most expected him to seek from his skimpy $16,000 salary of 1971. Finley might give him a car, which he did, and a gasoline credit card, which he did, and clothes, which he did, but $75,000 or $85,000—this was something else.

Like most self-made men, Charles O. Finley is a demanding boss. He pushes himself at a prodigious pace and expects his employees to keep up. But they do not have his financial involvement with his teams. They are working for ordinary money, and after working for Finley for a while they usually go to work elsewhere. There is a constant turnover in his front-office staff. He is a perfectionist who will push many who do not jump of their own accord. In twelve years with the A's he has had twelve managers. Half were fired in midseason. One was hired and fired twice.

Charles O. Finley is a remarkable man. He has made his own way in the world and flourished where others failed. He has overcome the harshest sort of poverty and illness and it has given him a sense of strength that frightens those around him. He has power in his professional life and he wields it, but he has earned that right. He owns his teams and he can run them as he sees fit. If he felt he had bought his A's the best players available and deserved better from them than his managers were getting, he had the right to make changes. Some say he should leave his teams to the professionals, but if they owned the teams would they?

He is a person of deep passions and stubborn convictions, a man of uneven temperament and a personality that seems to shift with the winds. One hesitates to guess what he is going to say or do next, but he is a never-ending source of fascination to those who listen to him and observe him. And an enigma to those who turn a part of their lives over to him as Vida Blue did, when, by virtue of accepting his bonus and signing his contract, he became a member of the A's, of the Finley family, and, as a professional athlete, not free, as would be, say, a writer or a salesman, to go to work for a competitor if he wished.

Finley flew Blue into Kansas City, gave him one of those gaudy garbs, introduced him to the writers and broadcasters and photographers as his "next, great star" and gave him a seat on the bench from which to observe the A's in action. It was felt there was not enough time left in the season to break him into the minors, so why not show him the majors, why not give him a look at the big time?

Says Blue, "It was scary, from Mansfield to the majors in one flight. I wasn't playing there yet, but I was practicing there. I was on the field with big-name players before games and it was hard to believe. When you're younger, the major leagues was something to be proud of. You wondered how the players got so good. You learned you had to practice. And one day you're play-ing with kids on some little, beat-up high school field without fences and the next day it seems like you're in a huge, fancy major-league stadium and you wonder if you practiced enough, you wonder if you're good enough, or ever will be. You get to pitch batting practice and you're so scared you wonder if you're going to kill someone with a pitch."

One who faced him, Ken Suarez, says, "He threw so doggone hard, nobody wanted to hit against him." Vida Blue had just turned eighteen when he was given a major-league uniform in Kansas City and turned over to the team's new manager, old Luke Appling. Alvin Dark had just been fired. Before the new season would begin, Appling would be out, too. The A's would be gone to Oakland. And Blue would be in Burlington, Iowa.

CHAPTER FIVE

The A's assigned Vida Blue to an instructional league in Arizona the winter after signing him. Here they went to work to polish up their diamond in the rough. In charge of him in Phoenix was William John Posedel, a 61-year-old scout from San Francisco who was coming on to Oakland to coach the pitchers. As "Sailor Bill," he once pitched Portland to a Pacific Coast League pennant, but served only five seasons in the majors and never won more than fifteen games in any season. He pitched for the old Brooklyn Dodgers and Boston Braves in the late 1930's and early 1940's and later scouted and coached for Pittsburgh, St. Louis, and Philadelphia. He had been around and learned his trade and as he says, "The best teachers usually weren't the best players."

Although Posedel taught Vida tricks of the trade, Blue believes he may have lost his curve ball in the process. Vida says, "He changed my whole delivery. He got me away from pitching straight overarm and my curve ball seemed to get away from me. He got me to throwing more three-quarters and I've been hunting for my old curve ball ever since. Other than that, I can't say it hurt me, I have to say it helped me. The main thing was, it helped my control. I was wild before. Now I still couldn't hit spots consistently, but I could get the ball over the plate consistently. And while I was hunting my curve, I could get by because my fastball was alive. That's the main thing. Lots of guys can throw hard, but their ball is straight as a string. I could throw extra hard and my ball moves. It's a natural thing and it's the thing which made me more than others."

He reported to spring training with the A's in Bradenton, Florida, early in 1968. They wanted to take a look at him before turning him over to their minor-league base at Waycross, Georgia. The new manager at the time, Bob Kennedy, says, "He was just a baby, but he could really burn that ball." He gave him one shot at major-league opposition, in an exhibition against the Atlanta Braves at Pompano, and Blue pitched two hitless and scoreless innings. "I was really impressive," he grins. He was somewhat disappointed when they still sent him on to Georgia, but they had no intention of moving him from Mansfield to the majors.

"I liked the way the guys lived in the big-league camp," Vida smiles. "Waycross was something else. It was smaller than Mansfield, I think. You couldn't live good there because there was nothing to do. I rode the bus to and from town. I played a lot of ping-pong and checkers and cards. I wrote a lot of letters home. I was homesick. I missed Mama and my brother and my sisters and my friends. I'd never been away from home before for any length of time. And it wasn't glamorous or exciting like you might think. Maybe I was a big bonus boy, but here I was in Waycross, Georgia, working out and waiting to be sent somewhere."

He was assigned for the season to the A's Class-A Midwest League farm team in Burlington, Iowa. The team was the Bees, the home ballpark was Community Field, and typical attendance was 300 to 400 persons. There was a turnout of 1,046 for the season-opener, however. The municipal band gave a concert, city officials gave speeches and the mayor threw out the first ball. When the ballyhooed Blue struck out seventeen of the Quad City Angels, he was hailed as a hero.

It was a Sunday, an April afternoon and chilly, so cold half the crowd was gone before the game was over. Vida, firing the fast one, struck out seven of his first nine foes, but soon stiffened from the chill. He had a big lead and a shutout until the sixth inning. After a single and a walk, he bore down to strike out two, but then the third baseman juggled a grounder and threw wide to first and a run came across.

After eight innings of three-hit pitching, he was within two of the team strikeout record, but player-manager Jim Hughes sent in another pitcher to pitch the ninth and wrap up the 6–1 victory. Later, Hughes said, "He threw 120 pitches. That was enough. There will be more games, you know." Managers, especially player-managers, do not have much help in the minors and they do not always keep count. He had kept count. He had his orders. This prize was to be protected.

"I was kinda shaky. I just threw the ball," Vida said later. The writer for the local paper, *The Hawk-Eye*, wondered if anyone ever threw it harder. What interest there was in baseball in Burlington turned to Blue. Throwing fastballs almost exclusively, he got off to a swift start, striking out a lot of batters and winning some games. In late May and early June he began to throw a lot of curve balls, too, couldn't control them and began to lose games. However, when he returned to his fast stuff, he regained his winning form.

On the night of June 19, Burlington hosted the Appleton Foxes in a twinight twin-bill and in the seven-inning first game, Blue pitched a no-hit, no-run game, winning, 4–0. He had help. In the second inning, manager-shortstop Hughes made a good stop behind second and threw out the batter. In the fourth, Marty Olson backhanded a ball behind third and threw out the runner. In the sixth, Blue himself knocked down a drive, almost fell, recovered and threw to first for the out. At the final out he was mobbed. "It was some kind of nice," he concedes. "This was Burlington, not Oakland, and that was Appleton's Foxes, not the Baltimore Orioles, but it was pro ball and it was a no-hitter and it was Vida Blue."

He was not always so successful. He lost, 1–0, to the Quincy Cubs, giving up only four hits and fanning fourteen batters in seven innings. John Cox, an infielder for Quincy, says, "Boy, that Blue could really blow the ball by you. He was the fastest pitcher I ever faced in the league. But a batter never knew where his fastball was going and neither did Vida. He'd strike you out on three pitches one time, then the next time he'd throw one in the dirt, two behind your back and one over your head, and then the next time he'd strike you out on three pitches again. He was brutal. About the only thing a hitter could do was to stick the bat out over the plate and hope a pitch hit it."

The curve began to come, and after he beat Cedar Rapids, 4–0, on four hits and thirteen strikeouts, he said, "I got my curve across the plate for the first time in my life. I don't think I could get by forever on just my fastball." Catcher Joe Tassone wasn't so sure. He said, "Blue just blows his fastball by hitters." Manager Hughes said, "The fastball is so good, if the batters ever get to worrying about maybe getting a curve ball, they'll never get around in time to hit the fastball. He has streaks of wildness, but fewer of them all the time. His control actually is unusually good for a hard-throwing young left-hander."

It is more than a myth that young left-handed pitchers tend to be wild. Young pitchers tend to be wild. Control comes with practice and the grooving of a smooth pitching style and the mastery of different pitches. Presumably, young left-handers simply do not get to use their left hand as much in life as young right-handers; many things in life are fashioned for right-handers. Presumably, it takes a left-hander longer to groove his style and gain control. Sandy Koufax is an ideal example. He may have become the best left-handed pitcher of all time, certainly of his time, but he was so wild in his early twenties managers were afraid to use him in games.

At eighteen, in his first professional season, Vida Blue struck out 231 foes and walked only eighty. All the control usually asked of young pitchers is that they strike out twice as many men as they walk. The hard-throwing Vida struck out almost three times as many. He had a smooth style for a youngster, a delivery that was not awkward, and while he was wild sometimes with his fastball and most of the time with his curve ball, he got the ball over the plate far more consistently than most young pitchers his age, and he got it over faster and it moved more than most. However, he lost more games than he won. He lost eleven games and he won eight.

He says, "I was trying to throw too hard and I'd wear out after five or six innings. I was inexperienced and didn't know how to pace myself." He was inconsistent. And sometimes when he was good, he did not get good support. "We did not have a good team," he says. Still, he not only led the league in strikeouts, but had the lowest earned-run average, 2.49, and was selected an All-Star.

Fresh from high school, he never had worked hard through a long season, and while he was not overworked and while the Midwest League did not play a real long season, he still pitched 152 innings over 24 games and was worn out at the finish. It had been a long, lonely summer for him. "I was learning. The skipper, Hughes, was helpful. Just pitching regular was helpful. But losing a lot of games—me and the team—was depressing," he says. "And there wasn't much to do in town. Burlington was just another town. About 40,000 people. I lived in a boarding house. Off-hours, I'd shoot pool, go to movies, go to the park and sit and do my thing with kids. We rode buses or cars to the games. The living wasn't plush and the games weren't big there, but the people were nice."

He was pleasant, extremely personable and lively, and less inclined to kid people at eighteen than he was at twenty-two. He was under less pressure than he was later and felt more relaxed and could be more natural. He made a good impression on the locals, but then, he has made a good impression wherever he has gone.

Hawk-Eye columnist Jim Eland was impressed, both personally and professionally. He wrote:

> *Blue is as articulate off the field as he is on. He is a sharp dresser, not flashy, but neat. His speech is the same. One would think him a veteran of ten seasons. . . . If he doesn't throw his left arm by a hitter someday, he should be one of the top pitching stars in the major leagues in a couple of years. Blue has a great chance because he isn't a temperamental pitcher. He has a blazing fastball and occasionally he'll break off a curve that will light up a few eyes. . . . If you haven't gotten the idea by now, I'm a Vida Blue fan. I'd almost pay my way through the gate just to watch him frustrate hitters. He's got a fast ticket to Oakland, and he's holding it in his strong left hand.*

But the ticket Blue really held in his hand just then was one taking him back to Mansfield. "I was so glad to be home," he says. He kissed his mother and the kids and rushed to the ball-field to find out what was happening in football. They wanted to hear about his baseball, but he wanted to throw the football and work out some new plays with the boys. Suddenly, summers no longer were for vacation and fooling around on the ballfield and winters no longer were for school and playing football. Suddenly, winters were for vacation and for watching others play football and summers were for playing baseball.

Early in 1969 he went to his second spring-training camp with the A's, who had finished sixth, just two games above .500, their first season in Oakland. Finley had fired Kennedy and brought back Hank Bauer for a second shift as skipper of the A's. The tough ex-marine was looking for pitching help and he took a long look at Blue, but he could see he wasn't ready, anyone could see it. The batters saw it and slammed him for eight home runs in a few exhibition games.

Vida explains, "I couldn't get my curve over. When I did, it hung, it didn't break. It just wasn't even a fairly good pitch for me yet. My fastball was very good, but no matter how good a fastball is, you can't beat major-league batters with just a fastball. Major-league batters are quicker with the bat than Midwest League batters and when they start to see they can stop worrying about other pitches and start laying for your fastball, they've got you. You can strike out the first six batters with just fastballs, but then the seventh will get you. And I couldn't get anyone out with my curve ball." He grimaces and says, "I was rotten."

He had to go back down to where he was better than the rest, to sharpen up to where he might be ready to take on the best. He was assigned to Birmingham of the American Association, which is Double-A ball and a big jump up from the Class-A Mid-west League. Here the manager was an ex-catcher, Gus Niarhos, and one catcher was a veteran, Elmo Plaskett, a chubby thirty-year-old from the Virgin Islands. The other catcher was young but talented Gene Tenace. "They helped," Vida says. "I got good receiving in games, the level of play in the league was good, and between starts I could throw to Gus or Elmo, who were old hands and could tell me little things to improve me, like when I wasn't holding the ball right or following through right or striding right."

He had good support here, too, for it was a good team, until the A's called up some players later on and the club fell from first place. The home field was Rickwood Park and only 374 turned out to see his debut, a 13–3 breeze past Montgomery, but as Blue kept breezing past foes, more fans started turning out to see him, but minor-league ball is not big in Birmingham and there still were only 954 fans on hand when he one-hit Savannah, 15–1, in mid-June, and many of these were lured by an offer of free safety razors to the first 100 inside.

For Blue, "It was back to the boardinghouse routine. Birmingham is Alabama and Alabama is the South and Vida Blue is black and southern towns aren't black men's towns. I'm from the South, but Mansfield's my hometown, and I know it, and this was a strange town to me, I didn't know it, and I felt out of place here. It was all right. There were no incidents. I was pitching good, but I wasn't being put up for mayor. I was getting older, stronger, smarter, maturing some, but I had a long way to go. I didn't really see it because I still didn't see how much better the big-leaguers were than the minor-leaguers and how much better I had to get. I went breezing by those boys in Birmingham and I began to think I was the best."

He won ten and lost only three. He struck out 112 and walked only 52. He had a 3.20 earned-run average. The A's had gotten him into the army reserves by then and he was beginning to work off his service obligations with once-a-month flights to Oakland for four-day duty-hitches and then he'd fly back and go back to pitching and he got in 104 innings in fifteen games before mid-July, when he was summoned to the majors.

There had been orders from Finley for Blue to throw his curve as much as possible, but Niarhos reports, "His curve still wasn't right, and his fastball remained his 'out pitch,' but he could get them out in our league with it." The local writers, like Alf Van Hoose, were excited by him and called him "True" Blue, a nickname Finley encouraged. Finley was getting excited and calling the manager and the pressbox for reports on him and calling the writers to build him up. "He'll be my left-handed Blue Moon

Odom," predicted Finley, Odom being hot for the A's just then before a sore arm arrested his progress, and, as it turned out, that was a premature, but eventually conservative prediction.

Finley had been pressuring his manager, Bauer, to bring up Blue, all the while preparing to fire Bauer and move in another manager, John McNamara. The A's improved to fourteen games over .500 that season, but they still hadn't caught up to Minnesota in their division and Charlie O. wanted to unveil his flashy new pitcher for the future. The A's weren't drawing in Oakland and "True" Blue might be box-office bait. Birmingham wasn't drawing, either, so why worry about the fans there?

Blue pitched his last Southern Association game July 16, stifling Savannah, 7–2, on five hits and eleven strikeouts. Finley called the pressbox three times during the game for progress reports and by game's end he was more enthused than ever. He called up Benny Marshall, the Birmingham *News* sports editor, to say, "The fans who didn't go to see 'True' Blue pitch just passed up the opportunity to look over the next Sandy Koufax."

Two days later Blue was called up. In the *News*, Van Hoose wrote, "Vida 'True' Blue flew west at high noon today with a one-way ticket. Birmingham won't see him again. The farm lad has become the man." But Birmingham manager Niarhos wasn't so sure he had attained full maturity yet, though he seemed sure he would star when he did. "This kid is some kind of prospect. What I wouldn't give for a future like his," he said. "But I wrote the A's manager Hank Bauer and the pitching coach Bill Posedel that it might be wise not to put too much pressure on him for a while, that it might be wise to tell him to simply rare back and throw and only occasionally try his curve ball. The curve may not be ready yet." Remembering the spring, he was cautious. So was Vida. "I'm happy about being called up, but not out of my mind like I guess I once thought I would be," he said. "We'll see what happens. I don't think that I've got the boys knocked. I do think I deserve a chance up there."

"Do you think you're ready?" he was asked.

"Do you think I am?" he answered.

No one knew. He didn't. And, as it turned out, he wasn't. Not quite. He was still a year away. He was just turning twenty and was not yet a man. In his first start he lost to the Angels, 5–3. In his next start he beat the Yankees, 6–4. He started two more without winning or losing, then went on relief. Whatever, he was hammered for thirteen homers and a sizable 6.21 ERA in 42 innings.

When Joe DiMaggio, then with the A's, first saw Vida, he said, "Blue throws smoke and throws it for strikes. What more does he need?" After he had seen him in action a few times, he knew. He needed a curve that would work. Later DiMaggio said, "It was a shame to bring up a kid like that when he hadn't pitched two pro years. He throws as hard as anybody, but he hasn't learned to pitch yet. Bringing a kid up to get shelled like that could ruin his confidence."

Instead it served to steel Vida's desire. He could see what his problem was, and it was one he could overcome. He says, "Everyone in the league soon knew I couldn't control my breaking ball, so they'd just lean back and wait for my fastball. It's amazing how fast word gets out. They're very smart up top. One team sees you, spots your weakness and spreads it around. Before they've left town the whole country knows. If I can get them to guessing it might be good breaking stuff, my hard one is tough to handle. But these guys are so good that if they feel they can ignore the other pitches, they can hit the fastest pitch. They didn't get a lot of hits off me, you know. And I didn't walk too many. But they got some big hits. They bombed some Blue-blazers."

Al Kaline hit three-straight home runs off Vida. Harmon Killebrew hit a grand-slam off him. These are outstanding hitters. For a while, Blue saw them in his sleep. He says, "I used to dream about being in the bigs. But the dream turned into a nightmare. It was like walking in a foreign mine field and not knowing where to step. It was discouraging. But it didn't bust my spirit or anything like that. I knew I had room for improvement. I knew what I needed and it wasn't anything I couldn't get. In a way the experience may have helped me. It showed me what I needed. It knocked some overconfidence out of me. It taught me humility. I hadn't been all that much in love with baseball, but now I had new respect for it and I could see I'd have to work and probably keep on working forever to beat it, and I wanted to beat it, I wanted to make it, I really wanted to be a big-league pitcher like I'd maybe never wanted it before."

Bill Posedel and John McNamara encouraged him. Posedel says, "He was close, as close as people thought he was when they brought him up and a lot closer than a lot of people thought after he'd been up awhile and banged around awhile. It sounds like hindsight now, but I saw it then. He just needed variety, a better curve. He had an overpowering fastball. I figured if the experience didn't scare him, he'd soon be overpowering them the way they had been overpowering him. But he didn't scare. He's made of good stuff. I could see that, too. He's a tough sonofagun." McNamara says, "He can take setbacks, which everyone can't take. We were unsettled and he went through a very unsettling time, but he didn't break, he didn't even bend, he just went back to work."

"The hell with it is what I said," Vida says. Hard lights glint in the corners of his eyes.

That winter he went to Fort Bragg, North Carolina, to take infantry training. It was a relief to be away from the pressure of producing in baseball, of living up to a big buildup. "I enjoyed it," he says. "There's nothing there to enjoy, but I enjoyed it. I wasn't going to have to go overseas to fight or anything like that. I did good. I was a squad leader. My name didn't mean anything. Not then. Not yet. They knew I was a ballplayer, but not a big ballplayer. If anyone looked it up, they found out I was just a fancy batting-practice pitcher in the bigs. I served 'em up and the Killebrews put 'em in the seats. In the army I was just another soldier. But a good one. I called cadence. We sang our way through our drills. It's a grind, but it was OK."

Then he went home and tried to explain why a guy his pals never saw lose couldn't win in the majors. That's a hard thing for a kid to handle. Almost all pros were stars in high school days. Most must adjust psychologically to being something less in pro ball, very often not good enough to make it at all. "I'm gonna' make it," Blue predicted.

In the spring he was back in training camp, now in the hot, dry desert-land of Phoenix. Posedel worked with him. Then Warren Hacker, a 45-year-old veteran of eleven years in the majors with

Chicago, Cincinnati and Philadelphia. Like Posedel, he never won more than fifteen games in a major-league season in his career, but he had learned his trade and was now the A's minor-league pitching coach. Although Posedel and Blue thought he had improved enough to be kept, Blue was assigned to the Iowa Oaks of the American Association at the top minor-league level of Triple-A and based at their preseason camp at Mesa and it turned out to be a break for him.

Juan Pizzaro, a 33-year-old Puerto Rican left-hander who had enjoyed one or two big seasons in a thirteen-year major-league career but had never quite fulfilled his enormous early promise and had kicked around, had landed with the A's, his seventh big-time team. He reported late, was left behind when the A's broke camp, was assigned to Iowa and befriended Blue. He helped Vida in Arizona and he continued to help him in Iowa.

"He helped me more than any single person in my career," says Blue. "He is very smart and he had a way of showing me how to do things. He took time with me. It's unbelievable, but with all the coaching I'd had, I really didn't know how to hold the ball to throw the curve right. Juan showed me. He showed me how to move the fastball in and out. He showed me how to conceal my grip on the ball. I think I was tipping off my pitches my first time up in the majors. Maybe minor-leaguers don't catch on, but major-leaguers do. He helped shorten my stride. Hacker helped. Sherm Lollar helped. But Pizzaro helped most of all. And he didn't have to do it. It wasn't his job. He had his own job to protect. He had his own worries. He'd been kicked around some and he'd slipped back to the minors. But he is a good person and he was good to me."

Pizzaro lasted just long enough in Iowa to help Blue. Soon Juan was on his way to Hawaii, then back up to the big leagues with the Cubs. And, as it happened, while the 22-year-old Blue was becoming the sensation of the majors, the 34-year-old Pizzaro was something of a lesser sensation in the National League, in the late going, tossing three shutouts, including a one-hitter. "It did my heart good," Vida grins.

In 1970, with Pizzaro's help, Vida Blue did Sherm Lollar's heart good. Lollar was the 45-year-old former catcher who had played eighteen seasons in the American League with Cleveland, New York, St. Louis and Chicago and now with Hacker had the task of applying the final touches to this talent. Lollar said, "I don't see how anyone can throw harder than Vida." Few could.

Blue missed the first eight games of the Iowa Oaks' season while in reserve duty. He debuted in Des Moines' Sec Taylor Stadium spectacularly the end of April, striking out fourteen and ahead, 7–1, when lifted for a reliever in the seventh. The crowd of 1,240 fans booed the move by Lollar, but Blue had not pitched since a four-inning exhibition stint nineteen days earlier and had run out of steam.

The only run off him came off a homer by Cesar Cedeno, a bright prospect now with the Houston Astros.

One week later Blue flew at dawn from four more days reserve duty in Oakland to pitch against Tulsa. The Oaks were on a winning streak and Vida stretched it to eight with a three-hit shutout of the Oilers. Next out he fanned fourteen in a 3–2 conquest of Evansville as the largest crowd of the season in Des Moines, 3,831, roared for the flash. Former basketball All-Star Cotton Nash did reach him for a home run. "It was one of my best curves," Blue grinned.

He kept winning. His fifth-straight was a four-hit, eleven-strikeout 2–1 triumph in Omaha. His sixth-straight was another fourteen-strikeout show in a 7–2 conquest of Omaha at Des Moines. There were 6,703 on hand that late May game, but there was a reason beyond Blue, it being Farm Bureau night and fans getting in on free tickets. Vida finally was beaten, 5–4, when Washington's nineteen-year-old, $88,000 bonus-baby Jeff Burroughs blasted a two-run eighth-inning home run for Denver. Another streak was snapped when no foe fanned in the fifth inning. Until then Vida had struck out at least one batter in each of fourteen-straight innings.

In his next start he went right back to winning, stopping Evansville, 4–3, and fanning Nash for the final out before 5,083 at the Taylor ballpark. Following this he trimmed Omaha, 2–1, fanning fourteen and permitting only two hits. Next out was his second shutout, 2–0 over Oklahoma City, striking out twelve and giving only four hits. He ran a streak of consecutive innings without an earned run allowed to 22 before finally being bombed, 7–6, by Tulsa in his last start in June. But next out, another free night, this one in Omaha and luring 11,687, Blue captured his tenth victory, 5–3.

At this point he was the most spectacular performer in the minors. Finley was on the phone all the time keeping track of his rising star but reluctant to risk a setback such as Blue had suffered at the end of the prior season. Lollar conceded, "Vida has been just awesome." Indeed, his foes were awed. Wichita outfielder Rich Scheinblum, who had put in a hitch up top with the Indians, said, "Blue's about a foot faster than Sam McDowell." Vida's curve was cracking, making foes defenseless against the fastball.

He was having fun, though frustrated by the A's failure to recall him. He was often in Oakland, but only flying in and out for reserve stints. Missing one, he almost was drafted, which Finley had fixed. Vida seemed to be really enjoying baseball now. Later, looking back on it, Lollar recalled, "My favorite memory of Vida in Iowa is coming out on the field and seeing him already there hitting ground balls to a bunch of kids. He was always the first player at the ballpark, in uniform long before he had to be. There were always several boys around. Some helped the ground crew. Others came with their gloves just to play around. Vida would get them organized for infield practice. He'd coach them, too. He'd show them how to field grounders, and he'd hit to them until it was time for our batting practice. He taught them a lot of baseball and obviously enjoyed doing it. You could see how much they admired him. He really likes the game and he really likes kids."

"I like living," grins Blue. And he was living pretty good at the time, on the verge of a return to the big time, swinging in a big town with his pick of plenty of pretty girls to date, winning regularly. Only at this time, suddenly, he stopped winning. His arm started to feel sore, but he did not say anything through a couple of starts. After a game in mid-July, a puzzled Lollar pointed out, "Vida seems to be forcing his pitches, not following through naturally." Blue admitted, "My arm has been tender the last couple of times out." Lollar promptly sidelined him, checking in with Finley, whose orders were to keep him sidelined a while. The league badly wanted Blue in its All-Star game in Des Moines the third week in July, but on Finley's orders Vida was held out.

Rest rapidly repaired the problem and soon Vida was pleading that he was ready to pitch again. The A's wanted to see for themselves. On Finley's orders Blue was recalled to Oakland, where McNamara and Posedel watched him warm up, then cautiously buried him in the bullpen. At this point the A's were in the pennant race but did not dare use Blue. For eleven games he went to the bullpen and waited, but night after night he was not called on to throw as much as one pitch until the final game, when he was told to warm up and got to throw one pitch while out on the field the opponent was retired at that moment and he was told to sit down again. After the game he was told he was being sent back to Iowa.

"I'm going to go home instead," he snapped. He was deeply disappointed and disturbed. However, he was talked out of his threat. "It was all emotion," he concedes. "It was a waste. My arm was fine. I was ready. They could have used me. They didn't. I was disgusted. But I really wasn't ready to quit."

Reluctantly, he returned to Des Moines and promptly was returned to action. But the season there was almost finished, a month before the majors ended their season, and while he had been gone the Oaks had slipped from first. On August 28, making his first start since July 16, Blue was brilliant, blanking the Triplets at Evansville, Indiana, 5–0, on just two hits and two walks, striking out eleven. After a six-week rest, his arm was strong, the fastball flowing, the curve breaking. There was time for just one more start and it was similarly great. On the first of September he shut out the Royals at Omaha, 3–0, on four hits, striking out sixteen. He had a no-hitter until two were out in the sixth. When he nailed the last out in the ninth his mates mobbed him. But they finished a game out of first.

Blue concluded his campaign at the Triple-A level at 12–3 with 165 strikeouts, the most in the circuit despite his long layoff, and only a third as many walks, 55. In 133 innings over seventeen games, he had posted a 2.17 earned-run average. "I knew now I was ready," Vida recalls. "It was still a mine field up top, but now

I knew where to step. I'd pitched in the big leagues and then watched for a week or so. I was real hungry. I had the stuff now and I wasn't scared or awed anymore. I was ready to go right back up." And right back up he went, more ready than even he realized.

CHAPTER SIX

Across the bay from the vain and aging jewel that is swinging San Francisco sits by stark contrast rough, hard-rock, rebellious Oakland. The first has most of the area's wealth, the second most of the area's poverty. Those in the first span the spectrum from hippies to high society, those in the second seem mostly to be middleground, hardhat and beer-drinking. San Francisco does not have Oakland's black ghettoes or its hunger, but Oakland does not have San Francisco's pretensions.

Along the Nimitz Freeway sit the twin sporting palaces of the Oakland-Alameda County complex—the glass-walled indoor arena and the concrete-and-steel outdoor stadium. Hockey's California Golden Seals and basketball's Golden State Warriors play in the arena, while football's Oakland Raiders and baseball's Oakland A's play in the Coliseum. All but the Raiders are struggling before sparse crowds. Pro football flourishes and the Raiders are a successful franchise.

In San Francisco's windswept Candlestick Park, the pro-football 49ers prosper, too. But the Giants have been having hard times since the A's moved in across the way to divide the sector's baseball enthusiasm. San Franciscans see themselves as too sophisticated to turn themselves over to pro sports without reservation. They have not been able to bring themselves to buy a modern indoor facility. Professional hockey and basketball interests turned from the town, turned to the common man and fine new facilities of Oakland for support, but without success. The sprawling peninsula population is large, the potential large, the turnouts small.

In the hills beyond Oakland it is beautiful, but in the city it is homely with congestion and people turn to the waterways, the forests, the golf courses, the parks, their suburban homes and swimming pools and their television sets for escape. They do not stay in the city or return to the city to buck the traffic jams of the freeways to find fun in a ballpark at the high cost of tickets, parking, food and babysitters, and those who are stuck in the city seldom can afford the fees of fun.

Trying to promote his struggling, expansionist hockey team, Finley gave out free tickets to the games at his baseball games. But his hockey team was a bad team and the crowds were worse. Sighing, he said, "You can't promote a funeral." Before the 1972 season began, he said, "We're so bad, I won't judge our coach until we get him better players." A week after the season began, he fired the coach.

Trying to promote his rising, pennant-contending baseball team, he gave out free bats, helmets, T-shirts, even cars at fan-appreciation day, but telling his few fans he appreciated them did not encourage the rest of the public to turn out. Some promotions produced good turnouts, but then the crowd count would go back down again. The best promotion is excitement on the playing field, but baseball is not by its nature a continually exciting game. It is a skilled and graceful game, but not a fast and rough game, and it takes individuals of uniquely colorful capacity to lend excitement to it. These are few, but Vida Blue was one.

The A's had a good team, but when Blue returned to their roster in September of 1970 they were not quite good enough. He had been wasted in the minors most of the season, and there were eleven days in August when he was wasted in the majors and Minnesota's Twins pulled far ahead in the divisional pennant race.

Promoted by Finley and a constantly changing corps of publicists, the A's had some exciting and skilled players. The third baseman, Sal Bando, was a husky, heavy hitter. The shortstop, little Bert Campaneris, was a base-stealing champion. The right-fielder, Reggie Jackson, was a home run-hitting champion, and a strikeout champion, too. The powerful, explosive, moody Jackson was exciting in everything he did, especially swinging the bat, even when he missed the pitch, but he had not quite caught the fancy of the fans, he did not cater to them, he went his own way. The pitchers, "Catfish" Hunter, "Blue Moon" Odom and Chuck Dobson were young and had shown signs of brilliance. But it was the new pitcher, Vida Blue, who brought real brilliance and captured the fancy of the fans.

They returned him to the majors on the road, in Chicago's old Comiskey Park, and he was nervous and his performance was uneven and he made his greatest impression with, of all things, his bat, hitting a three-run home run in the fourth inning of the first game of a Labor Day doubleheader, helping his team to a 7–4 victory. He did not get credit for the victory. He surrendered seven hits and two walks and four runs and was knocked out in the fifth inning. He says, "I was trying too hard." He sat in sweaty disarray in the dressing room later, swearing at himself, vowing to just be himself, to just pitch his game the next time.

This came four night later in Kansas City, where the expansionist Royals had run off four-straight victories. The A's staff gave Vida a rundown on the Royals' strength and weaknesses at bat before the game, but he says he disregards most scouting reports. "I hadn't been around long, but I'd been around long enough to know it didn't matter what a batter usually did, only what he did against you. Maybe he can't hit someone else's curve ball, but he can hit yours. Maybe he hits fastballs, but he can't hit yours. I got a good memory for such things, but I hadn't seen these guys enough to memorize anything. Maybe one's a good high-ball hitter, but you're a high-ball pitcher, what do you do, try to do something else, something you can't do? I decided to do what I did best, throw the ball hard. I'd show 'em enough of my curve to make 'em careful, then I'd try to blow the ball by 'em. I was prepared to match my strength against their strength."

In the first inning he got Pat Kelly and Cookie Rojas on grounders to second and struck out Amos Otis. In the second inning he got Bob Oliver and Paul Schaal on flies to center and in-between Lou Piniella on a liner to second. In the third he got Ellie Rodriguez to ground to first, he got Rich Severson to fly

to left and he fanned Wally Bunker. In the fourth he retired
Kelly and Rojas on flies to left and had retired eleven in a row
before he walked Otis, but then he retired Oliver on a grounder
to second to retire the side. In the fifth he covered first to put
Piniella out on a grounder to the first baseman, then stopped
Schaal on a grounder to the second baseman. He hit Rodriguez
with a pitch and then walked Severson, but struck out Bunker
again to bail out.

"I knew I had a no-hitter and it made me nervous and I was
wild for a while," he recalls. "All pitchers know when there
haven't been any hits off them and after four or five innings you
can't help thinking about it a little even if you try not to. There's
a danger in getting too careful, especially for someone like me
who doesn't throw so much to spots. I kept telling myself to
just pitch, just throw the ball. It was tense while it was scoreless, but it got a little better when I got a lead." In the sixth
Tommy Davis doubled and Jackson singled him home for the
first run of the game. In the last half, Blue walked Kelly, but got
two outs on grounders by Rojas and Otis and the third out on a
strikeout by Oliver.

There was a stirring in the stands among the sparse gathering
of 6,993 fans. All fans want to see no-hitters, though their interest
is rather sharply divided when it is developing against the home
side. By the seventh there was a lot of sound on every swing and
Blue got by, striking out Piniella, getting Schaal to hit to first and
Rodriguez on a grounder to shortstop. Now only two innings and
six outs stood between him and the no-hitter. And in the first of
the eighth, three hits and an error brought the A's two more runs
and Blue a 3–0 lead. Vida was sweating now and felt better when
Severson flied to right to open the eighth. Then pinch-hitter
Taylor struck out and the fans screamed. But then Kelly picked
out a pitch and lined a clean single and the crowd roared and
the pitcher's shoulders sagged.

"It was a disappointment," Blue recalls, "but what was I going
to do about it, run out to the outfield and get it back, stop play
and say let's do it again? It was gone. But the game was still
there. I said, 'All right, Mister Blue, back to work.' And I went
back to work." He got Rojas to hit to short to retire the side, ac-

cepted condolences in the dugout, then went out in the ninth, walked Otis, fanned Oliver, retired Piniella on a fly to center and finished Schaal with a grounder to third to wrap up a one-hit shutout, 3–0.

In the dressing room his manager, the coaches, his teammates and the writers told him how good he'd been and not to feel bad and that he'd have other chances. He is a calm sort who resists riding the rollercoaster of emotions, who resists giving himself away, who holds himself in. He says, "I don't like to get too high or too low. I didn't feel too bad and I also didn't run right out and celebrate. I felt I'd accomplished something, proven something, but I knew I'd have to do it again. I figured a big thing had gotten away from me but there wasn't much I could do about it and I would, indeed, have other chances."

He had no idea the next big one would come so soon. After his next start, in which he wasn't sharp and was finished in the sixth inning of a 6–5 victory at Milwaukee, he came home to take on Minnesota in his seasonal debut in Oakland. There were only 4,284 fans on hand, but it turned out to be a big night, though for reasons that were not anticipated. This was the night of September 21, the night Minnesota expected to clinch the Western Division pennant in the American League, eliminating the A's, and the pressbox and photographers' loft were jammed with newspaper and television journalists who wished to preserve for posterity the historic moment.

Champagne was chilled on ice in the Minnesota dressing room. Jim Perry, a 23-game winner destined to win the Cy Young Award as the league's best pitcher that year, was pitching for the Twins that night. He had pitched twelve-straight victories over the A's and had not lost to them in four years. The green rookie Blue was going for the home side. Despite his one-hitter against Kansas City, against the Twins he was the underdog. These were not expansionists but the best team in the division.

Blue began by striking out Cesar Tovar. Leo Cardenas flied to right. Then Vida struck out massive Harmon Killebrew. In the home half the A's got him a run when Campaneris tripled and came home on a ground ball. In the second inning, Blue retired Tony Oliva, Brant Alyea and Rick Renick on ground balls. In the third he fanned George Mitterwald and Perry around a ground-out by Danny Thompson.

He was throwing fastballs nine pitches out of ten—they were really humming and darting around—and tempting batters with a curve ball here and there. He says he felt very strong but not especially sure of himself. In the fourth he got Cesar Tovar on a ground ball and Leo Cardenas on a fly ball, but he got too careful working on Killebrew and walked him trying a curve on a 3-and-1 count, the first foe to reach base after Blue had retired eleven in a row. He then got Oliva to ground out to get out of the inning.

Later Vida said, "Killebrew was the one man I was afraid of. He hits the ball a long way. We were only ahead by one run and I didn't want him to tie it with one swing. I didn't want to give him anything he could hit good." And later Killebrew said, "He wasn't giving me anything I could hit. I wouldn't have hit what he was throwing. I never saw the ball. I just heard it hit the catcher's glove. He wasted the walk." Blue did not waste any more. In the fifth he disposed of Alyea on a fly, then struck out Renick. He fed one to Mitterwald that was a bit fat and the catcher ripped the pitch toward left, but shortstop Campaneris darted to his left, leaped and backhanded the ball as Blue breathed a sigh of relief and the fans roared.

By now everyone was thinking no hitter again but no one was saying anything about it. Blue recalls, "I was thinking about it. How could I help it? I couldn't believe I was right back in this spot again. I thought about losing the other one. But this one was early yet. I didn't want to make myself nervous. I wanted to just go on throwing the ball right. More than anything else I wanted to win the game. I didn't want to lose it and let Minnesota clinch the pennant off me here in Oakland. There was no one in the stands. It was just me and them."

Perry was getting the A's out, too, and the score remained 1–0 as the small turnout roared on every pitch.

In the sixth, Thompson popped up, Perry grounded out and Tovar hit a foul behind the plate that catcher Gene Tenace nearly fell into the Minnesota dugout to catch. In the seventh, Cardenas grounded out to shortstop Campaneris. Blue blazed

them to Killebrew, who missed them, striking out. Then Oliva
fouled high off third and Bando went to catch it and almost
missed it, barely snagging it in the tips of two fingers of his glove.
In the eighth, Alyea struck out. Renick hit a grounder wide of
first, Don Mincher fielded it and Blue hustled over in time to
take the throw to retire the runner. Then Mitterwald banged a
hard grounder to third baseman Bando. Sal stabbed it, but it
bounced out of his glove. He recovered rapidly and fired to first
just in time to beat the runner. Now the fans were roaring louder.

The athletes themselves were tense. Blue, sitting silently in
the dugout, was soaked with sweat. When he batted he went out
quickly. But his teammates increased his margin in the last of
the eighth with a five-run flurry, highlighted by a three-run
homer by Campaneris, to up the count to 6–0 against Perry, who
was permitted to remain for the pounding. There was some concern that Blue might have cooled off during the rally. He'd set
down thirteen in a row and had only three to go to get his no-
hitter.

"I was very nervous," he admits. "I made up my mind to just
rare back and fire." Blue was blazing. Thompson struck out. The
fans roared. The tension thickened. Pinch-hitter Bob Allison, a
tough veteran, came up and struck out. More roaring. More
tension. Now it was Tovar, a master with the bat. Vida got a
strike past him. Then another. He admits, "I was shaking so much
I didn't want to throw the ball." Somehow he steadied himself
enough to throw it again, a fastball up and away. Tovar swung
and popped it in the air in foul territory off first and Mincher
moved nervously under it and grabbed it and bedlam erupted.

Vida's teammates mobbed him and helped him off the field
and down into the dugout, where the writers and broadcasters
surrounded him and flashbulbs started popping in his face. The
rookie had hurled not only a no-hitter, but nearly that rarest of
baseball gems, a perfect game, permitting only one batter to
reach base. He sat in his soggy and gaudy green-and-gold uniform, too excited to undress, but, strangely, seemingly the least
excited person in the place. People were yelling and screaming
and he was saying softly, "It's very nice, very nice indeed." People were telling him how great he was and he was thanking

Campaneris and Bando for the fielding plays and hitting behind him that made it possible and telling them how great they were.

Charley Finley was on the phone excitedly calling from Chicago to congratulate him and tell him he had a $2,000 bonus and Tenace, the catcher, he had a $1,000 bonus for helping, and then Blue was sitting back down telling everyone matter-of-factly as if he'd been there a long time and knew all about this thing, "He gives little awards like that for no-hitters, pinch-hit home runs and other such feats. I hope to get more phone calls like that." He smiled, his face shiny with sweat. He would, of course, maybe more than he wanted, though he could not be sure of that. Someone asked with surprise why he didn't seem shaken up. Calmly, he said, "I am. A thing like this would shake up anyone." Then he went to phone his mother.

Over in the Minnesota dressing room, manager Bill Rigney, gray-haired and gracious, had grabbed a bottle of champagne, was holding it unopened in his hands now, and was saying, "That kid has a golden arm. If nothing happens to him, he is going to be one helluva pitcher. He is just great." Then he thrust the bottle to someone to send it over to Oakland for their unexpected celebration. The Twins' celebration would have to wait. And A's manager, McNamara, on his way out, was saying, "Guys pitch no-hitters sometimes. They're not all great. But this one was special. This kid can be great."

And Blue was waiting for the fuss to cease so he could shower and change into civvies and get away from it, which he did after working his way through the autograph-seekers who descended on him outside. Later, much later, when there was time for reflection, he said, "A no-hitter is a funny thing. You don't realize what it means until later, but it gives you an overnight reputation and something you have to live up to, which most can't live up to, and it can be forgotten fast if you can't follow it with some flashy things.

"It's a team thing, you know. It means you pitched good, maybe great, but not necessarily. Usually you had a great fielding play or two behind you along the way. I did. Later, I maybe pitched better in games that weren't no-hitters. I mean maybe I didn't get a great fielding play. Or maybe an ordinary hit went between people instead of right at someone. There's a lot of luck in this game. It's easy to get carried away by things and I think most do, but I try to be a realist. I was very young and I'd done something great, but I didn't want to be carried away by it. I'd rather pitch a ten-hitter and win than pitch a no-hitter and lose. This was nice. I got the no-hitter and I got the win and I knew for sure I belonged, but it scared me that I was so nervous goin' for it and I didn't want my emotions to get away from me over any one game. I want to pitch a long time and I want to be cool about it. That's the big thing. Doin' your job and bein' cool. I got a long way to go."

He went next to Anaheim, where he blew his cool and was thrown out of the game by an umpire for arguing too vehemently after being called out on strikes while at bat in the fifth inning while in the lead, 2–1. He said some things he shouldn't have said and was ejected and went storming down into the dressing room, more angry with himself than with the umpire. They are not fast to take a pitcher out of a game and he knew it. He sat stewing by his locker, tongue-lashing himself while his team went on to win, 4–3. Later he said, "It didn't matter if the call was right, I was wrong. I lost the no-hitter early, but what'd I think, I could pitch a no-hitter every game? I nearly lost my team the game. I let myself get a little swell-headed. I kept telling myself I shouldn't and wouldn't, but I did, but it was the first and last time. I intend to profit from the experience."

On the first of October, the last game of his season, at home against the Milwaukee Brewers, he went seven innings and did fairly well but did not get the decision as his team won, 5–4, finishing nine games behind Minnesota, but sixteen games over .500 and a threat for the future. Blue finished at 2–0 with a 2.08 ERA, 35 strikeouts and 12 walks for 39 innings over six games, with two of the games most memorable ones. He packed up and headed home for Mansfield, knowing he would be back in Oakland in 1971, back in the big time for sure for the first time, and a big reason his team was established as a pennant-contender.

Vida Blue was the first black man ever pictured on the front page of a weekly newspaper in the Mansfield area. There is no photographic record of his early career. But on the fourth of

December, 1970, it was "Vida Blue Day" in Mansfield and he was hailed as a hero. He says, "I didn't want them to give me a day. I didn't want to have anything another black man there, a school-teacher or a clerk in the bank couldn't have. I hadn't done that much yet. I didn't think I deserved it. But everyone said I should be nice about it because it would be a nice thing for the town. And it was nice, nice to be a part of something bringing black and white people together."

What he wanted to do more than anything was to get down to the school where the football team was practicing or to the vacant lot where the young kids were playing pickup games. He filled up on his mom's soul food and headed for the football field. "I just go out to give them some hints. And before I know it, I find myself diagramming plays on the blackboard, giving a little chalk talk here and there."

The former Little League coach bought some neighborhood boys some stuff, putting them through plays even in rain and mud, and organized them into a football team, frequently taking over the T-formation attack and flinging some footballs to the fellows himself. "It's funny," he says, "but when I'm around fourteen-year-olds, I feel fourteen years old. And that's just fine. Fourteen is a fine way to feel, a fine time of life.

"At the same time, it sometimes makes me feel a lot older. I just want to show them some things I know. Show them how to do things right. Not just baseball. Things off the field, too. Things about life. I'm learning. And maybe I can teach them."

He comes alive with kids and seems to relax with them as he seldom can with his elders. It is a cliché that some men are kids at heart, but it is true in Vida's case. He really enjoys himself when he is with youngsters and he grins and romps with them.

Saturdays and Sundays he'd sit in his darkened living room with friends, eyes glued to the television screen watching football, rooting hard, second-guessing, imagining himself on the field flinging that football.

When the football season ended he passed most afternoons in jeans and sweatshirts working out with the DeSoto High basketball team. And nights there would be dates.

It is still winter in Mansfield when spring comes to the South

and Southwest and the major-league baseball teams go into training. The boys were still shooting basketballs in the gym when
Vida Blue packed his suitcase and got a lift into Shreveport for
the flight to Phoenix and the 1971 season, which was to be a season such as few athletes ever have.

In the anatomy of that season, there is the stuff from which
superstars are formed, though seldom so swiftly, and in picking it
apart, in picking the flesh off the bones, there can be seen the
things that otherwise are buried beneath the surface. It was a
grand time and he was grinning with gladness and there was a
great sense of strength and accomplishment and importance in
him. He enjoyed himself, but beneath the skin his insides inevitably began to twist from tension and on his skin invisible blisters
began to form from the scorching spotlight.

He swears he was just trying to protect a place for himself on
the big team's roster as he pitched impressively through the exhibition games of the desert spring, but the drumroll was rising
even then, and in retrospect it is remarkable how ready the
sporting world was to welcome a new idol and how swiftly this
extraordinarily talented man was hurried into headlines, projected
into pressure, shoved into the spotlight.

CHAPTER SEVEN

Vida Blue pitched the Presidential opener to open the 1971 season. He did not win it, but he won ten-straight after it. By then the A's were well on the way to the pennant.

No A's team had captured a pennant for forty years, since 1931, when the franchise played in Philadelphia and the owner and manager was Connie Mack. Owner Charles O. Finley's new manager in Oakland was Dick Williams, a taut, tough former big-league handyman who just failed to last ten years in the majors. The husky, handsome 41-year-old made his mark managing champions in the minors, managed the Boston Red Sox to the World Series championship in 1967, but insulted some temperamental stars with his tough tactics and was fired a year later after the club fell back.

Minnesota's Twins were favored to win their third-straight Western Division pennant in 1971, but Williams' A's were given an outside shot at supplanting them as the team that would get a shot at the reigning Eastern Division and American League champion Baltimore Orioles. The A's had players of exceptional talent who were maturing, as well as balance and depth, which they would bolster as the season progressed. Not all of their key players would have their best years this year, but they would get runs when they needed them, they would stop the opposition from scoring when they needed to, the proper pieces would fall into place to string together victories, while Minnesota's Twins were coming apart, dropping below even the rising Kansas City Royals.

The A's infield was flawed only at first base. Don Mincher eventually would be traded for Mike Epstein, who would take over part-time and hit hot for a while before cooling off. Mike Hegan moved in sometimes, mostly for defensive purposes. Second baseman Dick Green and shortstop Campy Campaneris formed a fine double-play combination. Green was an exceptional fielder and a dangerous if not a good hitter. Campaneris was an erratic but flashy fielder and a lethal lead-off hitter, clever with the bat and brilliant on the bases. At third base, Sal Bando was the club captain, the team leader, good with the glove and power-ful with the bat. Larry Brown was a steady reserve.

There was some platooning in the outfield, especially in center, where Rick Monday, a speedy fielder, alternated with Angel Mangual. Monday slugged in runs in spurts, but had slumps and frequently was removed by reserve Army duty. Mangual, a rookie, came on with consistency. In right, Reggie Jackson was superb. His once uneven fielding smoothed out, his throwing remained potent and, while he struck out a lot and did not have his best year with the bat, he was one of the most awesome sluggers and clutch-hitters in the game. In left, Joe Rudi was a solid regular. However, the veteran Tommy Davis, deadly with men on base, also played there as well as at first base. Curt Blefary could fill in and pinch-hit, too.

Behind the plate, Dave Duncan, defensively outstanding and a smart handler of pitchers, opened as the starter, but improving young Gene Tenace eventually started to share the spot.

The pitching staff was thin but talented. Before Blue blos-somed, Catfish Hunter was regarded as the ace and he was in form for his finest year. Chuck Dobson had a sore elbow, which would sideline him awhile at first and then again at the finish but in between the pain passed sufficiently for him to be exceptionally effective. Sore-armed Blue Moon Odom and veteran reliefer Diego Segui were available for starting chores. The bullpen had two sharp relievers in converted starter Rollie Fingers, whose sinker produced strikeouts, and southpaw Darold Knowles, who

would improve as the season progressed, and the bullpen would
be bolstered when smart, tough old Mudcat Grant was reacquired later on.

Vida gave the big boost. His spectacular success was inspira-
tional and he was the "stopper" who snapped losing streaks before they began and ended frustrations wherever they arose. The
major-league minimum salary is $12,500. He was not, as has been
reported, receiving this. He signed for $14,750. He says, "That's
what I was offered and that's what I took. My no-hitter and one-
hitter of the year before didn't mean much. I was still almost like
a rookie. I had no manager or agent or adviser when the season
started. I didn't argue. I just signed." He was not regarded as a
rookie, because by major-league standards rookies cannot have
pitched more than 45 innings up top in the past and Vida had
pitched 80–42 in 1969 and 38 in 1970—but he really was a
rookie, even though he performed like a veteran.

In the spring, starting early and continuing through late
March, Blue went from good to bad. He no-hit San Diego for
three innings, then two-hit the Lotte Orions of Japan for three,
then Cleveland clubbed him a couple of times and the Angels
attacked him effectively a couple of times. Sometimes the teams
were fooling around with a Finley innovation in some exhibitions
in which the pitchers were only allowed three balls for a walk
instead of four. And, of course, you don't have to be around pre-
season exhibitions in any sport very long before learning to re-
gard them as meaningless. But, still, it seems now as though it
must have been divine intervention that caused A's manager
Williams to go with Vida in the season-opener and especially
again after that.

There were 45,061 fans in the D.C. Stadium on the afternoon
of April 5 to see the Washington Senators open what they did not
then know was to be their last season there. President Nixon
wasn't there for this traditional lid-lifter, but Secretary of Defense
Melvin Laird was there representing him and a former Vietnamese prisoner of war, Master Sergeant Daniel Pitzer, threw out
the "first ball" for him and the mayor of Washington, and Bowie
Kuhn, the commissioner of the major leagues, and Joe Cronin,

president of the American League, and Bob Short, owner of the Senators, and Charles Finley were there, and national sporting attention was there.

Blue confesses he felt as though he were coming unglued at the coming-out party. He tried to throw the ball past the first hitter, Toby Harrah, and the rookie shortstop hit it back past him for a single. Vida got cautious with the second batter, Curt Flood, and wound up walking him. Blue bore down to strike out big Frank Howard, but then Mike Epstein, later traded to the A's, singled to score one. Joe Foy hit to shortstop, but Campaneris made a bad play on it and another came in. Taking no chances, Vida fanned Elliott Maddox to get out of the inning. An inning later, however, after Tim Cullen flied out, Blue walked the pitcher, Dick Bosman, and after Harrah flied out, he walked Flood, and after Campaneris made another error, on Howard, Blue walked Epstein, and then Vida was out of there, walking to the showers, removed by the manager.

He was charged with three hits, four walks and four runs in less than two innings and his team wound up walloped, 8–0, and afterward he admitted he was awful. "The spring was something else," he said. "I threw too many curves, but that was the time to experiment. This was the opener of the regular season and I should have been ready and I wasn't. I was just a thrower, I wasn't a pitcher. I tried to throw too hard and it made me wild. I wasn't natural. I wasn't relaxed. I was nervous. Everybody was. I just wasn't right. And I let the team down. I gave myself quite a talking to. I didn't have nothing made. I had to go out and do it."

He did four nights later, in Oakland against Kansas City. He struck out the first two batters to face him. He gave up a single to Lou Piniella in the second, but struck out two of the next three. He walked one in the third, but struck out three others. After Otis reached base on Campaneris' error in the fourth, Vida fanned two more, Paepke singled, but Schaal grounded out. Blue walked one in the fifth, but struck out another. In the sixth he gave up a single to Otis, but struck out three-straight. He was leading, 5–0, when a rainstorm erupted, washing out the rest of the contest, and it was his first victory, a three-hitter, and he had tied the club record with thirteen strikeouts despite the abbreviated length of the contest.

He says, "After the long spring away and on the road, it felt good to be 'home,' and after the loss in the opener, it felt good to win. I felt relaxed and I was throwing loose and they were swinging and missing. I knew I was getting a lot of K's, though I wasn't trying for them. I wanted the win and was glad to get it."

The A's then had to take off on the first road trip of the season. They had started slowly, but they did not seem concerned. They flew into Milwaukee, having fun on the plane, and when they got off the plane a player took a battery-operated megaphone with him, and when they got on the bus he began to boom wisecracks. Williams stood up in the front of the bus, stuck his hands in his raincoat and said something to the effect that, "If you [obscenities] do not wish to take this seriously, you will find I do. Some of you think you can be awful. Well, I can be worse than any of you. I have rules I will enforce with fines, and I have no small fines. I suggest that you stay in your rooms between games the entire trip and think about playing baseball. And if any of you want to phone Mr. Finley to complain, I have three numbers where he can be reached."

The troops straightened up and went on to win twelve of their next thirteen starts, including the very next one, a 5–0 shutout pitched by Fingers, and the one after that, a 2–0 shutout pitched by Blue. The Brewers got only two hits off Blue, a pop single by Bernie Smith with one out in the fifth inning, and another single by Phil Roof in the eighth. He walked just two and fanned five. Two of the four men to reach base against him were removed by double plays and he wound up facing only 29 batters. "It's funny," Blue says, "but I wasn't sharp. My success amazed me. For the first time I began to realize that if I pitched right I didn't have to be at my best to beat some people. This impressed me. You're one of the best when you can beat the best without being at your best."

Less than 5,000 fans had turned out to see him pitch in Milwaukee, which was a lot less than would turn out later. For his next start, midmonth in Chicago, more than 18,000 were on hand, but this was for a doubleheader. The A's were fighting for first and the White Sox were winning at that time. Blue blanked his foes for five frames to run his streak of successive scoreless innings to 23 before the Sox scored in the sixth on a double by Mike Andrews, a single by Bill Melton and a single by Rich Morales. In the end, Blue breezed to an 11–2 victory, surrendering just six hits and hitting a two-run double himself. Bando batted Segui to a 6–1 triumph in the nightcap for a sweep. Next out, in Anaheim, Hunter blanked the Angels and the A's took over the league lead.

The writers were beginning to say very nice things about the young pitcher, but he had not begun to read them. "I'm more apt to read newspaper accounts of games I lose to see who they blame and what they say about me when I'm bad than I am to read about my wins," he smiles. "I don't have to be told how nice it is when I win. Not that I mind hearing nice things said about me."

In the A's dugout before a game in Anaheim, one of the Oakland players said, loud enough for a writer to hear, "Well, I guess they'll be calling up Vida Blue any day now." And when the writer took the bait and asked, "How can they call him up when he's already here?" the player grinned and said, "He's too good for this league. They'll have to call him up to some higher league." In retrospect, it really is astonishing how swiftly everyone jumped on the bandwagon. Were they waiting for someone like him?

Blue was not at his best but still beat the Angels, 7–3. He gave up five hits, including his first home run of the season. Jim Spencer hit the homer for one run, doubled in another and walked and scored the third on Alex Johnson's double. Afterward, Vida was dissatisfied with himself. "I don't like giving up home runs," he said. "I don't like giving up hits with two strikes on the batter or two outs in the inning, because that means maybe I let up and I don't want to do that. Spencer is a left-hander and he shouldn't hit me that hard."

The Los Angeles *Times* headlined BLUE IS BEAUTIFUL, but Vida said, "I got to do better." And he did in his next start, at home against Baltimore.

Before the game, Blue asked, "Who's pitching for them?"

Someone said, "Pat Dobson." Vida asked, "Is he left-handed or right-handed?" Someone asked, "What the hell do you care?" And switch-hitting Blue said, "I care 'cause I'd rather hit left-handed." And someone said, "Good Lord, man, you're not going to beat them hitting against them, you've got to beat them pitching against them. They're the world champs." And Blue said, "I'm concerned about my hitting. I can help myself with my hitting." And someone laughed and said, "You're the worst hitter I ever saw. You may make us rich pitching, but if we have to depend on your hitting, we might as well go to the poorhouse right now."

Vida was on his way to wealth, however.

In the first inning, after a walk with one out, he struck out Merv Rettenmund and Frank Robinson. In the second inning he struck out Brooks Robinson and Dave Johnson. In the third he struck out Dobson and escaped unscathed despite an error behind him. And in the last of the third he got his hit off Dobson, beating out a bunt. Campaneris also beat out a bunt to advance him to second. Vida then was thrown out trying to steal third, but Campy took second on the play and scored on a single by Jackson, and that, as it turned out, was all Blue needed.

Another error in the fourth did not rattle him and he struck out Brooks Robinson again to retire the side. He set the side down in order in the fifth. He worked out of a sixth inning jam that developed when Don Buford singled for the first hit off him and Rettenmund walked by getting the dangerous Frank Robinson for the third out. He struck out Blair and, for the third-straight time, Brooks Robinson in the seventh. He got three in a row in the eighth. He gave up hits to Rettenmund and Frank Robinson with one out in the ninth, but got Blair and Brooks Robinson on fly balls to finish off his fifth victory and third shutout.

In their dressing room the Orioles seemed awed. Brooks Robinson said, "His fast ball was rising, really hopping. I was swinging and missing." Frank Robinson said, "That's the best stuff I've seen in a long, long time." Manager Earl Weaver said, "If we could have looked for the fastball leaving the bench we'd have been all right, but we couldn't do that. He kept getting the curve over and we didn't know what to expect. And when you have to wait on a fastball like that kid throws, forget it. We got four hits and were lucky to get those."

In the A's dressing room, manager Dick Williams said, "This kid is another Koufax and he's at twenty-one what Sandy was at twenty-six. He's five years ahead of himself. He works at improving himself, he doesn't rattle, he has poise and confidence and a rare arm." Captain Bando added, "He's just starting and he's already the best left-hander in this league outside of Sam Mc-Dowell and in a few more games I may be ready to say he's better than anyone."

Later, Blue said, "That night was a turning point. A lot of people made up their minds about me that night. Few people came out to see me pitch, less than 7,000. Those that came wanted to see what the mighty Orioles could do with this little rookie. The Orioles wanted to see. I think my own teammates wanted to see. I guess I wanted to see, too. Well, we all saw.

"I was getting all my stuff together by then. I was strong and throwing the fast one hard and getting a good enough curve over enough to keep them off balance and guessing, and my control was good. They came at me pretty good and I could tell by the expressions on their faces they knew I was for real after a while. I could tell by the way my own teammates looked at me and acted around me they really realized for the first time I was for real.

"I knew, too," he smiles.

Among the most impressed was Finley, who wanted to cash in on his new star's bright light. Charlie O. called him in and made him an offer. As Vida remembers it, Finley said, "Baseball is a business and we have to sell it. People buy colorful personalities. A colorful nickname will help you. An unusual real name will help you even more. Why don't you change your middle name to 'True'? We'll call you True Blue. We'll tell our broadcasters to call you True Blue. We'll even put 'True' on the back of your uniform. How's that?"

Vida was startled, taken aback. He said, "No, sir. I don't think I'd want to change my name."

Finley said, "I'll make you an offer. I'll give you a $2,000 bonus if you'll go down and get your name legally changed. It will be a great thing for us and for you. It will make you famous faster."

Vida said, "No, sir, I'm sorry. I really don't want to do that, not for any amount of money. I don't like nicknames or funny names. I like my name, Vida Blue, just the way it is. It's an unusual name as it is. It was my father's name. It means 'life' in Spanish. I'm proud of it. I'd like to keep it just the way it is."

Not used to being refused, Finley shrugged, "All right, have it your way. But if you change your mind, let me know."

Later Vida wondered, "Why doesn't he change his name to True O'Finley?" When writers asked him about it, and he thought about it, Vida spoke resentfully, as though he felt he had been insulted.

Finley insists he meant it as no insult. He says, "It's true I asked him to change his name. I thought it would be good for business and good for baseball and good for him, and I still do. But I wasn't trying to buy him off or insult him. And I'm hurt that he tells people about it and that this story has gotten out in such a way as to make me look bad.

"I think youngsters of today don't understand what the old saying 'true blue' means. It means something that is good, something you can count on. It would be a good name for him and I only meant good for him."

Vida shrugs and says, "I guess he meant good."

There were times he was not so sure. Warming up to pitch a few nights later, he noticed that on the message board in bright lights was the information that the starting pitcher for the night was someone called "True Blue."

Vida stopped, shook his head and asked a writer standing nearby, "You see that?" Assured he had, Vida said, "I just can't believe he's serious."

Finley was serious. He had asked the team's radio and television announcers, Monte Moore, Red Rush and Bob Elson, to refer to Vida as "True Blue." Vida asked them to stop.

He asked the team's publicity director, young Michael Haggerty, to keep "True Blue" off the message board and out of the press releases. And he asked some of the writers to lay off it.

The veteran Elson thought the term "Blue Boy" appropriate,

repeated it regularly on his broadcasts and suggested it as the title of the book on Vida, who shuddered and suggested he skip that one, too.

Vida didn't even like it when his own mother persisted in calling him "Junior." He was a junior, but usually when the senior passes on, the "junior" is dropped. Vida said, "When I'm called 'Junior' it makes me feel like a little boy, and I'm not a little boy anymore."

He admitted he liked his last name, Blue. He said, "Blue is my favorite color. I buy a lot of blue things, including a lot of blue clothes. I have a blue comb and even a blue toothbrush. It's sort of special. But I don't like all those nicknames and all that playing around with the name—'True Blue,' 'Blue Boy,' 'Blue is beautiful'—it drives me up a wall.

"I like the name 'Vida Blue.' I feel as though I am honoring my father every time I put it in headlines. He is gone now, but his name lives on through me. I think when Mr. Finley suggested I change it to 'True Blue' he was being selfish. I don't think he realized I'd have to live with it. Well, I wouldn't have any of it."

When Finley signed a black schoolboy pitcher out of Detroit named William DeVault Daniels and announced his nickname was "Sugar Bear," Blue would not believe this was a name which the youngster had acquired in Detroit and felt it had to have been hung on him by Finley. When Daniels reported to the A's for publicity purposes, Vida refused even to pose for a newspaper photo with the youngster unless the photographer agreed to leave the nickname out of the caption.

Blue also did not like being called "The New Sandy Koufax" or "The Black Koufax." When one night someone said to him, "You remind me of Sandy Koufax," Vida acted surprised and said, "Do I? Gee, I didn't think I looked Jewish."

He was also being compared with flame-throwing Sam McDowell who'd enjoyed a big 1970 and was just beginning to slide into what would be a little 1971. Toward the end of April, Cleveland came to Oakland and McDowell was matched against Blue. McDowell had six-straight victories over the A's over two years, but Blue was going for his sixth-straight of this year and his reputation was growing. Cleveland's Ken Suarez, a reserve catcher for five years and normally pleased when given a start, was told he would start that night. But when he picked up a paper and saw that the opposing pitcher would be Vida Blue, he admitted, "I said to myself, 'Vida Blue! Gawd, what am I doing here?'"

Before the game, Oakland sportswriter Ron Bergman asked Vida if he'd read Cleveland's team batting average, only .190.

Suspiciously, Blue asked, "What're you trying to do, psyche me out?"

The teams were scoreless for five frames. With one out in the sixth, Vada Pinson doubled and Chuck Hinton singled for a run off Blue. Vida walked two before bailing out of the jam. But he stayed behind until the last of the seventh, when Green singled. Vida himself singled. Brown sacrificed. Rudi walked. Jackson whiffed. But Davis cleared the bases with a double for a 3–1 lead. That was all Blue needed. He stopped the Tribe on six hits. He had permitted just six earned runs in his six-straight victories.

He lounged back in his locker area receiving the press with a grin, funning with the fellows, and Rick Monday looked over and said, "It's frightening to think that he's his age and has all this poise. I still get nervous and I've been up awhile. He just got here and he acts like he's been here forever. Well, maybe he should have been. He sure belongs."

In the manager's room, Williams was saying, "All I knew of him before this season was what I heard around the office this winter, but I didn't believe it. Then I saw him in the spring and right away I saw that he was special. Not that he did anything special, but if you've been in this game awhile, you know. I said to myself, 'This is a special kid.'"

Blue was saying, "I'm having more fun than I ever had in my life. Where has this been all my life? Big ballparks, fancy hotels, nice people. The big leagues sure are nice. When you're winning. And I'm winning. You go first-class. Everything first-class for Vida Blue. The writers run you ragged, but you got to give 'em the time, they put your name up in lights. The fans always want those autographs, but you got to sign, they pay your salary."

Before games he stood in front of a mirror in the clubhouse complaining that his uniform was not tapered enough, tugging at his shirt and pants until he got them just right. He rubs his chin.

"The biggest mistake I ever made in my life was spending a dollar-nineteen on a razor. Now I have to shave every two weeks," he says, "just like clockwork."

He was relaxed before games, riding up and down the press and players' elevator, pressing the buttons, teasing the elevator girl, Terry. He was relaxed enough before games to lie down on the training table and nap for 35 to 40 minutes before he had to go out to warm up.

In the clubhouse he ran T-formation plays with the clubhouse boys. "Beware the blitz," he yells. In the outfield he runs pretend pass-patterns. Reaching up to grab a phantom football in full stride, he shouts, "I not only am the world's greatest passer, but the world's greatest pass-catcher." Tommy Davis says, "Too bad you can't throw to yourself." Vida Blue says, "If I could, I would." He is but a boy, and having fun, the time of his life. He gives off great gleams of joy.

He says, "On the field, I am all business. My hero is Bob Gibson. He doesn't mess around on the mound. He just goes out there and gets the job done. It's a mental thing. He knows he's going to do it and he makes you know it. He don't waste many pitches. He don't waste nothing. I don't want to imitate anyone. Not their style. It's nice being compared to a Koufax, but if I take it to heart I might get to striding like he did or throwing like he did and mess myself up. The only thing I want to imitate is an attitude, like Bob Gibson's. I don't mess around. When I go out there, I'm all business. I just want to do my job and maybe get a raise."

So he goes out there chewing on a toothpick or maybe a wad of bubblegum. "They're part of my equipment," he says. And the big No. 35 runs to and from the mound. He has been described as the first pitcher in major-league history who runs to and from the mound. Happily, he says, "The A's are a hustling ballclub. I figure I should be in there hustling with the rest of them. They say pitchers ain't athletes, but this one is. If they can run on and off the field, so can I. It's like a trademark." He runs with that high-prancing gait, almost rapping his rear with his heels. He bounces, as though with joy.

Leading the league by 2½ games, the A's opened a road trip in

Detroit. The Tigers set Dean Chance to face Vida. In 1964, when Chance was twenty-three years old, a tall, strapping farmboy from the Midwest, he won twenty and lost nine for the Angels. He led the American League in complete games with fifteen and shutouts with eleven and set a record by winning six 1–0 games. He had the best earned-run average in baseball, 1.65. He was better than Koufax that year. And a couple of years later he won twenty again and led the league in innings pitched and hurled a no-hitter. And now, just a few years later, still only twenty-nine, he was pitching for his fourth club in four years and having his fourth-straight bad year.

A nice guy, a fun-loving guy, but tough, hard as flint, he stood in the Detroit dugout and looked across at Blue and said, "He has to know it can happen to him, too. It comes fast and it can go fast. It's all in the arm. One day you can throw tomatoes through brick walls. The next day you can't dent a pane of glass with a rock. It hurts but you hang on hoping it'll come back." He grinned, "Oh, well, it's a helluva ride, the one on the way up. You only live once and I wouldn't have missed it for anything. I hope he enjoys it. The ride down is a lot rougher. I don't guess he wants to hear about that now."

In the Oakland dugout, told this, Blue made a face and said, "I know, I know, but I don't want to know."

Billy Martin, the tough, fiery little Detroit manager, had his Tigers worked up. Opening up, Mickey Stanley worked Blue for a walk. Jim Northrup flied out, but Vida, remembering the three-straight homers Al Kaline hit off him in 1969, was extra careful with Kaline and walked him, too. With two on, Blue went to his blazer and struck out burly Willie Horton and Bill Freehan to retire the side. Ed Brinkman singled to start the second but was thrown out trying for two. Jim Northrup singled with two out in the third but was also thrown out trying for two. In an effort to even the odds against Blue, Martin's men were gambling and losing.

Opening the fourth, Blue walked Kaline again, then Horton, but then struck out Freehan, Rodriguez and McAuliffe in a row. In the A's half, Jackson singled, stole second and scored on Bando's single to give Vida a lead. In the fifth, Stanley beat out a bouncer with two out but was stranded when Northrup flied out. In the A's half a four-run outburst drove Chance to cover and made it 5–0.

Angry with himself for having been so cautious to Kaline on his first two trips, Blue went strength to strength with the veteran star to open the sixth and struck him out. Horton singled, but Vida got the next two. And the next three in the next inning. And the three after that, including Kaline on a second-straight strikeout. And the last three, including Horton on a second strikeout, to end the game.

While Chance was losing his sixth-straight, Blue was winning his seventh-straight, his fourth shutout, a four-hitter. Williams said, "He was like a guy who was trying to throw through a wall all night . . . and could do it." The manager shook his head as though to get it straight and said, "I'd be lying if I said this spring I expected him to come this fast. I expected him to be a starter but not a star, not yet. He's fooled me, he's come so fast. No one coulda seen it." Rival manager Martin snapped, "He's hot, that's all. He'll cool off."

Blue sat, smiling, soaking his arm in a tub of ice water to speed the healing of the blood vessels that are burst by the exertion of pitching, towels draped around his dark, damp shoulders, his body lean and powerful-looking, and he said to the writers who surrounded him, "Your Tigers were talking about how they were gonna do this and that to me, so I said, 'We'll see,' and we saw, but don't get me wrong, I respect them. I walked Kaline a couple of times because he hit some out on me before. It's no disgrace when a guy like that hits some out on you. It's gonna happen. I respect them. But I want them to respect me, too." His smile widened. "Down deep now I think they do."

The writers were coming to see him in every city. The newspaper writers were doing columns and stories and two-part and three-part stories on him. And *Time* and *Life* and *Sports Illustrated* and *Sport* magazine and *Newsweek* had assigned writers to him who were preparing cover stories or major stories on him. He didn't understand that this wasn't the usual thing, that some good players played ten years without many, if any, major stories being written about them, that some of these magazines seldom did major stories on sports figures, but the other players told him, they teased him.

"Hey, Vida Blue, can I ride on your coattails?" asked Tommy Davis, who was living with Blue and Spider Hodges in an Oakland apartment.

"If you don't muss the material," grinned Vida.

He was trying to fit all the writers in, but no more than he finished with one than another turned up. There wasn't room on his schedule for them all. He had to be at the ballpark even on nights he didn't pitch. He had to prepare for pitching on his off-nights and he wanted to be free to concentrate on pitching on work-nights. He wasn't drawing distinctions between writers for the major magazines and those for small newspapers. He wasn't that interested. He treated them all alike. He answered their questions, and they all seemed to ask the same questions. In every city there seemed to be a dozen radio stations that sent interviewers with portable tape-recorders pleading for five minutes with him, and he sat still for all of them and the minutes mounted into hours and hours and hours.

After a television interview, a broadcaster complimented him with, "You have a lot of poise for a young man."

Vida smiled and said, "Well, I'm not Sidney Poitier yet."

He was fast becoming famous. The team went into Baltimore for a series between the divisional leaders. In a coffee shop there, Blue was having breakfast with fellow ballplayers Reggie Jackson and Steve Hovley when a lady decided they probably were ballplayers here in the hotel where the visiting teams stayed and approached them and said, "I'm a baseball fan. I live and die with the Orioles." She pointed to a balding man standing in the corner. "My husband, Sam, there, couldn't care less." She pushed a pad at them and asked for their autographs. Steve signed. She looked at his signature and her expression did not change. Reggie signed and her eyebrows arched. Vida signed and she suddenly squealed, as others turned in their direction, "Oh, my God! Sam, Sam, Vida Blue, Vida Blue!"

After two rainouts a Sunday doubleheader was set between the two teams, aces set to go in both games. Catfish Hunter was to face Mike Cuellar in the first game, Blue was to duel Jim Palmer in the nightcap. Blue was the big gate-attraction. Baltimore fans wanted to see their side show up this young man who had stifled the Orioles in Oakland. Baltimore is not a big baseball town. The Orioles have not drawn the way other winners have in other towns. But 43,307 fans turned out this time. The next game there would draw 5,577.

In the opener, Hunter coasted to his fifth win on a four-hitter, 6–2, as Cuellar caved in with wildness. In the nightcap, Blue blazed to his eighth win on another four-hitter, 2–1, as Palmer suffered his first loss after five-straight triumphs.

Blue gave up one run in the fourth inning on a walk, a single by Brooks Robinson and a sacrifice fly by Dave Johnson. And for a while it appeared it would be one too many. After allowing a lead-off single by Campaneris, Palmer retired eighteen A's in order. The A's struck in the seventh. Rudi and Jackson singled and moved to second and third on a wild throw from the outfield. With Epstein up, Palmer made a wild pitch, Rudi coming home. When catcher Andy Etchebarren ran the ball down and threw back to the plate he threw wild and the daring Jackson ran home with the winning run. Vida fanned Johnson for the final out.

After the game a Baltimore writer asked Blue, "Don't you think Palmer outpitched you?"

Blue looked at him for a moment, then shrugged and said, "Yeah, but I outwon him."

He'd had a sore throat and a touch of the grippe and had gotten out of bed feeling bad and gone to the mound feeling bad and worked hard, throwing many more pitches than usual, 132, and now he was exhausted, and he went back to his room to play dominoes with Mangual. They had dinner sent up to their room. Blue didn't want to go out. He had beaten Baltimore again, brilliantly, but the shine seemed to be coming off his pleasure. The writers still were coming around constantly. He didn't want to see them, but he saw them. The phone was ringing all the time. He didn't want to answer it, but he answered it.

"Are you happy?" he was asked.

"I don't know about being happy," he said. "What's happy? I can get things I want now. Now that I can get them I don't seem to want them as much."

On the road, *Oakland Tribune* writer Ron Bergman was complaining to a hotel desk clerk about his room. Blue came up behind him. "Bergman, have you ever lived in a ghetto?" he asked.

On the road, traveling secretary Tom Corwin handled press requests concerning the A's, which, although they were in first place, mainly were for time with Vida. The A's publicist, Michael Haggerty, did not get to travel with the team. An energetic young man from Chicago, he was besieged by press requests concerning Blue and kept in touch with the team by telephone. Mr. Finley also kept in touch with him by phone. It might ring at any hour of the day or night with a request which, of course, had to be honored. Haggerty considered disconnecting or destroying it. Sometimes, to get some sleep, he simply took it off the hook. He would not last the year out, but then A's publicists seldom do. He would quit just before the season ended. Most of the season he would be besieged. "I see Blue more than I see my wife," he sighed.

Monte Moore, the team's lead broadcaster for ten years and a loyal organization man and a good man, also helped handle public relations and publicity requests, which were now mainly about Blue. Other A's broadcasters did not last long. Al Helfer had come and gone in one year. Harry Caray had come and gone in one year. Red Rush had come in now and he would be gone at year's end. Bob Elson had also come in now and he also would be gone at year's end. He had lasted thirty-seven years with the White Sox in Chicago, but he would last only one year with the A's in Oakland. Elson was saying, "It's some kind of year to be here. It's been some years that I've been in baseball and I've never seen anything like this Blue boy. Did you know I call him 'The Blue Boy'?"

From Finley came orders that the team was to be called only the A's, never the Athletics. They were Finley's A's, not Connie Mack's old Athletics from Philadelphia. Moving them from Kansas City, he spent $500,000 to publicize them in Oakland, where they drew only 700,000 fans in 1970. But now it was 1971 and the team was leading the pennant race and Vida Blue was leading in the pitching and publicity race. Finley was planning a cow-milking contest, a hot-pants day and even a Vida Blue Day. The story was spreading that the hottest property in the game was making a mere $13,000 for the season, which wasn't true, but which wasn't far from the truth and which Blue did not deny and which Finley did not deny. There was speculation that Finley might tear up Blue's contract and renegotiate a new one for him, but this was not true, either, for if Finley did this, he would then have to open negotiations for the following season on the new, higher level, which he did not wish to do.

Not that Finley would not do something for his player. Blue was Finley's boy and Charlie would take care of him. Charles O. Finley sat back in his leather-covered chair in his Michigan Avenue insurance office in Chicago and said so, sweat staining circles on the armpits of his shirt as he worked in his shirtsleeves on a hot day with the air-conditioning turned low, answering the phone and shouting at his secretary and talking to writers like Leonard Shecter of *Look* and Armand Schneider of the Chicago *Daily News* and others who were seeking interviews and would continue to do so as long as Finley's A's were hot and his hottest player was the most underpaid superstar in baseball.

Finley, talking on the telephone: "How many shares can we get? Good. Get 'em!"

Finley, talking to his secretary: *"Roberta!"*

Finley, propping his feet in white loafers up on his desk: "First pair of white shoes I've had since high school. The kids on the club said, 'Boss, why don't you get with it?' So I got these white shoes."

Finley says, "Most of the things I proposed to the baseball people they resented because they live in the dark ages. Some of the things they have adopted or begun to adopt—night All-Star games, night World Series games, colored uniforms, special promotions—but only after waiting until it looked like their own ideas. Other ideas of mine they have not adopted but should have adopted.

"All teams in the same region should be in the same league. It is stupid that the Cubs and the White Sox, the A's and Giants, the Angels and Dodgers, the Yankees and Mets do not play each other regularly. These are great natural rivalries and these teams

should be competing with one another for honors. It would cut
travel costs and increase gate receipts. It would also stimulate
attendance if all teams in all leagues met each other at least a
couple of times each season. It is stupid that a fan in Kansas City
never gets to see a Willie Mays in the flesh all his career, that a
fan in St. Louis can't see my Vida Blue."

Finley says, "We in baseball know what our problems are and
we can correct them, literally overnight. Overnight! It's stupidity
that we don't. Gross stupidity, which is 144 times worse than
plain stupidity. And stupidity I can't stand. Laziness and stupidity. My God, when you're in business and you know sales are
slipping and not keeping pace with the increase in the population and you do nothing about it, that's stupid. When you see
other games have more excitement than yours and are taking
popularity away from you and you do little to add excitement to
your product, that's stupid."

Why doesn't he turn up the air-conditioning? He is not afraid
to sweat. He says, "Sweat plus sacrifice equals success. The three
S's. Life is that simple. But everyone isn't willing. I've put a lot
of sweat and sacrifice into success in business and I've put a lot
of sweat and sacrifice into success in sports, and I'll succeed in
sports as I succeeded in business. If you want to see the sunshine,
you gotta weather the storm. Well, my early years in baseball in
Kansas City were awfully stormy, but now in Oakland I can
finally see through the clouds and now I'm looking for that pot of
gold at the end of the rainbow. The sun is starting to shine on me
now."

He said, "I've lost a lot of money and I've lost almost all my
hair. I've been ridiculed. I had to ask my family to make sacrifices. I had to make sacrifices in my business. My team wasn't
good enough to bring out fans while I was in Kansas City and I
couldn't survive on $56,000 a year in radio and television money.
I brought a bunch of babies to Oakland but at least I got $5
million in radio and television money for five years to help me see
the storm through. I've been making money there ever since, and
now that our youngsters are maturing to the best in baseball I
hope the fans will begin to support us."

He sighed and said, "I've been ridiculed for firing managers but I've paid them well and as in any other business that is run with good sense if men don't do the job the boss feels they should do he should replace them with someone who may do a better job. I have a good manager now and we are winning with him as I thought we should have begun to win a few years ago. I feel the players I've given my managers were ready a few years ago. I was ridiculed when I became my own general manager, but I've brought my team good players.

"I work at the job. Take the year I went to the College World Series to look over Rick Monday of Arizona State. Monday looked fine and we signed him for $105,000. But I saw this boy Sal Bando out there, too, and I told my scout, 'If he's still around in the second round, take him.' We did and gave him a $35,000 bonus to sign. Reggie Jackson came from Arizona State, too, and we gave him $80,000. I've never been slow to spend money to get the best. I paid $100,000 to get Larry Brown just to give us a reserve infielder for our bench. Esposito and Knowles cost us $300,000, Locker $75,000. I offered $500,000 for Sam McDowell a few years ago. On the other hand, I let a valuable property go, Ken Harrelson, because he was hurting us, I just gave him his release.

"I paid $65,000 for Dick Duncan, $35,000 for Mike Hegan, $25,-000 for Dick Green, $25,000 for Joe Rudi, $25,000 for Pat Dobson.

"Sometimes it takes more than money to get someone. Campy Campaneris was a bargain at $500 because of good scouting. You know how I signed Blue Moon Odom? I went down to Macon, Georgia, and I sat there in the first row of the auditorium in that Negro high school the night he graduated. That day I'd rented a half-ton truck and loaded it with vegetables and chicken and all kinds of food and took it out to his house. That night, I signed him for $75,000 a half-hour after graduation. I went to Hertford, North Carolina, to sign Catfish Hunter for $75,000.

"These are my kids, my babies. When I bought this team the cupboard was bare. We started from scratch and have built a giant. And this is a young team which is just beginning to develop its muscles. It will get better. Last year Vida Blue told me he was going to win twenty games his first full year in the majors. I knew right away this was the kid for me. I'd never met a player so determined and aggressive. With kids like this, we're going places.

"But all I hear about Blue now is how much money he's not making and how much he should make. There should be more to this than money. We are in the midst of a season, going for a pennant, which should come first. There is pride of performance. We paid Vida a handsome bonus. Now he must produce, which I say, frankly, he is doing. If he does it over a period of time, he will be paid accordingly.

"I am a businessman and this is a business. We operate in a businesslike manner. Take Tommy Davis. We sold him and his $72,000 contract to the Cubs last year. Then the Cubs released him and he's playing for us again for $37,500 and he's doing one great job for us. He no longer is a $72,000 player, but he will be paid properly based on the job he does."

The graying owner sighs and says, "Too many players, too many people expect something for nothing. I pay for value received. I pay a lot to sign a player and I do not expect him to hold me up for a veteran's salary the second he does something good. When players request ridiculous raises right away they never remember the big bonuses paid them.

"If someone isn't willing to sweat and sacrifice for the success of this organization, let them go. If they don't go on their own, I'll see that they go. I don't care how many people come and go. The team and the organization come first. Those that produce will share in any prosperity."

Finley said, "Vida Blue is beautiful. He is what baseball needs. I am going to promote him and he is going to get publicity and he is going to be great for the entire game. Don't you worry about him making money. He is going to make money. He is going to get more than money. He is going to get great things from this game. I am going to see that he gets great things. I am going to protect him."

A writer asks A's manager Dick Williams, "How many games can Blue win?"

Williams smiles and says, "How many games can he pitch?"

Finley suggests to Williams that he pitch Blue only every fifth day instead of every fourth day as he originally was set to do and as most mound stars do. "We must protect him. We must save his arm. He is our future," Finley says.

Williams agrees. Williams is a tough man. He can work with a boss. He recognizes that a boss has rights. But he will fight for a manager's rights, too. In this case, there need be no fight. He agrees.

Blue disagrees. "I am young and strong and healthy. I have a good body and my arm is strong. I am learning. The more I pitch, the more I learn. The more I pitch, the more I can win and the more I can earn. I don't need any extra rest. I want to work regularly."

Later he admits, "I had begun to think winning in the majors was easy for me. I had begun to be carried away with my winning. It's only human nature, I suppose. No one was challenging me. Everyone was telling me how great I was. I began to believe it.

"I never thought I was a superstar. I always figured you should wait two or three years to see what type of ballplayer you really are. But I was beginning to see where I might wind up being one.

"People were beginning to talk about my winning thirty, which is a magic figure. I thought twenty would be plenty. That's what most pitchers aim for. Reggie Jackson earlier told me I was good enough to maybe win fifteen my first year. That seemed like a lot then, even to me. He underestimated me, but so did I. It wasn't his fault, but I thought about fifteen as a sort of ceiling for a while, like it wasn't possible to win more. And now it was only mid-May and I was already going for number nine."

He went for it in Kansas City and he wasn't sharp. "I was too relaxed," he says. Three singles brought in a run off him in the third. A single, a walk and a double brought in another in the fourth. A triple and a fly plated third in the fifth. He gave up only those three runs and the A's rallied to win, 5–3, on two-run hits by Davis and Campaneris, but Blue was removed for a pinch-hitter in the eighth inning and Bob Locker got the victory. Vida had pitched eight-consecutive complete games. He had given up no more than six hits in any of them. He had given up eight hits in seven innings in this one. And he went home with the team and was wiser than before.

"The Royals weren't a bad team. They were in second place. They were playing well. They let me know they were out there. It knocked some of the cockiness out of me. It brought me back to earth," he says. "All the way on the flight home, way up there in the air, I was thinking I got to keep my feet on the ground. It was just another game. It wasn't even a loss. But it wasn't a win for me and I'd begun to think they all would be."

The next one was, on the ninth in Oakland against Milwaukee. Vida gave up a single to Roberto Pena in the third, a single to Danny Walton in the seventh and a single to Ron Theobald in the eighth and that was all. He shut them out, 3–0, for his ninth-consecutive victory and his fifth shutout.

He says, "This one was significant because I warmed up bad and wasn't able to throw hard. I don't know why. You never do. But sometimes you warm up bad and throw good and sometimes you warm up good and throw bad. You learn it's unpredictable. Sometimes you feel bad and throw good and sometimes you feel good and throw bad. This time I was throwing bad, but I was able to throw the ball where I wanted to. I walked three but I had good control. I got by on good control. And maybe them being scared of me some. Having a big name helps some."

Next out came number ten. Minnesota came to town the third weekend in May and 28,537 fans turned out on a Sunday afternoon to root for Blue. The next night, 2,868 fans would show up to see the A's play. On Sunday the sun shone brightly, but the breezes blew across the field. Minnesota remained barely in the pennant race, and the Twins were tough. Blue scattered six hits over six separate innings, all singles. One produced a run when it followed a walk and an error by Campaneris in the sixth, but that was all Blue gave up. The A's got two runs when Jackson doubled and Epstein homered in the fourth and another when Jackson walked, Bando singled and Monday hit a sacrifice fly in the sixth. Blue won, 3–1, to run his record to 10–1, and the Twins were falling from contention.

Stories had spread that Vida carried a couple of dimes in his uniform pocket when he pitched. It was supposed that these represented twenty victories. Vida said, "To tell you the truth, I only went out with one dime when I went for number ten. But I won't tell you the truth about why I carry them because a man can't tell all his secrets. I can't tell you writer guys everything now or there won't be anything to talk about later. When I go for twenty, maybe I'll carry five pennies. If I go for twenty. You guys got me winning thirty already. The number is only ten. Last I looked, they weren't putting anyone in the Hall of Fame for ten."

But Blue was being immortalized nevertheless. May was his month for fame. He was the cover subject for *Sports Illustrated.* On the cover he was described as the "Hottest of the Hot Ones." Inside, the story by Roy Blount was entitled "Rhapsody In Blue." He was the cover story on *The Sporting News.* He was featured in *Newsweek* in a story entitled "Is Vida Blue Really True?" The very same week he was featured in the May 24 issue of *Time* in a story entitled "The Blue Blazer." *Time* quoted him as saying, "When I'm going good, I don't believe there's a batter who can hit me."

Vida shudders. He says, "I don't want to say things like that. I may think them. I can't help that. I'm human. But I don't want to say it. I don't want to say the wrong things. But it's hard to say the right things all the time. I don't know what all the right things are. And I'm asked to say things all the time.

"I've been telling people I've been having good luck. That's just my way of being modest. I'm not just lucky. But I'm lucky to be with a good team. I'm getting good support. I'm lucky not to be unlucky. I could be pitching just as good and getting a lot more bad breaks. As little as I've been around, I've been around enough to see that.

"I try not to think of publicity as pressure. I try to take it in stride as good for baseball and good for Vida Blue. I enjoy it. I think it's great for any ballplayer. And I think it's great when a ballplayer can help his game. It's always something to have people want to talk to you and want your autograph.

"I just never knew there were so many of them," he sighed.

Wells Twombly wanted him for a story for *The New York*

Times Sunday Magazine just then. And a man from *The New Yorker* wanted him, too, which, as someone said, would soon introduce the little old lady from Kokomo who has never read a sports page in her life to the life of Vida Blue.

CHAPTER EIGHT

The room remains dark and shrouded by sleep when the first telephone call comes ringing. Dutifully, Tommy Davis raises himself and gropes for the receiver. Reaching it, he takes it gently from the cradle and speaks in subdued tones. In the other room, Vida Blue is resting and must not be disturbed. He is baseball's new *Wunderkind* and he must not lose sleep.

An important newspaperman is calling. Journalists sometimes forget about time zones. It may be midmorning on the sidewalks of New York, but in Blue's Oakland neighborhood it is just breakfast time and athletes who play night games sleep late.

The number is unlisted, but this means nothing. Small children have it. Young ladies get it. Sportswriters demand it. One gives it to another. The calls come. The phone keeps ringing, day and night.

"No," Davis says firmly, like a protective parent, "he's sleeping. He pitched last night. Certainly he'll talk to you. Vida's good about that. Can he call you back? Certainly he'll call back. He's a great kid."

Later, Vida called back to Milton Gross of the New York *Post*.

"You have stirred up the country," Gross said.

"Oh, I have?" Vida said, as though surprised. Then he whistled and said, "Good for me."

This was roughly the way Wells Twombly described it in *The New York Times Sunday Magazine* and it was roughly the way it was. At the time, Vida still was returning calls. But there were too many of them and in time he stopped.

He was living in a fair-sized, two-story apartment in a house in a modest middle-class black neighborhood in Oakland. The apartment belonged to Raymond "Spider" Hodges, a former merchant mariner who was working for BART—the Bay Area Rapid Transit system. Hodges lived there. In season, Tommy Davis lived there. Davis brought Blue there. Later, when reacquired by the A's, Jim "Mudcat" Grant moved in, too.

Hodges likes sports and music and the sports figures who moved in with him moved in music with them too. Each had his own hi-fi and records. Davis even had a flute. When he practiced, Blue would run in protest from the room. When Mudcat would practice, no one would protest. Singing and dancing, he performed professionally between seasons with some lovely ladies as "Mudcat and his Kittens."

"The Spiderman" said, "Sometimes this is a quiet place and sometimes this is a noisy place. Sometimes there is no movement and sometimes it is dead. It is the way the people here want it to be whenever they want it to be that way. Some of us are married and some of us are single. For some of us there are sometimes ladies around and sometimes there are not. Our friends are free to come and go. This is my place, but it is our home and it belongs to all who are living here at a given time and we try not to intrude on one another. Tommy and Mud are like me. We are not kids and we've been around. Vida is a baby, but he has the bearing of an old man. I am not impressed by his fame, but I am impressed by him. He is good people. I hope we are good for him."

Davis says, "I try to guide Vida, but I don't have to do that much. He's a 22-year-old who acts like a man of thirty. He's from a small town, but he don't seem lost in the big city. He's under a lot of pressure, but he responds to it perfectly. He is leading us to a pennant. Leadership is a heavy load for a young man, but he brought that on himself with his performance. He has to accept it, but the way he accepts it impresses me. He just goes out and does the job. He may be impressed with himself, but not as much as others would be. He still works to improve himself. He's not so sold on himself it would break him if he ran into bad times. I'm sure he's stronger than that. Some of the guys are a little jealous of him, but he just shrugs it off and teases them and laughs a lot. He wins you over.

"He's just himself. He's what he seems to be. There's no false front. He's young and he loves young ladies and he wants to have fun and there's nothing wrong with that except that it's getting harder for him to go out with a girl and be left alone by other people. Life isn't as much fun for him as it was before he became famous and every writer and every broadcaster wants to take up his time and take him apart and try to figure out what makes him tick. Half the people in the world want a piece of him. He handles the writers better than veterans twice his age. Some of 'em are tough. They keep coming at you. They keep digging. Sometimes he'd just as soon sit with a bottle of soda pop and hold hands with a young lady and listen to music. But his time isn't his own anymore. He sees that and he accepts it as best he can, which is better than most could."

Davis was a brilliant Brooklyn basketball and baseball star who signed with the Brooklyn Dodgers and joined them in Los Angeles. He led the league with 153 runs-batted-in, 230 hits and a .346 batting average in 1962. He led the league in batting again the next year, when he hit .400 as the Dodgers won the World Series. He was making $72,000 a season and had settled his wife, three daughters and son in a $60,000 suburban home. Then he broke his ankle and when he came back he had lost his speed and his agility. He came back and showed he could still hit, but the big operators had lost their faith in him. He began to bounce around, from one major-league team to another, from Los Angeles to New York to Chicago to Seattle to Houston, to Oakland back to Chicago and back to Oakland.

He was released by the Cubs on Christmas Eve and with this release went his fancy salary. He was sent the notice on a slip of paper. He says, "I was hurt. No phone call. No words of sympathy. I thought I had meant more to baseball than just a slip of paper. I went into my den and cried. I had a wife and four kids and a house and no job. I wasn't prepared for this." Oakland offered him a chance and he took it. And he gave value in return, a part-time player who came through in the clutch and counseled their kid superstar. He was thirty-two and in his fifteenth year as a pro and he had lost his illusions. "All I want to do is survive," he said.

He could show this to Vida, that no matter who you are and what you are it comes down to survival in the end, that there is no sentiment in sports and if you don't make and save the big money when you can, the time will come when it stops coming in. "I am a friend and adviser to him," Davis smiles, "but he wants a friend more than he wants an adviser. I can warn him whore the rough spots in the road are. I've been there. I know. But if he don't want to listen, I can't make him. He's like all kids, he has to find out for himself. But he's not like most kids in that he's smarter than most. He wants to do his own thing, but he doesn't do much that is bad for him.

"The worst thing he does is start cussing and running out of the apartment when I pick up my flute," Tommy smiles.

Vida vows, "Some day I will hide that flute where he'll never find it. He is a bad flute player, but a good man. He's a good baseball player and he teaches me a lot about the game. And he's a good man who teaches me a lot about life. But I'd like to learn for myself.

"Sometimes," Vida smiles, "he's like an old mother-hen, clucking and gabbing. He don't understand that some mistakes is fun to make."

Mudcat says, "That young man is not going to make any mistakes he doesn't want to make. He knows where they are. He knows where it's at."

Davis says, "Vida is nice to the people he feels he should be nice to. If he feels someone doesn't deserve anything from him, he doesn't give 'em anything. I respect him for that. He's tough. He's best with the kids. The mothers around here can't believe how the ballplayers treat the young boys of the neighborhood. We treat 'em as equals. They treat us the same. We treat 'em nice. But Vida's best with them."

I suspect Vida does not yet feel fully comfortable with white people. He grew up in a segregated black community in the

South and he has been thrust into a world of black and white athletes run by white men and he is suspicious of them and not sure of them and not at ease with them, and when he is on his own, he tends to stay with "his own," and when he can he goes home to "his own."

He felt comfortable living in a middle-class black neighborhood and most of his friends are black, though he has white friends. Normally, he has no racial rages running through him, he is not militant, he goes his own way without concern that he must adopt current styles, black or white.

He treats everyone as though they were his equals. He is aware that all the clubowners and all the general managers and all the managers in baseball are white, which makes the sensitive black athlete feel like more of a performer than a partner in this profession. He is aware that most of the writers who interview him are white, with the occasional exception of a Sam Skinner, a skilled San Franciscan who runs his own syndication service, or a Brad Pye, a fine columnist for the Los Angeles *Sentinel*.

Occasionally, Vida is given to tongue-in-cheek comments about the racial situation, such as when asked if a stack of telegrams contained any from his hometown and Vida said no, and he really didn't expect any, and when he said he got a lot of fan mail from Mansfield, but none from the white mayor, and smilingly suggested, "Maybe I'll run for mayor there—that oughta raise a little hell."

A newspaper in the Mansfield area printed a story with some editorial comment on the side about how disappointed they were in this attitude and the white mayor, Walter Calbert, pointed out, "We had a Vida Blue day here, and right this minute we got a man down in Baton Rouge introducing a resolution in the Legislature commending him. We're proud of him and we'll let him know. His being black has nothing to do with it."

Blue felt bad about the whole bit because he does not enjoy being the center-point of controversy and was relieved when it blew over. He says, "I am proud of being black and I am aware that if things are much better in Mansfield and in the South and all over the country than they once were, they still are far from what they should be for the black man. Mansfield is probably 60 percent black and I don't think it has a black city official. And it bothers me some that people who recognize me treat me better than they would another black man. But I want to know whites and be able to live with them in peace. Race prejudice on either side is stupid. I'd prefer a world in which color was no concern to anyone."

A waitress in a coffee shop called him "boy." He reacted with rage and began to tell her off. She began to cry. His rage evaporated. He said, "Let's forget the whole damn thing." He says, "I saw how stupid the whole thing was. She wasn't thinking. She didn't know any better. She should have. So should I."

He relaxes in the apartment by playing the black music of "The Temptations" and Stevie Wonder and Marvin Gaye and other such artists. The kids are always in and out of the apartment. They run errands for the ballplayers and kid around with them. They are ten and twelve and fourteen years old and are accepted by the players as friends.

Perhaps I am reading something into this which isn't there, but it seems to me that successful black men such as ballplayers see how important they are to black youngsters and welcome their attention more and treat them more as "equals" than do whites.

On the other hand, Vida Blue turns on to white kids as well as black. He is not suspicious of kids and does not recognize color where kids are concerned. He has been forced to grow up faster than he wanted to and he welcomes it when he can be a boy again.

As he says, "When I am with fourteen-year-olds I feel fourteen. And it is not a bad feeling."

"Hey, Vida Blue, you gonna win tonight?"
"Hey, you, you gonna get me a loaf of bread today?"
"You gonna give me some money?"
"For the bread?"
"Naw, for me."

He calls his mother, "How you doin', M'dere?" using a Bayou term. "Is there anything you need, Mrs. Blue? Why, I am just fine, Mrs. Blue. Well, now, if I wasn't eating right and getting the proper rest, how could I be winning all these games?"

The phone keeps ringing and he keeps complaining. Someone suggests he take the receiver off the hook. "If I do that, how will I be able to get my calls?" he grins. If someone doesn't call him, he calls them. If it is a lady, he brightens immediately. "Are you more beautiful today than you were yesterday?" he asks.

Chatting with his roommates, he has a way of talking with broad respect about other players. "Mr. Willie Mays, Mr. Henry Aaron, Mr. Frank Robinson, Mr. Brooks Robinson, they deserve to be called 'ballplayer.' I use 'Mr.' with them because a young buck like me has to respect my elders," he smiles. "I use 'Mr.' to you because it puts you at a disadvantage."

Frequently, he puts on outsiders with broad black southern accents.

He tells Tommy Davis, "Warden, I am goin' stir-crazy, and I am gonna bust out of this joint. And if you try to stop me, I'll shoot my way out. Tell the guards in the towers to lay off."

Davis smiles and says, "If you wait until I get the key, I'll free you from your shackles. But your pass expires at three. We got a game tonight."

"Poker or pool?" Vida asks.

He may go to shoot some pool or drive some golf balls at a range, both of which he does right-handed. Sometimes he'll go to the playground to watch the kids play some ball or coach them or umpire their games or shoot a few baskets.

Perhaps he will drop in to chat with Billy, Lonnie or Andy Taylor at Taylor's Parlor of Tonsorial Art, cutting up with the cats at the haircutting and styling salon, which, if you didn't know better, you'd think was a barber shop.

"Hey, man, ain't you ever gonna lose?"

"Not if I can help it."

"I got news for you, you cain't."

Or a number of other such places.

There are places all over town where he knows people and a lot more where they know him. He hasn't lived here a year yet, but he is big here and at home here already, although it is not really his home. He sometimes feels strange here and, for all his friends, he sometimes feels lonely. "Just moving to a place doesn't make it home," he sighs. "I am far from home, a grown-up man out in the big wide world and I will just have to get used to it, the way it is."

He says, "I have friends I didn't know I had. There's people I meet in the meat market and the clothing store and just walking down the street. There are people from the South, from my home state, from my hometown, even from my high school, who show up who I never saw before in my life. And then there are just people, thousands of them, who are always telling me to call them if I need anything."

He sighs and says, "I can see how some stars are trailed everywhere they go by buddies. They go in groups, like gangs. They run errands for the leader. They pull his chair out for him when he wants to sit down. I want to sit down by myself. I don't need a whole lot of people around. A lot of them want loans. I'm not making any money yet and when I make some I want to still have some when I go. I just want to be Vida Blue. And I just want people around me who'd want to be around me if I wasn't some kind of star."

He is handsome, his smile is enormously personable and when he dresses up in mod duds he is a knockout, but he'd just as soon travel the town in his green and white Joe Namath football jersey and a pair of old pants and loafers, and he frequently does. Still, he turns the ladies on with his looks, his personality and his fame. He says, "I am interested only in those who are interested in me and not my fame and not the money I may make, but it is tough sometimes to figure out which is which. I pass judgments."

He smiles and says, "I thought when I got famous, pretty ladies would come falling like rain out of the heavens around my feet. It hasn't been that way, but it's OK."

He puts it down. "I am more impressed with a nice lady than with looks, though if a fellow is fortunate enough to have a choice he's just naturally going to pick the looker. I like girls. I am nice and natural in that way. But they are more impressed with me than I am. I like to have dates when others are not staring at us. I like to hold hands, you know. I don't get carried away with it. I have to save myself for my pitching. I can't be running around all the time. I might get more privacy in my own home, but I don't want it that badly that I want a wife. I am not looking to get married, not for a long time yet. If it comes soon it will surprise me more than anyone."

Yet everywhere he goes, he goes to see ladies he knows—at banks, supermarkets, insurance companies, airports. He just stops in to rap with a lovely for a while and it seems to brighten his worst moods, though he has a bright outlook on life and is not by nature a moody man. He moves about, light on his feet and smiling. One young lady says, "You soon see he is not a picture in the newspaper or on your television screen. He isn't a face on a bubblegum card. He's no cardboard cutout. He's the real thing. He's very real. If you can get him to relax with you, you relax with him. He's like a man lost in a crowd, you know, a little lonely. And he's got a little-boy quality."

Most writers react favorably to him. A reporter in Cleveland described him as "a warm and decent and friendly human being, soft-spoken and modest, but articulate; a joy to interview." Bob Jauss in *Chicago Today* wrote, "Vida is honest as well as humble." Brad Pye in *Cause,* a magazine "dedicated to the reality of equal opportunity," wrote, "A beautiful Blue! He's true blue. His personality is as beautiful and as blue as the Mediterranean Sea." Such things were written about him as would turn the head of a monk.

Kansas City manager Bob Lemon observed, "I'm convinced it won't be on the mound where Vida will have his trouble, it will be off the field. That will be his true test. Now everybody's hanging on his shirttails. He has a million glad-handers hanging around him. The press is hounding him. They're telling him how great he is. When they tire of this, they'll lay in wait for him to slip so they can say something more sensational. I wonder how he'll take all this. This is what a superstar has to handle and it's hard."

Vida said, "It's a weird scene. You win a few baseball games and all of a sudden you're surrounded by reporters and TV men

with cameras asking you about Vietnam and race relations and
stuff like that. I don't even know who I am yet. I'm young. I
don't have a whole philosophy of life set down. I don't have a
whole lot of experiences to relate. They all want something different and I haven't experienced that many different things to give
them. I just want to answer their questions, but the more questions they ask the less answers I have and it gets harder and
harder. I know I've done a good job handling the publicity so far
at my age and I don't see why I should change. Just be nice and
treat people the way you want them to treat you. The problem,"
he sighs, "is they don't treat you the way you want to be treated."

His pet peeve is "Bogartin'," and he says this is when a guy
walks around like he owns the world, acts superior and begins to
push people around. It is, he says, "when you suddenly become
a star and you begin to act like one. You can get cocky awful
fast. Well, I don't think that's the way to be. I think a lot of stars
have been spoiled by letting success go to their heads. It's hard,
but I think I don't want to think of myself as a star because as
soon as I do I may stop being one. I mean, I've got to have confidence in my ability to do the job, but I can't be cocky about it.
You can't be thinking about how good you are. You have to be
modest about the whole thing, never bragging about anything
you've done.

"I keep telling myself, 'Don't get big-headed. Be good to the
writers. Talk to the kids. Sign autographs. Don't brag. Throw a
ball into the stands once in a while. Don't go Bogartin' around.'
I think a man who has a hero image should remember that when
he is out in the public. But I'm not going to present myself as
something I'm not. If people don't like the way I am, the way I
come across, I can't help it, that's me. I think I owe the public
something. Not everything, but something. I can't sign all the
autographs, but I try. I don't ever want to forget the 'little people.' I don't even want to think of anyone as 'little.' If God didn't
give me the ability to throw a ball hard, what would I be?"

A busboy at the Edgewater Hyatt House motel, where Blue
used to live when he was moving in and out of Oakland, says,
"He still comes over here a lot, and when he does he says hello

to everybody. He remembers you." A lady behind the office counter says, "He hasn't changed. He's a doll, a dream. We love him. He promised to get us some tickets."

In the dressing room, Vida Blue says, "The last thing I want to do on this earth is act superior to my teammates. Lordamighty, I'm not superior to them. Some of them have been here awhile and have done some things I may never do. They're superior to me. But right now I'm doing some things some of them may never do and I know it and they know it and it's hard to keep things the same between us. It's hard to keep things the same when there are ten writers and broadcasters around me and none around them. It's hard to keep things the same when it's 'Vida Blue Wins' in headlines, not 'The A's Win.' I'm tryin' to be natural. I just want to be me."

His roommate on the road, Angel Mangual, says, "He is a good man. He has a good heart. He thinks about people. He is the success suddenly but he sees it for what it is and he sees it can go, poof, as fast as it come. Everyone has something to say about him or to him and he listens to everyone, but it no bother him or change him. He good roomie. He causes problems, but nothing I mind. He gets lots of calls and I answer the phone lots of the time because no one wants to talk to me. We tired, we lock off the phone and sleep a lot. We get along great. He never get mad for nothing. He never say he feel bad. He just lives. He says, 'I gonna work hard. I gonna be best.' I think maybe he will be. He tell me I be best, too. I know better. He say, 'Angel, some season you drive in 525 run.' I laugh. I know is his psychology. He like old man. He tough. No one mess him up, I betcha. But they may drive him crazy."

Tommy Davis says, "The pressure can only get worse the better he gets. It grows and grows and grows. I've seen it happen. Sandy Koufax turned inside of himself. He didn't want to give anything of himself to anyone. It disturbed him deeply when people poked into his private life. He came to like baseball and I think he liked being with the players, but he hated the spotlight and he never came to like fame. There's a feeling that everyone wants to be famous, but it just isn't so. Those who aren't want to be famous. Koufax may miss pitching, but I guarantee you he doesn't miss fame. But he's an introvert. Vida's somewhat extroverted. At least, he's more outgoing, more fun-loving. He's more open, more willing to give. This makes him more vulnerable. I only hope he doesn't get hurt. Let's see how he does. Let's see how he takes care of himself. Let's see."

Will success spoil Vida Blue?

Mike Epstein said, "He's a nice likable kid. Let's see if the world can make him into a monster."

CHAPTER NINE

Later, Reggie Jackson said, "I think it began to change for Vida when we went back East, first to Boston, then to New York, the end of May, the beginning of June. The news media is centered in the East. There are more newspapers in Boston than in any city in the country and it is a red-hot baseball town. And most of the network television and radio people, the wire services and the syndicated newspaper columnists and the national magazine people are based in New York. They'd been sending people out to see him, but now they had him in their backyard and they almost smothered the breath out of him.

"He was hot. He hadn't lost since opening day, he'd won ten-straight in less than two months and he'd been brilliant. He was young and good-looking and he had a colorful name and he was a new star on a pennant-contender. Everything was just right. Baseball needs excitement and when someone really exciting comes along, the press and the public smother him until it becomes hard to breathe. I know because it happened to me a couple of years ago when I was ahead of Babe Ruth's home-run pace for a while. You still have to perform, you know. They'd ask me if I could hit sixty home runs, and I didn't know. The harder you try for them, the harder it is to hit them. They'd ask Vida if he could win thirty games, and he didn't know. And it made it harder to get the next one. Everyone was shooting for him.

"I got to feeling I was a trophy, not a person. I got carried away by it. And I wasn't as hot as Vida. I doubt that they ever went after anyone the way they went after him. And I stood by and watched and saw what was happening. He didn't get carried away with it, but he did begin to feel like a trophy, and he didn't like it. I didn't just stand by. I tried to tell him how it was going to be. I tried to warn him that it would get worse. I tried to warn him that if he slipped, they'd turn on him. I went through that, too. And he was smart enough to see that.

"But it began to get to him. He's not soft, but they just literally take your life away from you. They don't really care about you, see. They don't know you. They don't want to know you. They just want you to be some perfect superman who can hit sixty home runs or pitch thirty victories. And they keep coming at you until you want to turn and run. All of a sudden it goes sour.

"He lost in Boston, but still they kept coming. Then he won in New York and they came at him harder than ever. And suddenly it began to be too much. He handled it beautifully, I thought, better than I did, and I was good, too good for them. But it's too much for anyone to handle. No one can take it. No one. It's just too much."

As *Life* magazine wrote it:

> *Vida Blue is walking around the visitors' clubhouse in Boston's Fenway Park, naked to the waist. It is an hour before he is to pitch against the Red Sox, and his voice is filling the air with a terribly out-of-tune version of a folk-rock hit.*
>
> *Occasionally, he pauses and leaps high and straight into the air, his left arm shooting out, sending an imaginary basketball on its path to the imaginary basket. "Don't you do anything right-handed?" a visitor asks.*
>
> *Vida Blue stops and gives the questioner his special are-you-kidding look, head cocked to one side, right cheek resting on his right shoulder. Then the corners of his mouth quiver, his eyes light up and a broad smile splits his face.*
>
> *"Shoot marbles," he answers. "I just might be the very best right-handed marble-shooter in the major leagues."*
>
> *Ever since mid-April, Vida Blue's life has been one long press conference. The reporters and the photographers are*

at him constantly. Smile, Vida. Snap. *Would you blow a bubble, please?* Snap. *Another bubble, please.* Snap. *Make a fist.* Snap. *Tell me who your heroes are.* Snap.

The pictures appeared in the magazine. What did not appear was the fact that he did many things right-handed, some of them to save his left arm, and the sarcastic comment of a teammate that "Vida sings right-handed." Nor the fact that he might as well have pitched right-handed that night.

The reporters were all over him, right up to the time he had to pitch. The fans waited for him. There were 35,714 of them there and old Fenway Park seats only 33,370. Some were standing and several thousand others were turned away at the gates. And they started screaming as soon as he showed up on the field. Some screamed from precarious perches atop billboards. And thousands more stood outside with transistor radios, roaring when they roared inside.

Some writer had asked him if he had ever dreamed big-league victories would come to him as easily as they had. And he had drawn back and said, "Easy? Look at me sweating out there. Is that easy? It's a lot of hard, hard, hard work. It's going to be that way the next time out and the time after that and the rest of the season and the rest of my career. It may look easy, but there's nothing easy about it."

Now, he stood on the mound in Fenway Park where left-handed pitchers seldom win because it is only a little more than 300 feet to the Great Wall in left field and right-hand hitters reach the wall with soft fly balls. He said, "It feels like the wall is about to fall in on you. It's like pitching in a matchbox and you have to make an effort not to get psyched out.

"I resorted to smoke. I tried to overpower them with fastballs instead of setting them up for the fastballs with curve balls. I just wasn't smart. And it wasn't the left-field wall which beat me, it was me. My mind was out in left field. My mind wasn't on the mound. The writers were beginning to distract me. I was talking more than I was pitching. I didn't do much good pitching that night."

Reggie Jackson gave him a lead in the first inning when he

nailed his ninth home run, a tremendous 430-foot drive to right off Sonny Siebert, the unbeaten Boston pitcher who was going for his ninth-straight triumph but had been around awhile and was not drawing anywhere near the attention being paid Blue. After that night, in fact, he would win only six of sixteen. But this was his night. Blue blew the lead. In Boston's half of the first, Reggie Smith singled and Rico Petrocelli lined the ball into the bleachers in center and Blue was behind. In the sixth, Petrocelli pounded another, high into the screen in left. In the eighth, Smith singled, Petrocelli walked and George Scott singled and Blue walked off the mound, relieved by Williams, as the crowd waved white handkerchiefs at him.

Boston won, 4-3, as Blue lost his second against ten victories, having given eight hits, including two big ones, and two walks, and the writers surrounded him afterward, pressing in on him until he felt pinned to the wall, and they asked him if he'd had his best stuff, and he said they had just beaten him, that's all, and they asked him what Petrocelli hit, and he said just pitches, that's all, and they asked him how he felt when Petrocelli hit the homers, and he said he felt bad but it was no disgrace to have a man like Rico Petrocelli hit homers off you, and they asked him if he had set any goals for himself, and if he still thought he could win thirty, and he said no, he didn't set goals, and he never said he thought he could win thirty, he had no idea how many he could win.

They come at the hot player in waves. They're not all there at once. Some come and ask their questions and then others come and crowd in and ask most of the same questions and then more come and ask most of the same questions and then the television people want you to repeat the answers to those questions for the cameras and then the radio people want you to repeat the answers to those questions for the tape-recorders and you give the same answers until you feel like you're in a long-running stage hit repeating lines, until you feel like giving different answers just for the hell of it, but Blue, sweating and tired and disappointed sat there and answered all their questions.

He says, "Losing was all right. It was something I had to learn to do. I took it with a smile. I took it the way I figured a true professional athlete should. I figured if I lived very long I had to learn to live with losing as well as with winning. Losing is hard. Winning is easy. It's no trick to be gracious when you win. The trick is to be a man when you lose."

Then someone wanted to leave the ballpark with him to interview him on the way back to the hotel and someone wanted to interview him at the hotel and someone wanted to buy him dinner and talk to him. They asked him who his hero was and how much money he was making and how much money he was going to ask Finley for and about the dimes he carried in his pocket when he pitched. Someone asked him if there was anything special about the dimes. He said, "Yes. They say 'In God We Trust' on them."

Outside the ballpark, the fans waited, and they pressed in on him, pressing pens and scraps of paper and programs and autograph books at him and shouting his name and he stood there and signed and signed and signed until he thought there would be no end to it, the sweat running down his face and staining his white shirt. When, wearily, he finally got into a hotel room the phone was ringing. "What would it be if I'd won?" he asked.

Back home in Mansfield his mother's phone was ringing, too. And reporters were coming to see her. And the poor woman was holding up wonderfully well. A large, handsome woman with a lovely smile and a lovely laugh, she was somewhat mystified by the fuss over her son, but she accepted it and she accepted the questions and answered. "I knew he'd do it if he got a chance. You see, he's always been a very, very poor loser, and poor losers always try harder," she said. "No, I've never seen him pitch in the major leagues. I saw his face on the TV news the other night when he won and I got a wonderful feeling. I'm not a person who cries easy, but for a few seconds there I wanted to. It just didn't seem true. But there he was on TV. . . ."

And on the first of June he was in New York and the writers were coming around and calling up and he couldn't get away from them. And they were asking him who his hero was and how much money he was making and how much he was going to ask Finley for and about the dimes he carried in his pocket when he pitched and how he was able to pitch so well so soon and if he was surprised by his success and who the toughest batter he faced was and what goals he had set for himself and if he thought he could win thirty, and he kept answering the same questions over and over and some different ones, here, too, prying ones, about his private life, about his love life, about being black, about how his teammates were taking his success, about life with Finley.

He says, "They're the best, I guess. The New York writers. They're good. There are good and bad writers everywhere, in New York and everywhere else. I'm not talking about the writing. I'm no judge of that. I'm talking about getting what you say down right and putting it in the paper right and not shading it wrong and not putting their own things into it, which some do, which makes you mad, which makes you not want to talk to the rest because it follows you around, they all pick up a misquote from one bad one and keep using it.

"There are probably more good writers in New York than other cities. They ask the same questions, but they ask other questions, too, hard questions, questions I don't want to answer, but questions I'd want to ask if I was a writer. They've done their home work. They know about you. They have the stats and they tell me things I don't want to hear but things I'd want to write if I was a writer, like I was two games ahead of Dennis McLain's pace when he won 31 a couple years ago. They're sharp. You try to shake them, but they track you down. They find you in a restaurant with a phone call. You hate it that they do, but you admire it, too."

The writers came and the television people came with their cameras and bright, hot lights and their microphones and the radio people came with their tape-recorders. And then the game came, a Tuesday night game, and 30,052 fans came out to Yankee Stadium, the largest night game in this tremendous, triple-tiered antique in nearly three years, to see this bright new star, Blue, for the first time in the big town. Bando doubled, Monday singled and Duncan singled to give him a two-run lead in the second inning. Bobby Murcer doubled and Felipe Alou singled to cut the lead in half in the home half. But Rudi singled and Jackson homered for two more in the next inning, and Rudi doubled and

Epstein doubled for another in the seventh. In between, Blue was working fast and effectively. He has thrown harder, but he had good control and was getting both the fastball and the curve over and the Yankees were hitting out.

In the eighth, Alou doubled and Michael singled for a run off him, but that was all and it wound up 5–2 and he wound up with his record at 11–2. Running on and off the mound, working fast, not wasting much, very businesslike, bearing down all the way, not at his sharpest, but sharp enough, he set them down with six hits and one walk and got back to the dressing room. Finley got to him first, with a phone call, and Vida said, "Thank you, thank you very much, but, damnit, they shouldn't have gotten the two runs." And then the writers got to him, asking those questions and at one time he was surrounded by eighteen reporters and sat there, half-stripped and hot and sweating, with his left arm freezing in a tray of ice-water, feeling trapped again, and finally he said, "I can't stand it. I won't be able to stand this all season." And then he shut his eyes and was silent for a moment, then he said, more softly, "It's going to be tough. I'm going to try. But I don't think I can do it."

In Washington, Senators' vice-president Joe Burke said, "In baseball these days we're resorting to all kinds of special days to bring people to the ballpark—bat day, ball day, poster day, Honor America Day—but give me a day with Vida Blue and 20,000 people will find their way into the stadium." He under-estimated Blue. He got a Sunday with Blue and 40,246 found their way into D.C. Stadium, where 6,221 had turned out to see the league-leading A's with Hunter humble the home side the day before. The Senators scared no one, but this was the team and the place where he had been put out on opening day, and foe Denny McLain of thirty-game fame had beat the A's ten-straight times over almost five seasons, so Blue was trying a little harder. In the third he walked a couple and a sacrifice and a single by Elliott Maddox brought in a run off him, but he got tougher after that and didn't give them anything else of consequence and only three other hits and didn't walk another man and with the help of home runs by Monday and Tenace mauling McLain, Blue breezed, 8–1, and the large turnout left turned on by the Louisiana lad, and McLain left, laughing sadly, "He's something else all right."

Later, Vida smiled wistfully and said, "It's tough to be me. Every man I face wants a piece of me. A man that doesn't have much wants something from me. I can make his whole career. Get a hit off Blue and it's a big deal and the home crowd will cheer him. I smile at him and he smiles at me."

The A's headed home the second week in June at a pace of two victories in every three starts with a lead that was up to seven games over Kansas City and Minnesota. Davis was the only batter hitting above .300, but Epstein, Bando and Jackson were driving home runs. Blue was 12–2 and Hunter was 9–3, and Dobson was sharp at this time and stopped Boston, 6–1, to give the team a split in a two-game series with Boston after the Red Sox had spoiled Oakland's homestand opener. The Yankees won the first of a three-game set on a Friday night and it was up to Blue to bail out the team the next afternoon before it got into trouble. Some 23,985—over 10,000 more than had turned out the night before—showed up to see.

The A's had been faced with a situation when, because of off-days, Blue in his regular rotation would work only once in the eight-game homestand and only twice in twelve days and his start at home would have come on a Bat Day, when a better-than-normal turnout was assured, anyway, so Blue was moved into Hunter's spot and Hunter was moved back to give Vida an extra start. Williams said, "He's enough of a promotion by himself." But the fine touch of Finley was seen in this.

Vida struggled some. In the first inning, Alou tripled with one out, but Blue struck out Thurman Munson and Roy White for the second and third outs. By the time he got into trouble again, the A's had gotten him three runs. In the fourth, Munson walked, was sacrificed to second and scored on a single by John Ellis. The next inning the A's got Blue five more runs. In the sixth he walked Alou and gave up a home run to White, only the fourth home run he had given up in 130 innings, but the A's came right back with two more in their half and they kept scoring. Rudi, Campaneris and Mangual had four hits apiece. Rudi had a home run and drove in three runs and Campaneris scored three, and with this kind of support Vida coasted to a 13–3 triumph.

"This was my thirteenth and it was a little lucky," he said later. "Maybe I was lucky the hitters were hitting behind me the way they were. And maybe it made me careless. My concentration has a tendency to wander sometimes. It's easier said than done that you should bear down on every pitch and be sure you're doing what you want to do. You work every fourth or fifth game, you pitch nine innings almost every game when you're going good like I've been going, you face thirty or forty batters every game, you throw a hundred or a hundred and twenty pitches, and you let down sometimes. Especially those times you get the big lead. I was ahead, 8–1 and 13–3, and I relaxed and before I realized it I was behind on the batters, I was throwing at 2-and-1 and 3-and-2 and you make it tough for yourself."

He said, "I'm tired. I'm just tired. All I want to do is go home, take the telephone off the hook and sleep for two days. I'm beat."

The Yankees hadn't noticed. Around the Edgewater they were talking about him all that night. Thurman Munson said, "The first time he faced us a couple of the guys were saying that, well, he wasn't all that fast and, so, he didn't seem to be all that tough, and then we get another look at him here and wow! He gets himself in a jam and I know he's going to have to come in with a fastball and I'm a pretty fair fastball hitter but he blew it right past me and then he blew it right past White and then he blew us out of the park. White whacked him for a home run, but you catch a fastball, you're gonna whack it, that happens, and he was far ahead and he may have let down a little. He may have been tired. When you're winning complete games like he's been doing, you're pitching more than most guys. And by the record he's been pitching better than he's pitched against us. But I want to say he showed us something."

All around the league they were talking about him. The other ballplayers were impressed. Ballplayers get excited by a hot ballplayer, too. They're not as easily impressed as writers are, or fans, but they get impressed, too, and Blue was making a big impression. Washington came to town and huge Frank Howard, the Senators' most menacing slugger, said, "This kid throws hard and his ball moves and he's got a curve he can throw and he gets over the plate what he throws and he's very hard to hit and he seems harder to scare." Ted Williams, the Senators' manager, a great hitter in his day and a great student of pitchers, said, "Blue is the best-looking young pitcher to come along in years." Others liked him, too. In Las Vegas the bookies had him a 3–1 favorite every time he pitched. By baseball standards, this was a tremendous edge. But he was winning. And acting like a winner.

Washington came to town with Dobson scheduled to start the first game of the series and Blue the second. Vida got to the ballpark early for the first game because he is happy there, where on nights he is not pitching he is fairly free from game pressures. He ran his pass-patterns in the outfield during the twilight pregame drills then retired to the dressing room sweating heavily "It's real easy for me to perspire," he observed. He removed several sweatsuits he had been wearing and balled them up and sent them spinning into a dirty-clothes hamper with basketball-styled jump-shots. Asked why he wore so much warm clothing in such warm weather, he thought a second, brightened and answered, "I guess I'm just a fool."

Some clubhouse boys were watching him. Vida said, "George, you my man, get me a soda pop. Steve, how 'bout wringing out my sweatshirt here. Chuck, get m' a dry sweatshirt." Well, George and Steve were clubhouse boys, ready for orders, but Chuck, last name Dobson, the starting pitcher for the night, and unbeaten, besides, was not. Chuck, with a straight face, said, "Get your own sweatshirt." Vida, with a straight face, said, "Oh, I *knew* I'd go too far." And then he grinned broadly and Chuck could not help smiling. Blue is hard to hate.

"George," Blue was saying, "I'm not drinking no red soda pop. Where you think I'm from, Louisiana?" George took back the red soda pop, strawberry, and brought back purple pop, fruit punch. Vida downed it in two swallows and remained thirsty. Smiling slyly, he said, "I got to Bogart me another soda water. Hey, George, you my man . . ." A few minutes later he was at quarterback and George and Steve were at other positions and they were running phantom football plays. And a little later, Chuck was on the mound, beating the Senators, remaining unbeaten, before 8,392.

The next night, Blue was on the mound, beating the Senators

before 19,893. His fourteenth was a five-hitter, 5–1. Again Mc-
Lain was his foe. Again Blue started shaky. He walked two men
in the first inning. He struck out Howard, but let down to Dick
Billings, who singled to score a run. Vida did not let down again.
He did not walk another batter and he did not give up another
run. Meanwhile Rudi and Epstein hit homers off McLain in the
first inning, Duncan hit one in the second and Rudi and Epstein
hit the damn thing out of the park. Blue was good, but he better
McLain growled, "It's amazing. I had good stuff and they just
hit the damn thing out of the park. Blue was good, but he better
know it's not always enough. You got to be lucky, too. Maybe
he'll win thirty like I did. And maybe he'll win twenty. And
maybe a year or two later he'll find himself trying not to lose
twenty." It was McLain's twelfth loss in sixteen decisions and
he would lose 22 out of 32 before the season finished.

A dozen red roses arrived at the Coliseum, sent to Blue, com-
pliments of Liz' Florists.
Seeing them, someone asked, "Who sent them, some girl?"
Vida said, "No, Liz."
"Isn't Liz a girl?"
"No," he said, "She's a florist."

It was back to the road, back to the airports and the planes and
the motels and the hotels for a week, which opened with the A's
winning three out of four games, one a 2–0 shutout by Odom,
in three days and nights in Milwaukee without an appearance by
Blue, but with complaints by Milwaukee management about it
because with him the Brewers could have made some money.
The team flew on to Minnesota at the end of the third week of
June and Blue drew the assignment of opening the series there
on a Monday night and drew 23,334 fans there and millions more
to their television sets, as this one was nationally televised.
Campaneris got him a run in the first when he singled off Ray
Corbin, reached third on two walks and came home on a ground-
out. But Blue gave Minnesota two in the third when Reese
tripled, Corbin singled him in, and, after Vida got the next two,
Killebrew singled in another. But, as often is his way, he seemed

to get stronger after that and shut out the Twins the rest of the way. He got even in the sixth when Epstein doubled and came around on singles by Bando and Duncan, and he got the lead run in the seventh when Campaneris came home from third when catcher Mitterwald threw wild trying to stop Rudi from stealing second. Blue won, 3–2, his fifteenth victory and fifteenth complete game, and he struck out thirteen to give him a league-leading total of 196.

The autograph-hunters hunted him out in seemingly endless numbers. He said, "I think I have already signed some scrap of paper for every man, woman and child in the United States. What do they do with all those scraps of paper with my signature on it?" And someone said, "They ball them up and throw them in the wastebasket."

He said to one young man, "Hey, it seems to me I've signed three for you already."

And the lad smiled and said, "No, four."

After five victories, Vida had said, "I want to sign. I want to sign 'em all."

After ten he sighed and said, "You got to sign. You just got to."

After fifteen he said, "You don't got to sign. You don't got to do nothing but die."

And went on signing.

He went home happy because his mom was waiting. Finley had telephoned Mrs. Blue in Mansfield and invited her and her other children to come to Oakland when the team returned to spend the last weekend in June with her son, to see him pitch and to see him receive a special gift as a reward for his outstanding showing thus far that season, a new car.

As she settled in the motel with Vida's brother and his four sisters, the writers and broadcasters gathered around her, making her feel like a celebrity. The reporters asked her how her son's success had changed her life. She said, "I really hate to go to the mailbox these days. It always looks ready to overflow. And the phone, why, it never stops ringing."

They asked her how he seemed to her. She said, "He's a wonderful boy. He never changes. They make this fuss over him, but he's the same Vida. I know people are looking for success to change him, but I don't think anything could change him." She beamed and his brother beamed and his sisters beamed, and he hugged them and beamed some, himself.

At the Friday night game, which Vida was to pitch, they seated the family in box seats on the second level and the newsmen gathered around her again and heard her enumerate her son's virtues. She said, "He is single. He doesn't smoke. He takes only an occasional drink—a beer, perhaps. He is staying with a very nice man, this Tommy Davis. He dates only nice girls. And he calls home at least once a week."

Another virtue was that he could pitch exceptionally well. He was good, he was really good. He was young and as yet really inexperienced and under a lot of pressure, but even on a night like this, when, because of his family's presence, he especially wanted to be good, he was able to be exceptionally good.

There were 33,888 there for the affair and Blue did not let anyone down. His consistency was astonishing. He struck out twelve, walked only one. He surrendered just five hits. He escaped unscathed from his only jam in the seventh when Cookie Rojas and Lou Piniella got two of the hits, singles, but he got Bob Oliver to pop out and Dennis Paepke to fly to left. And although the A's spent a lot of time scoring, Blue wrapped up a 7–0 triumph—his sixteenth victory and sixteenth complete game, and his sixth shutout—in less than two-and-a-half hours.

Afterward Vida said, "You see, my team scores some runs and then I go out and don't let the other team score. It's simple."

And his mother said, "He comes from calm stock."

Vida added, "She had seen me pitch only once before in my life, in high school. That is, she saw the same person then, she didn't see the same pitcher."

And how did his mother like what she saw? "It was very nice," she said. But she did not say anything about the pride that showed through her fine, strong face, illuminated with satisfaction for her son.

She shepherded her twins, Cheryl and Jean, twenty, and Annette, fourteen, and Mike, ten, and Sandra, six, back to the motel, where they had dinner with Vida, who fussed over them, and they talked about their hometown and old friends and the old days.

The next day was Vida Blue Day, which was another way of getting 40,000 fans into the ballpark on a Saturday afternoon for Finley, who doesn't miss a trick. Blue was presented with a baby-blue Cadillac El Dorado with the License plates V-BLUE and his mother was presented with flowers as they stood with the rest of their family on the field and waved to the fans and were given an ovation. Vida thanked the fans and Mr. Finley, then he and his mother and brother and sisters were driven around the field in his new car. And afterward the A's won the game and everyone went home happy.

One of the A's pitchers asked, "If I win four games, do you think Charley will give me a Honda?"

And Tommy Davis did ask Finley if, since he was guiding Vida, he could cut in for 10 percent of his action, and Finley said, "Fine, and you can serve as his chauffeur."

Vida's sister Jean recalled, "My sister and I got our licenses before Vida did. We had to teach him to drive. Big brother didn't like that."

Vida's twenty-second birthday was a month away. His mother was asked what she was going to get him for his birthday. She said, "It doesn't matter what I buy for his birthday. He'll like it, whatever it is. He always does."

Before she left, Mrs. Blue said, "The only difference I see in Vida is how he paces the floor when I talk to him. He just keeps walking back and forth, kind of nervous and fidgety."

He took her and his brother and his sisters to the airport, careful to see that everything was taken care of for them. It was touching, how attentive he was to them. He fussed over his mother. He funned with his brother and sisters. Clearly, he has a strong family feeling. Clearly, he cares.

On Sunday it was back to business, the best weekend business Finley ever had in sports. He followed a Vida Blue pitching night and a Vida Blue Day with a hot-pants day and drew 33,000. It seems sex is the best gate attraction next to Blue. The visitors dropped a doubleheader as the A's swept the four-game series.

Before long it was revealed that Blue had blushingly bargained for a good deal to go with his car, smilingly sweet-talking his boss into tying some fancy ribbons on the package. Sometime later,

Finley offered details. He said, "I agree that Vida is the most underpaid player in baseball. At $13,000 he has to be. But there are some things that go beyond contracts. There are other considerations that can mean as much a great deal of the time as a new, lofty contract. I like to feel I treat my players as I would like to be treated if I were a baseball player, and we'll take Vida as an example.

"You know about that new car, that $10,000 job? He got that. The insurance for a 21-year-old driver is $1,200. I picked that up. Then he said to me, 'Mr. Finley, that nice car is fine, but that thing is going to take more than I make in a year to drive, what with upkeep and gas.' So I told Vida OK. The next day, Vida had a gasoline company credit card from me. A couple of weeks later, Vida came to me again and said, 'Mr. Finley, that nice car and all, it's great, but I don't look like a man who drives a Cadillac.' I said, 'In other words, Vida, you want a new wardrobe, something to go with the car, to dress like the owner of a new Caddie should.' Vida told me that was the idea. I asked him how much this new wardrobe would cost. Vida told me, 'About $500.' So I said, 'OK, stop in my Coliseum office and pick up a check.' When he stopped in to pick up the check it was for $1,000.

"Like I said, yes, Vida is the most underpaid player by contract in baseball. But as for tearing up his current contract and giving him another, well . . . Like I said, there are other ways."

Vida confirms all this, saying, "I was winning the games and bringing in the money at the gate. The car was very nice. I'd just as soon have had the money. And I guess I got what I could. It was sort of like a con game, me suggesting I might like this and him offering me that, and us kidding back and forth. It was very nice. He didn't have to give me anything, you know. I knew it, anyway. So if he wanted to play it like a game in which I got prizes, fine, I was willing to play along. I didn't have all that much in life, you know. And that man had control over what I was going to get."

Vida said, "Right now, he treats me like I was a gift from God, but I'm not going to win every game I pitch and some bills may come due some day."

When Vida got the car he smiled and said, "I'd rather have had a Grand Prix." He offered the car to his mother, who seemed shocked and asked, "What do you think I'm going to do with that big old thing?" It wound up in her driveway, anyway, because with the V-BLUE license plates it attracted too much attention. Vida got a deal from a dealer to drive a Grand Prix in the A's colors of green and yellow and he drove this car, which he called his "Green Hornet," most of the rest of the season. ARCO awarded him 100 gallons of gas free for every victory, so he did not have to depend on the credit card.

He had turned to Tommy Davis' lawyer and manager, Bob Gerst of Los Angeles, and was beginning to make money on side deals, filming television commercials and making some TV guest appearances. This took his time, but not as much as the writers and broadcasters did. And this was for Vida, not for the owner or the fans or the game. The attorney was a cautious man who relieved him of the responsibility of dealing with all the agents and promoters and businessmen who were descending on him at every turn. The press was pressuring him more than ever and he regarded gratefully any relief he received.

He went back to work before 33,378 when Minnesota came to town and it resulted in his first loss ever in the Oakland Coliseum after ten-consecutive wins there since his first brief appearances of a couple of seasons earlier, and his third loss of this season. He was not routed or anything like that. In the third inning, Cesar Tovar doubled in a run off him. In the fourth, Steve Braun hit a home run. The game was tied, 2–2, in the seventh, when Braun walked and Leo Cardenas hit a two-run homer. Blue was taken out for a pinch-hitter and the A's wound up losing, 5–3.

In the dressing room, Blue told the writers, "I don't know. I guess I made some bad pitches, but the one Cardenas hit was so high he shouldn't even have swung at it, and he sure shouldn't have been able to hit it. I guess these things happen in this game. There's nothing in the rule book says Vida Blue can't lose." The newspaper headline the next day read VIDA BLUE LEARNS HE CAN LOSE. The lead: "One pitch and one swing turned Vida Blue into a mortal."

Vida said, "That's good. I was beginning to get the idea I was a machine."

On the Fourth of July he was operating with machinelike efficiency again, stopping the Angels in Anaheim before a record crowd there of 44,631 by a score of 2–1. Blue gave up nine hits, the most he had permitted in any game that season, but he scattered them, he got the big outs with men on base, he didn't walk a single man, he struck out seven and he gave up a run only when rival pitcher Tom Murphy swung late and feebly on a fastball but popped it between the infielders and outfielders with a man on base who beat the throw home. Home runs by Epstein and Rudi beat Murphy and brought Blue his seventeenth triumph, and they were talking about him in the Angel quarters later while the fans watched a traditional and patriotic fireworks display outside.

Manager Lefty Phillips was saying, "He has as good a fastball as I've ever seen. His other pitches are average. He does have great control and poise and he has improved himself. When he gets the other stuff, he'll be in a league by himself. Like Koufax." And Jim Spencer was saying, "Some of the guys were saying they thought he'd be better, but when he comes up with a better curve and a changeup no one will ever get a hit off him. He made some mistakes to me and I hit the ball. I've been lucky against him. What you think when you go up to face him is of self-preservation. You think, 'Dear Lord, don't let him hit me with a pitch.'"

In the A's quarters, Blue was saying, "I was bad and I made some bad pitches." Someone asked Blue if he knew the stats showed Spencer hit him as well as anyone. Vida said, "Nah, I don't read stats. That's his job, to hit the ball. My job is to get him out. I didn't do it." Someone pointed out the only run came on a fluke hit and that at the time he seemed to be talking to himself out there. Vida said, "Yeah, I always do. Those little bloopers make you talk to yourself. They drive you crazy."

He sat with his pitching arm embedded in that bucket of ice and stared at his arm as if it belonged to somebody else, Steve Bisheff of the Los Angeles *Herald-Examiner* said later. He noticed how Vida kept looking down at the floor and shaking his head and how terse his answers were and he wondered about the pressure on him. Vida said, "I don't want to talk about the pressure." Someone asked him if he'd maybe had his mind on the

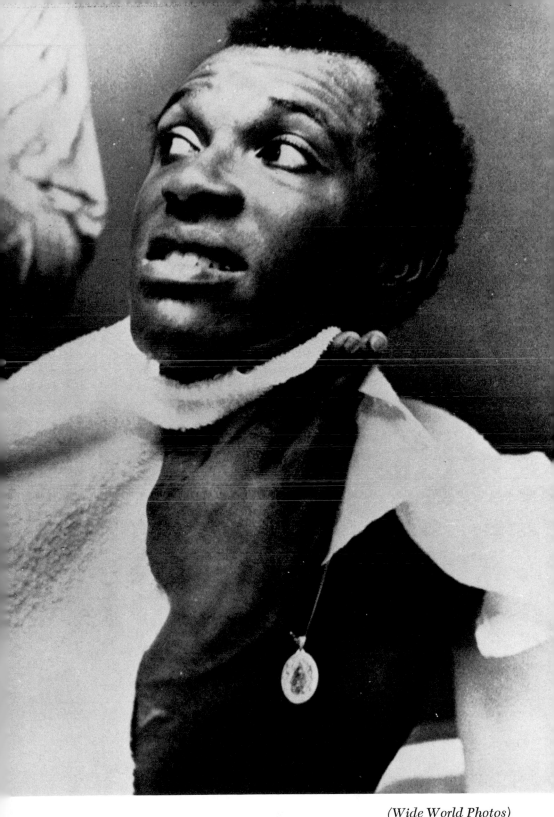

(Wide World Photos)

(Ron Riesterer, *Oakland Tribune*)

(Ron Riesterer, *Oakland Tribune*)

Vida in the A's clubhouse, matching muscles with Reggie Jackson (top), and running phantom football play with clubhouse boys. (John Zimmerman, *Life* Magazine © Time Inc.)

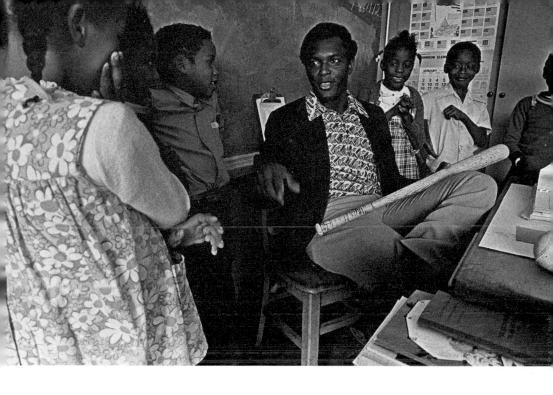

Holding class in a neighborhood school. (Christopher R. Harris)

(UPI)

A little extra lovin' for a fan.
(Christopher R. Harris)

The fans make demands. (Top—
Ron Riesterer, *Oakland Tribune*)
(Bottom—John Zimmerman, *Life*
Magazine, © Time Inc.)

At the airport, with teammate Angel Mangual and a future fan. (Fred Kaplan for *Sports Illustrated* © Time Inc.)

(Christopher R. Harris)

(Christopher R. Harris)

The moods of Vida Blue. (Ron Riesterer, *Oakland Tribune*)

With fans. (Ron Riesterer, *Oakland Tribune*)

Enjoying a special day at the ballpark with his mom. (Howard L. Erker, Pleasanton, California)

Taking official custody of the controversial Caddy. (Howard L. Erker, Pleasanton, California)

Raring back. (Ron Riesterer, *Oakland Tribune*)

With manager Bob Gerst looking on, Vida Blue signs a contract with Harry Granoff to endorse Regent Gloves.

With Willie Mays on Dick Cavett's ABC-TV show.

(Ron Riesterer, *Oakland Tribune*)

forthcoming All-Star Game. Vida said, "Man, how do you know I'm even going to be selected? That's what's wrong with the world today. Everybody takes too much for granted."

More writers and broadcasters crowded around and someone asked him how he rated this game against others he'd pitched. Vida said, "Let's not rate it. Let's forget this one and look forward to the next one. This one's history." Finally, he walked away. He hid in the showers, steaming the soreness from his body. He did not come out until almost everyone else had left. He asked, "What's gametime tomorrow night? Six o'clock? I think I'll come out around one to get away from that damn telephone and find me a corner somewhere and get me some sleep."

He finished drying himself off and began to dress. He said, "Mercy, you'd think I'd given up ten runs, you'd think I lost." He sighed and said, "I was a little lucky I guess. But sometimes in this game it's as good to be lucky as it is to be good." He finished dressing and looked around at the nearly empty locker room, littered with discarded dirty clothes and soiled towels, and he said, "Mercy, are we really only at midseason?"

And he walked away and out, and it took him a long time to work his way through the autograph-seekers who had waited patiently and excitedly outside. As he approached his hotel he thought about Disneyland, where the lights were twinkling not far away and the holiday crowds were gathered to frolic carefree amid fantasy. He whistled softly. "Wowee," he said, "don't all those people wish they were Vida Blue."

This traditionally is considered midseason. The A's reached it a big 11½ games in front at the halfway point in their schedule with a .654 percentage, the best in baseball at the time, on 53 victories and 28 defeats. Blue stood 17–3, Hunter 11–7, Dobson 6–0. Davis was hitting .310, Mangual .303, Jackson .280 and Bando .278. Bando had 49 RBI's, Jackson 41, Rudi 40 and Epstein 38. Jackson had 17 homers, Epstein 12, Duncan and Bando 11.

Vida Blue was baseball's winningest pitcher; had the most complete games, 16; the most shutouts, 6; and the lowest earned-run average, 1.54.

Behind all these statistics had been a torrid three months of effort, a blazing burst of national acclaim and unrelenting attention. He had already pitched what for most pitchers would be a full season and he still had a long, hard way to go. Smiling with wistful wonder, he asked, "Is this still 1971?"

He had one more start before opening the All-Star Game, and with this one they almost went into 1972. It was against the same foe he had faced in his last outing five days earlier, the Angels, only this one was in Oakland. Before 22,938 and an excited southern California television audience, Blue did not lose, but he also did not win, though he pitched spectacularly.

He spaced seven hits, struck out seventeen, did not give up a walk for the second-straight game and did not give up a run for eleven innings. Unfortunately for him, at the end of that time, Rudy May of the Angels had not given up a run, either, and he, while throwing a three-hitter and fanning thirteen, had walked six. It was scoreless, and Williams, worried that Vida's arm might come unhinged and follow his next pitch to the plate, mercifully relieved his tired and precious property at this point. May followed an inning later. The relievers dueled on and on and on, past midnight. Many lost much sleep. After five hours and five minutes, at five past one in the morning, in the last half of the twentieth inning—before the umpires would have called the contest because of curfew regulations—Blue's road roomie, Mangual, singled to give the A's and Knowles a dramatic 1–0 triumph.

"It's not wasted effort when the team wins," Blue insisted later. But he seemed worn'out by the effort and disappointed that it had not brought him the shutout triumph it warranted. He sat in the dressing room freshly showered, but not fresh, his sport shirt open at the neck, slacks neatly pressed, loafers brightly shined, date for the night long since disappeared into the morning, and he watched his teammates wearily celebrate. After a while he got up and limped off, going home alone. After games he always limps. Is it psychological? "I don't know," he admits. "I only know that after games I hurt some."

In a hotel lobby, Charles O. Finley was asked just exactly how many extra fans Blue was attracting with each start. "I'm not going to tell you," said Finley. "He's got enough salary leverage as it is."

CHAPTER TEN

"I'm Vida Blue. And this is Aqua Velva Ice Blue. You know, I started using Aqua Velva when I was back in Double-A ball only making $1,000 a year.
Now, you've probably heard I'm the lowest-paid superstar in America. Well, I am.
(Smile.)
But next year I'm gonna make a whole lot of money.
(Big smile.)
And I'm gonna start my day with a splash of Aqua Velva. Success isn't gonna spoil Vida Blue."

He is on camera for thirty seconds and he is beautiful. Everyone who has seen the television commercial, and there may not be a man, woman or child who has not, would agree he is beautiful. The Parkson Advertising Agency, which prepared it, and the sponsor, who bought it, agree he is beautiful, for he is selling the shaving lotion. He is natural, he speaks well, he is extremely handsome, and when he smiles he wins you over completely. He is a natural. The people who see it say he should be an actor, he is another Sidney Poitier.

He makes it look easy.

They shot two commercials, one for the 1971 season and one for the 1972 season. It took 92 takes over six and a half hours to get it the way you see it. That's how easy it was. He sweated over it and suffered over it, and the director sweated and suffered over it, and the agency people sweated and suffered over it, and the day under the hot lights dragged on and on and on. The director told Vida's manager, Bob Gerst, he never met a celebrity so agreeable, so willing to submit to retakes to get it right, so ready to keep working to get it right.

Gerst set it up, and when the agency couldn't get a suitable studio in San Francisco or Hollywood, they flew Blue and Gerst to Sacramento in a private plane and shot the main commercial and an alternate commercial at a studio there. Blue was paid $25,000 plus guarantees of additional monies if the commercial were used beyond contracted limitations. It is Gerst's understanding that close to a quarter of a million dollars was paid to put the commercial on during prime time on national network television throughout the summer alone.

Gerst sweated through it, too. That's what he is paid for and he earns his money. Blue says, "As soon as I got hot, not only the writers and broadcasters and fans started to come after me, but the agents and the businessmen and the friends who had deals for me and all sorts of guys wanted to represent me and I didn't know one from another and I didn't know anything about the deals that were being offered me and I was suspicious of everyone and everything, but I wanted to take some things because big money was being waved at me and I needed the money, but I could see how easy it would be to make bad deals and I could see I had to get someone to take care of me and get these guys off my back and get me something in the bank.

"I turned to Tommy Davis, who said he had a good lawyer in Los Angeles who managed his business affairs and who also was the attorney for Jerry West—who had been big for a long time— but who didn't handle a whole lot of guys and didn't tie his guys up in a whole lot of little deals and didn't take 'em for a lot of money. This was Bob Gerst. I had a T-shirt thing going that sounded pretty good to me, so I took it to Bob and he looked it over and threw it right out the window.

"I liked him right away, and he seemed to like me. He didn't pretend that I wasn't hot or anything like that. And he told me just what his take would be. He laid it all out for me. And I liked the look of it. So I asked him to take over all of my money and business affairs, and he agreed. I'm not tied to him for life, and he's not tied to me. If we get unhappy with one another, we can split. I'm happy.

"I'm a little close with a buck. Maybe because I never had much money, except the bonus, and I never spent much of that. When I got hot, I found I had a lot of long-lost relatives and friends and I didn't dig that much. I didn't even have any dough yet. With Bob I first began to make some. But I wanted to keep some, too. I'm no penny-pincher. Anything I have is my family's. I'll give to a charity a whole lot quicker than I'll give to a cousin I never saw before in my life. If I ever give a $50 tip I should get an Emmy award. If I win the Cy Young Award for the next fifty years, my style won't change.

"Gerst is a nice man. He's got a nice family. He's a family man. He's also a businessman. He's young and he's sharp and he's aggressive. No one's gonna push him around. He does his job down to a T. He asks me for my back business papers or contracts for all my life. I don't know where they are. I'm not that interested. I should be, but I'm not. But he wants them because he can do something with them, so he keeps after me. I got to have someone like him. He drives me crazy, but I like him. And I trust him as much as I trust anyone."

Bob Gerst is thirty-six. He was born in Chicago and moved to Los Angeles while a little boy. His dad, Hyman, has sold insurance for Metropolitan Life for forty-seven years and is a product of Tilden High in the Windy City. Gerst went to Fairfax High in the Jewish belt of Los Angeles. He was an excellent athlete and recalls with good humor that he was the school's No. 1 pitcher, ahead of Larry Sherry and Barry Lattman, and its No. 1 quarterback, ahead of Jack Kemp. But while he went into law, they went straight ahead into professional athletics. Gerst did play three years of baseball under Rod Dedeaux at USC. He played the infield and the team won titles in his time, but not an NCAA title such as it has won many other times.

Gerst graduated from law school in 1959 and passed his bar and went into practice in January of 1960 and now is a member of the firm of Weissburg, Jacobs and Gerst with handsome offices along the Avenue of the Stars in the swank Century City complex in L.A. He married Dorene while in law school and has two sons, David, born in 1958, and Daniel, born in 1962, and lives in a modest residential area in west L.A.

He was representing a businessman friend of Jerry West's who recommended him to West when Jerry was having contractual problems with an endorsement deal and Gerst wound up taking over most of his business affairs. Jerry is conservative and tough. He doesn't want just any deal. He doesn't need the money or the headaches of a lot of little deals that might depreciate his image. He wants only a few solid things. Gerst thinks along the same lines. He is a nice man, but in the clinches the lawyer in him comes out and he does not dismiss details lightly. He is tough. He is out to protect his clients.

Unlike many in this relatively new field of athletes' representation he does not have a long list of clients. He took on Tommy Davis and through Tommy he took on Vida Blue. He would take on others if the right ones came along, but doubts he would take on many. He says, "You can't spread yourself too thin and still do a job for the clients you're supposed to be representing. Many have been attracted to this field by the sort of money the superstars can command, but they all wind up taking advantage of those in the lesser income bracket. I'm not interested in getting together a long list of professional athletes whose few bucks I'm cutting. I'd rather have only those who have sufficient earning potential to need representation, for whom I can do a real job and merit a reasonable return."

Although some managers and agents take 25 to 50 percent of their athletes' total earnings or side-deal monies, the complicated hourly wage formula by which he figures fees due him from Blue has a ceiling of 15 percent. In return his basic responsibilities are to screen, research and discuss all offers with Vida and make recommendations, negotiate all contracts, manage his money and investments and tax affairs, and supervise his personal and television appearances and major interview situations.

These are detailed and demanding chores. The most difficult came later, in the negotiations of a new contract for Blue with Oakland owner Finley. Team owners and general managers may resent athletes having attorneys and managers represent them in

these matters, but the teams usually have top-level experts behind them while young and inexperienced athletes formerly did
not. In the meantime, Gerst sifted through hundreds of offers
advanced his new client and accepted enough to earn Vida an
additional $75,000 through the end of 1971, which for a youngster
on a $14,750 salary was most welcome.

Gerst went along on Vida's more important appearances and
commercial tapings and fought many of his fights for him "to
make sure he got presented in the best possible light." In con-
trolling Blue's returns, he did not immediately embark him on a
heavy investment program, explaining, "He was just beginning
to make money and needed a base from which to work. In his
position, it was important that his funds be liquid, that he have
money in the bank, money in reserve, money he could get his
hands on if wanted or needed. This year, when he's on more
solid footing, we'll look to take some of the excess and invest with
it in programs promising good returns for his future along with
solid protection for his present, but I want him to have a better
understanding than he now has of these programs and their prospects."

Blue had little understanding of the business side of life when
he was thrust into it after about two months of the 1971 season and as the demands on him became excessive he began to
hide from them. He missed some appointments and stopped
answering some telephone calls and became elusive even to those
tied to him. This writer recalls frustration at being unable to
corner the subject for agreed interview sessions, finally calling
Gerst's office in hopes of getting through to Blue and, before even
getting to speak, being asked by an associate "Hey, if you're
going to Oakland, will you ask Vida to call us. We're having
trouble reaching him also."

However, what seems to have been irresponsibility may have
been the desperation of a young man driven by demons, for he
had to find some way to concentrate on his main role: He still
had to produce on the field. Whenever he'd let you down, he'd
grin, hold up his hands in mock horror, back up from pretend
fear of your wrath and plead for forgiveness. "I'm sorry. I'm

wrong. I admit it. Please don't beat me. I won't do it again. I promise," he'd say, knowing very well he would, knowing you knew he would.

The harsh fact is superstars frequently do not honor their own commitments because they know they are important enough to get away with it. When their importance diminishes, they often find it hard to adjust to having to come through on a lower level. Blue always made it clear he felt bad when he behaved badly. And when he was cornered for commitments, he always behaved beautifully.

Gerst says, "He is beautiful and he has a beautiful future. He caused us some concern, but a lot less than most in his position would have. And when he posed problems, it wasn't because he was selfishly seeking some profit but because he simply had to get away from the pressures which were pounding at him. I tried to protect him from many of these pressures and tried to impose as few of my own as possible and still do some of the business for him he wanted us to do for him. He is very young and was in an incredibly demanding position and I really felt he reacted with a great deal of grace.

"Obviously, he's enormously talented. He's also intelligent. And while he's ambitious, he's not greedy. He's not so eager for the quick buck that he will do everything that comes along. He has patience and will wait for what's best for him in the long run. He should have a long run, long beyond baseball, and we have to think about that because a pitcher's arm is fragile and a professional athlete's career can't be counted on going beyond ten to fifteen years at the most and he has to do a lot of living after that. He's commercially attractive. He has the name and the talent, the rare good looks and tremendously appealing personality and the poise to go beyond baseball. People notice him, they look at him, they're drawn to him. Color doesn't matter as much as it once did, and where it might he may be the first one with the stuff to overcome any objections. He's very special."

Gerst says, "I do not have contracts with the athletes I represent. I can't understand lawyers, managers and agents battling against the reserve clauses which bind players to teams, then signing athletes to contracts which bind them to themselves. Where is that fair? If I'm not doing a job that satisfies Vida, I wouldn't want him to stay with me. If he ever became tough to work with, I wouldn't want to stay with him. Life is too short. I'm not that hungry for power and wealth. I want to do a good job for my clients and make a good life for myself and my family. As long as I do a good job for Vida and we're working well together, we'll stay together."

When word got out he was representing Blue, Gerst was contacted by many managers and agents who wanted to do Blue's business for him, but Bob was set to do this side of things, too. He says, "I don't believe there were very many major individuals or agencies in the field who didn't come at us. Some of them seem solid enough and some of them seem suspect, to say the least. Many of them are hustlers who cut the clients terribly. I know one major agent in New York who will get an OK from an athlete for $250 for the use of his name in something, then pocket most of the $1,500 check he got from the deal. My clients see all of the contracts.

"The T-shirt deal Vida brought me originally was the worst thing of its kind I've ever seen. There was nothing wrong with the shirt or even the money he'd have made but these vultures had written a contract that would have tied him to them for all endorsements and commercials for years, body and soul, far beyond T-shirts. A guy like Vida gets hot and he's promptly pounced on by parasites who want to pick his bones clean while the flesh is still warm. I have a large file full of dead prospects, dozens of deals we've rejected. These include radio commercials for a loan company, television commercials for a bar-b-q outfit, endorsements for leather coats, public appearances for quickie outfits. So-called close friends call up saying Vida promised to do this and that when he did no such thing. It's incredible."

Gerst says, money is far from the only decisive factor. He insists image is equally important. He says, "Vida's peak years in sports are limited and he has to make the most of them while he can, but he's going to live a lot longer than that, he has to live with himself and his public image, he has to be himself, and he has to be put in a position where he faces a comfortable future. We'd rather have a few, substantial things of quality than a lot of flimsy things of doubtful merit."

Aside from the Aqua Velva commercial, Blue did some TV spots for the California Milk Advisory Board, which have been shown regularly for many months. He did them for the first year for a $10,000 fee and a $1,000 donation to the Sickle Cell Anemia Disease Research Foundation and they were renewed for six more months for another $6,000 and because he really does drink a lot of milk and recommends it to youngsters and considers it a sort of public service. Singer Vikki Carr and others have done similar commercials that are shown regularly. The personality talks about milk, his talk is taped and portions of the tape are removed for the thirty- to sixty-second spots. In Vida's case he talked for two hours and eleven spots were taken out and approved for use. The finished products are not nearly as polished as the Aqua Velva commercials, but they capture the natural, informal quality that was desired and they capture a lot of his boyish charm.

> *Vida: Well, first of all, when I was at home, ah, I used to . . . my mother would have to keep me away from the refrigerator because I would sneak back in and get milk. And even now I find myself—when I go out to a restaurant —three out of five times I will have milk in my diet or with my diet. I'm sure no one wants to drink milk when you're in a group of ten or twelve men, you know, and I'm sure they would get on you about that. But, I don't think I would be afraid to order it; they would just have to get on me. I'm definitely a milk-man. These are the he-men of the group. I mean the ones that drink the milk are the ones with the good bodies.*
> *I feel as though I have a real fine body here and (smiling broadly) I think milk has played an important part in that.*
> *Announcer: Every body needs milk.*
> *Even Vida Blues.*
>
> *Vida: I do coach a Little League team, and it's in this same pasture that I used to play ball in. We'd come out after school and we play a little ball and we have fun.*

And naturally I'll take 'em to my house afterwards and I'll
treat 'em to cookies and milk. So I try to influence kids
about growing up and just knowing the difference between
right and wrong. I couldn't tell you how much milk I used
to drink. I'll take a rough estimate—maybe a gallon and a
half a day. That's quite a bit. . . . I still have that love for
milk. Maybe two and a half gallons per day now. At my
apartment I don't have to worry about anyone hassling me
if I order milk. . . . I can drink as much as I want. . . .
Announcer: Every body needs milk.
Even Vida Blues.

Prescott Sullivan, San Francisco *Examiner* sports columnist,
wrote:

> *Through a large part of the baseball season, Blue was*
> *on the air voicing the claim that he consumed an average*
> *of two and a half gallons of milk per day. It was too much*
> *for some listeners, as indeed it was for us. Mention of it*
> *was made in this column. Readers also questioned Blue's*
> *capacity to put away ten quarts of milk daily. Skepticism*
> *spread to the sponsors. They, too, found it hard to swallow,*
> *and Blue was asked to tone it down a bit. But, as subse-*
> *quent events were to prove, he was not exaggerating.*
>
> *At a banquet he attended in Modesto, two half-gallon*
> *cartons of milk were placed in front of him. It was in-*
> *tended as a gag, but Blue saw nothing funny about it. All*
> *seriousness and with eyes only for the milk, he took care*
> *of the first half-gallon before the entrée and the second*
> *after dessert. In so doing, he made believers of all con-*
> *cerned. Simple arithmetic convinced them that two and a*
> *half gallons a day were no trick at all for a guy who*
> *could, and did, knock off a gallon at one setting.*

Blue not only drinks milk and sometimes shaves and uses after-
shave lotion, he wears clothes, too, and Gerst set a long-term deal
with Jantzen that sends Jerry West and other prominent athletes
around the world with their families to wear their sportswear
and be pictured in magazines doing the same. This is a quality
concern, and Gerst was seeking one other top-drawer outfit Vida

might represent reasonably on a long-term arrangement. Blue also plays a bit of baseball and he signed with Regent to endorse a line of baseball gloves for three years.

Several publishers bid for a book on him, and this book, to be published by Prentice-Hall, was arranged for an advance and a percentage of sales. He is young yet to have a biography of his life in print, especially after only one full year in the majors, but it was felt that the season was so spectacular that a revealing work was possible, and he agreed to search inside himself for his true feelings and to permit the book to show him as he really was, and Gerst agreed. Others did other books on him, but not with him.

Vida really did not take himself as seriously as many others did, and Gerst did not mind him doing a "Laugh-In" TV show in which he did the usual series of quickie spots.

> *Questioner: When you were a boy, did you ever think you'd make the majors?*
> *Vida: Whattayamean? I am a boy and I'm already in the majors.*

When the show was shown, he missed it. Not that his team was playing that night, but a pro-football game was on television at the same time, and there was no way he was going to miss that.

He did a Dick Cavett late-night television talk-show which neither he nor Gerst felt came off well because Cavett did not seem tremendously interested in baseball, and though he had some questions ready he brought them out with an air of cynicism. He asked him about the fans, his salary, Finley asking Vida to change his name and the dimes he carries in his pocket when he pitches. Vida said things like "My name is screwed up enough as it is," sweating under the hot lights. Cavett said things like "Oh, he's *good-looking*" and "Is he for real?" and eventually confronted him with a couple of umpires, and it went downhill from there.

The fans really were interested in this new star. His appearance in one city was previewed in headlines with IT'S BLUE MONDAY and

the Yankees ran a large ad in such newspapers as the New York
Post proclaiming in bold block letters:

VIDA
BLUE
is pitching Sunday.
You coming out?
The Yankees are digging in to stop flame-throwing Vida
Blue and the rest of the red-hot Oakland A's. You coming
out?

Inevitably, there was a song written about him and recorded. It
was written by Tom Newton and Choker Campbell, published
by Luzar Publishing Company and recorded on the Tri-City La
bel with the same song on both sides, sung in country-and-western
fashion by Newton on one side and in rock-and-roll fashion by
Albert Jones on the other side, with Vida guaranteed a minimum
of $5,000 in royalties.

If you are looking for a hero
Exciting and new
There's a boy in Oakland
Name of Vida Blue

He throws a fastball
Like it's shot from a gun
Everybody's talking
That he's number one
That's Vida Blue

He's good-looking
Throws BB's, too
Vida's still a youngster
He's just a boy,
But let me tell you

He's the real McCoy
He turns it loose
Inside and high
Before the batter blinks
That ball's gone by
That's Vida Blue

Oh, that poor catcher
He needs a bigger mitt
Now all of the kids
And their parents too
Are rooting hard
For Vida Blue

They've heard of Feller and Koufax
And all the rest
But this kid from Oakland
Could be the best
That's Vida Blue
Vida who?
Vida Blue, thats who

It goes on awhile. Hearing it for the first time, Vida's face broke into a broad grin, his toes began to tap and he began to sing along.

Killebrew, Yastrzemski
And Gates Brown too
Can't buy a hit
Off of Vida Blue

Baseball is still
Our national game
But the last few years
Things were kind of tame
But now they're buzzing
From town to town
Ain't no hitter living
Put Vida down

Get his autograph, girls
He won't bite you
He's a gentleman
That's Vida Blue

Daddy, ain't Vida Blue
Ever going to lose again?
Watch your mouth, boy
That's Vida Blue
Ain't nothing he can't do
He's the greatest
That's Vida Blue

It was fun for him, hearing it, and he laughed at it, and left it, smiling and singing, "If you are looking for a hero . . . Exciting and new . . . There's a boy in Oakland . . . Name of Vida Blue. . . ." But when the other players heard it and they laughed at it and started to sing it, his good nature was truly tested. Shaking his head, grinning, he says, "They played it in Milwaukee and the guys got on me but good. While I was warming up, they stood on the steps of the dugout, looking up in the stands and sort of singing and sort of yelling to the ladies, 'Get his autograph, girls . . . He won't bite you . . . Go right on down . . . That's Vida Blue.'"

He still had to perform on the field.

CHAPTER ELEVEN

Vida Blue says, "When I'm throwing good, I don't think there's a man in the world who can hit me."

He smiles and adds, "I really feel that way. But I think you have to think that way to win. I think you have to think you're good to be good. I think you have to think you're great to be great. I think you have to think you're the best before you can be the best. Before I had won awhile in the majors, I didn't know how good I was. I thought I was going to be good. But I didn't know. Now I've been here awhile and I know. I can be the best. Because I've been beating the best. They don't come any better than they are up here. They are the best. They've done it. I'm not the best yet because I haven't done it enough yet. Maybe I won't. But I think I will. I'm close already. If I can put a little more to it. No one was as good as me for one year. If I can put some more years to it . . . But, you have to be lucky. Your arm has to hold up. Your support has to hold up. I got a helluva chance."

They called 1968 "The Year of the Pitcher." The batters were dominated, the writers were bored and the fans were frustrated. Baseball acted, lowering the pitching mound and reducing the strike zone. There even was a strong suspicion a livelier ball had been introduced. By 1970, batting averages had risen 16 points, homers were up 40 percent, hitters were dominating pitchers, interest was rising and attendance rose by nearly six million. A year later, Blue burst on the scene, almost single-handedly reversing the trend, and yet interest in him and attendance at his games was remarkable. Bucking the odds, Blue was brilliant.

Standing splay-footed while waiting to pitch, Blue looks awkward. He has a big motion. He rares way back, raising his bent right knee high in front of him and dropping his left hand with the ball low behind him. He thrusts his leg forward, delays briefly, then uncoils, bringing his arm around in a not quite over-arm motion. Here is a lot of motion for the batter to look at. And if it is not quite stylish, it has a smooth flow to it. He does not seem to be extending himself even when throwing his hardest.

Former Yankee left-handed pitching star Whitey Ford says, "If you think like a pitcher, the first time you see him, you have to say he can throw the ball. He has a loose, easy windup. He cocks himself and that way he gets the most spring out of his body. He's smooth and he comes right over the top with the ball. He's an all-around athlete. He has balance." Baltimore batter Dave Johnson says, "Vida has a nice, easy delivery. He has good control of his body. You like to hit against a guy who grunts out there because then you know it's coming hard. But Blue doesn't do any grunting. I think his arm will hold up."

Blue says, "My motion came to me naturally. It hasn't changed much over the years. Bill Posedel made me less overarm. Sometimes I get a little too loose out there, work too fast and stride too far. I have to close up, slow up, shorten up. Sometimes I'll go in the outfield during pregame practice and practice my motion and my follow-through to keep it grooved. Sometimes I'll release the ball too high or too low. Whatever I do wrong, I usually can tell. Posedel also tells me between innings. Sometimes he'll give me a little yell even when I'm on the mound. I can make adjustments even between pitches. It doesn't throw me off.

"I'm at the point where I throw fastballs eight out of ten. The other two usually will be curve balls. The curve is getting better, but it's not like something that drops off a table. The big thing is if I can get it over. They're usually looking for the fastball, so the curve ball is hard for them to hit. But the big thing is to get them to thinking it may be the curve so they can't plant themselves. The fastball remains my out pitch.

"They swing at a lot of first pitches on me. I've learned I can't throw full speed 100 pitches a game so I'll take something off the fast one from time to time. This way I always have the real hard one in reserve. It also gives the batters a different speed to worry about. I throw the curve hard, but sometimes I throw it a little slower. Once in a while I throw a changeup but I haven't got a real good one yet.

"Mostly, I don't try to finesse a batter. I blow him down. I just try to hit the corners or jam a guy and break his bat. I enjoy breaking a guy's bat. That means I'm throwing good. Sometimes I'm not throwing hard. There's no reason for it I know, it's just not there, the snap's not there. When I realize it, I hold the ball more across the seams so it moves more and try to hit the corners more. My ball moves a lot anyway. It's a natural thing and it's what makes my fastball so effective. I guess I throw as hard as anyone. But, also, my ball is alive and some fastball pitchers throw straight. I also hold my speed longer than most speed pitchers.

"I throw strikes. Another big thing I have is control. I can't hit a dime at 90 feet. I can't always cut the corners the way I'd like or hit spots every time the way some veterans can. And I didn't always have control. But it came fast, much faster than to most guys my age, especially fastball pitchers—and, from what they tell me, especially left-handers. I do get the ball over. And if you just get the ball over with any swift or anything at all on it you got a chance, the best hitters will go out seven times out of ten. Why, did you ever notice how many hitters pop up swinging at 3-and-0 pitches grooved right over the plate? Happens at least five times out of ten. The pitcher's got the edge to start with.

"So I throw strikes. So, throwing hard, with a live ball, I get a lot of strikeouts. I like strikeouts. So do the fans. I like to do it myself. If they hit the ball in the air or on the ground they may find a hole with it or the fielder may muff it. But I'll take an out any way I can get it. If I was sure I could get it on one pitch, I'd rather have that than the strikeouts. Strikeouts are hard work. You have to throw at least three pitches. Sometimes you can get three outs on three pitches. I don't care about records, just outs and wins. If I strike out 27 men but in-between some get on and some get home and they beat me, I'm unhappy."

Whitey Ford says, "It's something he has to start thinking about

now, his curve and changeup. He ought to work on it now because, if he gets to be as good as I think he's going to be, he's
going to be around a long time. And he can't afford to wait till
later till everything else is gone to start looking. I think he's
smart enough to know that."

Vida says, "Sometimes I think I don't want to think about other
pitches until I'm an old man and sometimes I think I want to
master them as soon as I can. If you ask me different times I may
say something different different times because it depends on my
mood. I'm afraid of messing myself up by fooling around too
much. And I know most of the time I don't need much else. It
doesn't hurt my arm to throw hard. Everything's fluid. My body's
flexible. But throwing too many breaking pitches, snapping your
arm and your elbow, that does damage. If I don't need it, why
do it?

"On the other hand, the more I pitch the more I realize there
are times when I'm not throwing good, when I need the other
things, when I need to have the ability to change speeds. I admire the guys who can throw the 3-and-2 changeup, the 3-and-2
curve. That's guts. That's some kind of pitcher to be. But those
are things I'll have to learn and acquire and I'm not sure I should
go after them right away. It does make me feel good to pitch a
good game when I'm not throwing good, as if I'm mastering
baseball itself. It's nice when the ball is doing what I want it to
do. It's nice to know I got something in reserve other than just
blowing the batters down."

Young as he is, Vida has fashioned a philosophy of pitching.
He says, "I go out there wanting the win, of course. You start
out trying to pitch a no-hitter. By that, I mean you're trying to
bear down on every batter. You don't want to walk anyone. You
don't want to give up a hit. You give up a walk or a hit, you try
not to give up another. You go for the shutout. They score one
run off you, you try not to give them two. Physically, you try to
pace yourself some, but you don't look too far ahead, you try to
take each batter in turn. Piece by piece, pitch by pitch, you build
the best game you can.

"You never know going to the ballpark or warming up, how
you're gonna be. Generally, I'm pretty good. I'm consistent. But

I'm talking about fine differences. If the fastball isn't smoking, I try to make it move more or I go to more curves or try for more corners. If I'm wild, I'm not going to go for the corners. I usually throw low and my ball rises. If I'm wild high, I'm in trouble. And when I'm wild, I tend to be wild high.

"I don't go too much by scouting reports. If a pitch someone hits is my best pitch I still figure I got to throw it. I figure I got to match my strength against them, even if it's against their strength. Maybe I can keep 'em off balance, but I haven't been around long enough to outsmart 'em. They can figure things out, too, they're good, they're trying to beat me and I can either beat them or I can't. I know they remember things I did. I try not to get into a pattern. The catcher helps.

"I try to stay cool. If they get a couple of hits off me, it doesn't kill me. I start out trying for the no-hitter, but I never expect it. I want to keep trying for the best I can get. I don't want to get rattled. If they get a run, two runs off me, I'm not going to cut my throat out there and I'm not going to throw the ball in the stands and go home. As long as I'm still in there and as long as we can still win I'm still going with my best. If they get a couple of men on, maybe they'll hit into a double-play. If they're rapping the ball on you, maybe it'll go right at someone. As long as you're in there, you just do the best you can and then there's no regrets later.

"I have pride. It's an asset. I don't give up. A lot of guys do. They get disgusted and throw it away. I don't throw anything away.

"I don't care who's at bat. You won't believe that, but I mean it. It doesn't matter if it's Harmon Killebrew or the pitcher. If I'm going good, I can get anyone out. And if I'm going bad, anyone can hit me. Sure Harmon Killebrew is going to get more big hits than any thirty or forty pitchers. But he may not get them off me. I may only face him eight, ten, twelve times in a season and he may not get a hit off me. Pitchers may get four or five or six. I been beat as many times by bad hitters as by good hitters. So I don't judge 'em. I just pitch to 'em. And I try to pitch tough to all of 'em.

"I'm not afraid to be mean. Not much has been said about me throwing at hitters, but I'm not afraid to move a man around at the plate. If a man takes advantage of me, he'll have to pay his dues. Any man is going to have to show me he can stand in there. If he crowds the plate, I'll move him back. I'll throw inside, knee-high, chest-high, head-high. Even if men are on, I'll still do it. It's a challenge to me to do it. My control is good. I want to let them know I'm there. They have to earn my respect. I respect them, I want them to respect me. I won't knock anyone down unless I have to. If someone throws at my teammates or at me, I have to throw at them. But I won't throw at a man's head. I throw too hard, there's too much of a risk to play tough guy. From what I heard, Drysdale was the last really mean pitcher. But it's an advantage. And I want every edge I can get. So I'll be as mean as I have to be."

He already has the opposition nervous. Whitey Ford says, "Once you get them worrying about you and looking through the sports pages to see if you're going to pitch the next series against them, you've really got something going for you. I think it's starting to work like that for Vida Blue now. That's just about the greatest thing in the world a pitcher can have going for him." Don Drysdale says, "If you can get them afraid of you, it's a tremendous psychological edge. If they're uncertain up there, holding back, lacking confidence, they're not going to get to you even when you're off form. Something like that happened when I put together my record run of shutout innings. When you get a streak like that going for you, the other guys figure you're hot and no matter what they say on the outside they don't expect to do anything to you." But Sandy Koufax says, "Even if a great history helps, you still have to perform. If this wasn't so, an outstanding pitcher would never get knocked out. Vida Blue is outstanding, especially for one so young. He throws exceptionally hard and his ball moves and he has control. He performs."

Opponents say Blue's fastball blazes, smokes, hops, darts, jumps, skips, pops, sails, slides, sinks, tails off and explodes. Boog Powell says, "Blue's fastball reminds me of Koufax's. It starts at the knee, takes off and goes by you chest-high." Blue laughs and says, "I've thrown some that started at the knee and wound up in the stands."

Paul Schaal says, "His ball seems to jump right over your bat." Roy White says, "His ball seems to speed up on you and then seems to disappear." Cookie Rojas says, "When he winds up I start to swing." Brooks Robinson says, "He throws so hard you haven't got long to make up your mind." Frank Robinson says, "Even when you know what he's going to throw, you still can't catch up to it. It tails in on you and then sometimes it doesn't."

Harmon Killebrew says, "He has yet to throw me a damned one down the chute. He's in, out, up, down, and everything has something on it." Carl Yastrzemski says, "What impresses me about him is his poise and control. He throws in and out, up and down, I think he could win even without that great fastball." George Scott says, "He's got good stuff. He's only a baby and he's gonna get better. I sure hate to think of him getting any better than he is now."

This was a youngster who didn't turn twenty-two until the middle of the season. Traditionally, left-handers develop late. Warren Spahn was twenty-five before he won a big-league game. Sandy Koufax was twenty-five before he was a winner. Rube Waddell was twenty-six before he reached his stride. Lefty Grove was twenty-seven before he settled down. Sam McDowell is supposed to have been the most talented southpaw of recent years and throws bullets but he was twenty-seven before he had a big year and at twenty-nine he's still wild.

There are no guarantees Blue is going to get better, or even remain nearly as good. Karl Spooner struck out twenty-seven men in his first two major-league games in the mid-1950's but shortly thereafter burned his arm away. Herb Score had a swift start but was hit by a line drive and was through at twenty-four. Even without injury or accident, some athletes never again live up to one big season. But Blue believes he will get better.

Vida says, "I think talent is 80 percent of pitching. The rest can be taught. I've learned a lot in one season. My knowledge of the game and the hitters is improving all the time. My knowledge of myself is improving all the time. I know my weaknesses. My concentration wanders sometimes. I talk to myself on the mound all the time to keep bearing down. I have to improve my stuff. I'm a perfectionist. Despite my record, I'm not satisfied. I know I can do better. I haven't stopped maturing and I haven't stopped gaining weight and strength. I'm going to be a bigger man. I may level off as high as 205 pounds. It's amazing that I've done as well as I have. I'm just learning to pitch. I haven't mastered my trade yet."

Dick Williams says, "Vida has complete control of himself. Since he has the ability, he will be what he wants to be. He's tough. He's just starting, but already when he gets his curve ball over he's as good as Sandy Koufax or Herb Score were, and he gets his curve over. He's in his first full season up here. Sandy had as much stuff in his first season, but he couldn't control it for five or six years. It took Sandy five years to pitch ten complete games. Vida is five years ahead of Sandy."

Bill Posedel says, "Don't give me the credit. We've all tried to help him, but he helps himself. He has the body and arm of a great thrower and the mind of a great pitcher. If he is not as complete a master of his craft yet as some pitchers, he is so far ahead of where others were or are at his age that it's scary. The first time I ever saw him he could get all of his pitches over the plate. He hadn't decided how he wanted to hold his breaking balls. Everyone doesn't hold them the same, you know. You can't teach just one way. Apparently, Juan Pizzaro showed Vida a way he liked. I've helped him with his delivery some and I keep on him to keep up his concentration, but these are only technical details which may have accelerated his success some, he's such a natural he'd be getting there on his own anyway. He makes a mistake, he recognizes it and sets about correcting it. He has amazing poise. I just never saw a kid come so fast. He's a once-in-a-lifetime pitcher. Maybe that's an exaggeration. We have a tendency to go overboard. But there was Koufax. And now there's Blue. And the rest of the left-handers haven't had this kind of talent."

Tommy Davis, who played with Koufax, says, "Sandy exploded, Vida glides. Vida has an easier motion, using lots of body, which saves his arm. He can throw hard for nine innings, which few can do. Sandy developed an arthritic elbow and had to pitch in terrible pain his last years. He still pitched exceptionally, but then he retired early. With luck Vida should last longer. Koufax didn't mature until he was twenty-five or twenty-six. Blue might rewrite the record books."

Whitey Ford says, "Sooner or later the arm goes bad. It has to. The arm wasn't meant to stand the strain pitching imposes on it. It's unnatural. Sooner or later you have to start pitching in pain. Koufax did. Blue will, too. That will be a test."

Blue says, "If I have to, I will. I don't want to think about it."

Vida adds, "It's nice to be compared to Koufax and other great pitchers like that, but I don't compare myself to them and I don't want to start trying to imitate them. You know Sonny Sixkiller, the quarterback? Someone asked him who his hero was. He said himself. What he really said was he didn't have a hero, he just did his own thing. If it turned out he looked like someone, he couldn't help that, but he was his own man. I admire that and I feel sort of the same way.

"I just pitch the way Vida Blue pitches. It's the only way I know how. It may not be the way someone wrote down. But it's my way.

"I wouldn't mind it if some day a new young pitcher comes along who is called 'The New Vida Blue.' "

His catcher, Dave Duncan, sat in front of his locker and talked about his prize pitcher. For all that's been said about him, why has he been able to come so fast when so many other strong-armed, talented and intelligent young pitchers have not? Duncan says, "I'm young myself, but I think I've seen some things that separate Vida from other pitchers, especially young ones. For one thing, he's faster than anyone knows. He doesn't come all the way all the time. Then when he needs it, he throws a ball that gets to the plate a foot or two ahead of the last one. And some of the balls move a lot more than others. They can't agree on what his fastball does because it really does different things different times. No one batter sees it all. I squat back there and I'm surprised at what comes up. And he has a tricky motion and the hitters don't see the ball quick. There's no way those batters can make adjustments in time. It's a very hard thing, hitting a little

round ball thrown hard from a short distance with a round bat.
And when you throw what Vida throws, the batter has to be
lucky as well as good.

"He already has a better-than-average curve. He can't throw it
right. It's a wrist pitch and it has to be thrown with the same
motion as the fastball to fool the batter, but it's a tough pitch to
learn to throw right. He has a tendency to throw it too hard. He
also has a pretty good changeup but doesn't have any confidence
in it, so he doesn't throw it much. And he hasn't needed it much.
But it will help as it comes. He has incredible control for someone who throws so hard and is so inexperienced. He gets the ball
over the plate and averages less than three walks a game. Some
games he doesn't walk anyone. Even better, he can often clip
corners and pitch accurately to spots, though he can't do this
consistently. But his control is so consistent that despite how hard
he throws and how much his ball moves, I know about where it's
coming and he's easy to catch. He throws a relatively light ball.
By that I mean it doesn't bruise my hand under the glove. It
seems to glide, it sort of sails and dips. For a batter, it must be
like trying to hit a paper airplane that's darting with the speed
of a jet.

"He sometimes has troubles in the early innings because he
starts out so strong he throws too hard and his control isn't as
sharp. As he tires a little he actually gets sharper. But he is strong
and doesn't wear out and often is pitching better in the ninth
than in the first. Lately, he seems to be tiring more. He's not
throwing quite as hard. By the All-Star break he'd pitched 184
innings, which was more than any full season in his life before.
His arm thought it was through and he still had half a season to
go. But I think it's as much a mental thing as anything. He's
never worked under such continuous pressure, and he's had a lot
of special pressures to deal with. His concentration isn't as sharp
as it was.

"Here's where I feel I help him. I know how he likes to pitch
and I know the batters better than he does. We talk things over
some and I know he's not afraid to go strength to strength. So I
call most of the pitches. I make it a point to do a lot of homework
so I can help a lot when he's pitching. I give him the sign and he

gives me the pitch. He has confidence in me and seldom shakes off a sign. Maybe after he's been around longer he'll be shaking off more, he'll be wanting to do some different things, but chances are we'll be talking it over and I'll still be able to give him what he wants to throw. I figure if I can free him to concentrate on his remarkable physical ability, I've done a job. He has a lot of things to think about out there. He hasn't been throwing long enough to have his grips and his motion grooved. Any thinking I can do for him, I want to do. And I feel a small part of his success. But, hell, I know better than anyone, he could do it all alone if he had to. You could put a high school sophomore who could catch the ball behind the plate and Blue would still be outstanding."

Blue says, "I've thought a lot about why I've gotten so good so fast, and then again a lot of times I try not thinking about it, as if to say if I figure it out it'll get away from me. It's a combination of things. The ability to throw a ball which moves in different ways different times at slightly different speeds and throw it pretty much where I want to most of the time is one thing. As I moved up I had to get more variety to stay ahead of the hitters, and my curve is just good enough and I can control it just enough to give me that variety. I may be tougher than some players. I have a lot of confidence in myself. I don't rattle easy. I know if I could pitch without all the side things off the field, I'd be better than I am. I'd feel fresher, my mind would be clearer, I'd be more rested. But would I want to pitch without publicity? And no one forces the side-money on me. I'll just have to make adjustments.

"I figure now if I can just get through this year, just survive somehow, I'll be all right in the future. I don't feel like I've got this league by the tail. I'm ahead of myself, but I have to stay ahead. I'm good, really good, but I got to get better. I've been ahead of the hitters, but they're going to catch up. I'll just have to figure out a way of getting ahead again. I've got it in me. But I've been getting a lot of breaks and I figure a few are bound to start going against me. I'm in for harder times, I feel it in my bones. This game just isn't this easy. Life isn't this easy."

Johnny Sain, the former pitching great, says, "The better you get, the bigger the crowds get, the more the batters bear down against you. It gets harder, not easier. You stand out there with this reputation and you get to feeling very alone. The noise of the crowd tells you that you have to do it. Not the eight other guys—you."

Blue admits, "It's lonely out there sometimes."

CHAPTER TWELVE

A spokesman for the commissioner's office smiled and said, "The All-Star Game will not be held if Vida Blue is not in the starting lineup." He was there, the most highly touted entry in the mid-season classic in years. The fans vote on the eight starters on each side but the managers pick the pitchers, and Baltimore manager Earl Weaver, managing the American League, picked Blue, who had held his Orioles to one run in two starts, to be his starting pitcher. Anything else would have caused a commotion.

Blue entered the July 13 game at Tiger Stadium in Detroit with seventeen victories, more than any other pitcher had ever brought into this annual event. Previously, Bob Feller's sixteen victories in 1941 had been the best. Denny McLain had fifteen the year he won 31, when he was twenty-four years old. He won 24 games the next year. But he got in trouble off the field, was suspended and has been struggling since.

Feller was twenty-two in 1941 and he wound up winning 25 that year. He won 27 in his best year. Although a right-hander, Feller probably was the pitcher most comparable to Blue at a comparable point in their careers. Feller was rushed right out of high school into the majors at the age of seventeen and he was good, if not great, right away, putting together seasons of 5–3 and 9–7 and 17–11 before having his first big year, 24–9, in 1939 at the age of twenty. Blue was a lot less experienced but eighteen months older when he put together his smasher in 1971, which, as it turned out, was very close to Feller's of some thirty years earlier. At twenty-one, Feller was 27–11, and at twenty-two, 25–13.

Feller was a fastball pitcher who could throw moving balls hard for nine innings and the curve he later perfected broke like it was rolling off the edge of a table. He had a motion, speed and stuff similar to Blue's and was similarly advanced early. Like Koufax, he was almost unhittable at his best. Sandy pitched no-hitters in four consecutive seasons, one of them a perfect game. Feller pitched three no-hitters and an all-time-record twelve one-hitters. Koufax struck out eighteen men in games twice, Feller eighteen once and seventeen once. Koufax struck out 382 in one season, Feller 348.

Koufax lasted twelve seasons and won twenty or more games only three seasons. He won 165 games in his career and for several seasons he was as dominant as any player has ever been. Not counting almost four years given to the service at the peak of his career, Feller pitched eighteen years, had six twenty-victory seasons and won 266 games. With less than one full year behind him, Blue was bound for a twenty-victory season, had struck out seventeen in a game—though an extra-inning game—had a no-hitter and a one-hitter and soon would get his second one-hitter. He had ten to fifteen years ahead of him to aim at immortality, but he certainly had made a swift start.

He admits he was a bit awed to be in the hotel, then in the dressing room, then on the field before a roaring night crowd of 53,559 fans and a national television audience and among the game's greatest stars. Before dressing for his start he recalled, "A year ago I was in the minors and I watched this game on TV. How could I have even dreamed I'd be starting it tonight?"

The spotlight shone bright and hot on him as he ran out to face the National League's best. Throwing hard, he retired the side on just seven pitches, all strikes, in the first inning. Leading off, Willie Mays took a strike, then went for one and grounded out to shortstop. Henry Aaron took a strike, then grounded out to third. Joe Torre took a strike, fouled one off, then popped out to second. Blue bounced off the mound to cheers. His side failed to score off Dock Ellis in the home half.

Opening the second, Blue got a pitch too close to Willie Stargell and hit him. Vida went in, out and low with fastballs to big

Willie McCovey and the third strike thudded into Bill Freehan's mitt. Vida threw one to Johnny Bench, the brilliant young catcher, and Bench popped it foul out of play behind the plate. Vida threw another high and outside and Bench was ready and got around on it and drove it high and far into the upper-center-field seats for a two-run home run. It was sudden and Vida scuffed his toe on the mound, bent his back and went to work. He got rid of Glenn Beckert and Bud Harrelson to get out of the inning. Again Ellis stopped the American League in its half.

In the third inning, Blue got by Ellis and then got Mays again on a fly to right-center, but Aaron then drove a pitch into the upper deck in right. The camera hung on Blue, who stood very straight, expressionless. He threw bullets to Joe Torre and struck him out. That was it, pitchers in this game being limited to three innings. He had walked none, hit one, given up only two hits, but both of them home runs, and surrendered three runs.

Luis Aparicio singled. Weaver sent Blue's teammate Reggie Jackson up to pinch-hit for Vida and the muscular youngster came around on an Ellis pitch and smashed it with frightening force on a rising line over 500 feet to a light-tower in right-center for a home run. It rebounded far off the metal tower and startled all observers. Al Kaline said, "It was the hardest-hit ball I've ever seen in my life." Frank Howard said, "If it hadn't hit that tower, it might have carried 600 feet. He crushed it." It seemed to unnerve Ellis. Rod Carew walked and, two outs later, Frank Robinson hit another homer.

Now the American League was ahead, 4–3, and Blue was still the pitcher of record, and since the lead held up, he wound up the youngest winning pitcher in All-Star Game history. Jim Palmer, Mike Cuellar and Mickey Lolich protected the lead as Harmon Killebrew and Roberto Clemente traded additional homers and the American League won, 6–4, ending a streak of eight-straight losses.

In the dressing room later, Jackson, who'd started the winning rally, grinned and hugged Vida and said, "Anything for a buddy." The reporters wanted a lot from him, but they still wanted a lot from Blue. They crowded around him and pressed him to express his disappointment. Vida stood right up to it and said, "I had good stuff, but it just goes to show you that good pitching doesn't always stop good hitting."

He laughed and said, "Look, I said a little prayer before going out there tonight. I guess The Man wasn't listening. Or maybe the other guys were doing some praying, too. I mean, these are the best hitters in the bigs. It's no disgrace when hitters like Johnny Bench and Henry Aaron hit home runs off you. I mean isn't Bench supposed to be the best to come along in years? And isn't Aaron an all-time great?

"You say this is supposed to be a hitter's park?" he laughed. "Man, every park I pitch in is a hitter's park. It is when they got hitters like this in them. Like, wow, you guys may have written that I'm a super pitcher, but I never said it. And if I am, these are super hitters, so they got to beat you sometimes, right? And they didn't beat me, right? We won, didn't we? They messed me up a little, I'll admit," he laughed.

He seemed almost to be having fun, like to have the image of perfection stripped from his shoulders was a relief. He liked the idea of showing the writers he could take it, too. Later, he said, "I don't want to be one of these pitchers who gets a hangnail or an upset stomach or the sun in his eyes on the way to a loss. I'm no alibi-artist. You lose, you lose. You win, you win. You pitch your best and sometimes you pitch better than other times, and if you're good you pitch good most of the times, but sometimes it works better than other times. The other guys are good, too. They're hungry, too. They're reaching into your pocket. They know where the money is."

Earl Weaver came back to console him for his disappointing showing and congratulate him for winning and Blue shook his hand. "You can shake it now," Vida said, "because you won't feel like shaking it after the playoffs."

Relatives and friends had crowded into Sallie Blue's large living room in Mansfield to watch Vida in the All-Star Game. Munching fried chicken and sipping orange soda and beer, they cheered during the first inning but moaned and groaned in the second and third when his foes got to him. After Bench's homer the phone rang. It was Vida's aunt calling from Los Angeles to console her sister. "Well, you can't win 'em all," Mrs. Blue laughed without a lot of happiness.

Someone said, "Oh, well, that boy's just startin'. He hasn't even begun to show his stuff yet."

As Blue left the mound after his last inning, his trousers seemed to be sagging some. His mother called out to the television set, "Junior, pull your pants up." And as Jared Lebow later wrote in *Look,* sure enough, Vida promptly did just that.

After the All-Star Game, Sandy Koufax said, "I'd still rather have his future than anybody else's past."

Back to business, and Blue's first start following the break was on the sixteenth at home against Detroit. Sal Bando had been saying, "Let's face it. Oakland is a horrible place for hitters. The Coliseum is a football field. There's too much foul ground. The wind's always blowing in your face." The Tigers took this tack, too. Billy Martin said, "It's like playing at an airport. I'd like to see Blue keep doing what he's doing back East, where it's hot and the humidity saps your strength." The Tiger manager didn't want his players awed by the pitcher. Tiger catcher Bill Freehan said, "I thought he'd be faster. He has the advantage of pitching in a pitcher's park."

Blue shrugged and said, "You still have to throw the ball." He smiled and said, "Hitter's parks, pitcher's parks, it's all nonsense. It's the hitter and the pitcher 60 feet, 6 inches apart and the hitter either hits the pitcher good or he doesn't. One maybe has an edge one way some places, another another way other places, and it all evens up and it all comes down to the same thing, a duel between the hitter and the pitcher. They can put me down or build me up all they want, I still have to throw the ball and they still have to hit it." The build-up was such that the tear-down was inevitable. Frustrated foes didn't want to give him too much credit.

There were 24,434 on hand to see the Friday night game, nearly 20,000 more than had shown up the night before and almost 10,000 more than would show up the following day. They wanted to see if Blue would be affected after his showing in the

All-Star Game. Blue admits he was bearing down a bit harder
than usual.

He walked Al Kaline in the first inning but struck out Aurelio
Rodriguez and Willie Horton. He retired three in a row in the
second and three in a row in the third, fanning Rodriguez for the
second-straight time. Opening the fourth, Tony Taylor hit a fastball up the middle for a single. But Blue got Kaline on an infield
pop, struck out Horton for the second straight time and finished
off Freehan on a fly ball. He got three-straight in the fifth, striking out two; walked one in the sixth but got a strikeout and a
double-play; walked one in the seventh but got another double-
play and a ground-out. He struck out Horton and Freehan and
got a ground-out for the third out in the eighth. He set down
three in a row on fly balls in the ninth. He won, 4–0.

Taylor's hit had been the only hit off him. Three had worked
him for walks. It was Vida's eighteenth victory, eighteenth complete game and seventh shutout, lowering his earned-run average
to 1.35.

Afterward, however, he seemed irritable, for the first time,
really. Oh, there had been moments of weariness or impatience
before, but now the pressure seemed to be staying with him all
the time. Possibly he became most aware of the burden he carried
in the All-Star Game, when he was expected to make miracles
and was unable to make any. He pitched well in the game, but
for many it was not enough, and now he was beginning to wonder if for many anything he would ever do would be enough.

He had done too much too soon. He pitched the best he could,
which was very good, and the victories came, but, young as he
was, he knew it wouldn't always be that way, and he couldn't
understand why others couldn't see that.

His early streak showed him, he said, that he could be one of
the good ones, maybe the best in time, but he knew that time
hadn't come, and he knew he was due for some bad luck behind
his run of good luck. When he came back after the All-Star Game
with the one-hitter he didn't want the pressure to start building
up again, and for the first time he began to assert himself. He
never treated the writers badly, nor did he blame them for all the

pressure he was feeling, but they were the ones he had to deal with. His left arm was soaking in the ice water and he slammed his right fist on the table when a writer asked him if he'd win thirty. "I don't know," he said. "I'm getting a little tired of all these questions about whether I'll win thirty or forty. What do people think I am—a robot? I was aiming for twenty victories when I started the season and I still am, and that's all I'm aiming at."

Someone asked him if the two dimes he carried represented the twenty wins. He said he didn't want to talk about the dimes. Actually, American League president Joe Cronin had given him a third dime he now carried, and this represented thirty, but he didn't always carry them. Another time, another place, he confided, "Of course the dimes represent ten wins each. Any fool can figure that out. They're supposed to be good-luck charms. And I guess I figured if I talked about it it would take the charm off it. But I'm not really superstitious and I didn't want to get to depending on things like that. What if I lost them? What would I do then, cut my throat? Anyway, how lucky can dimes be? Dollars got to be luckier."

Someone asked him if he was as fast as he'd been earlier in the season. He said, "I don't know, I don't measure." Someone asked him if he felt he should have had a no-hitter. He shrugged and said, "I wasn't real sharp. I just made them hit the pitches I wanted them to hit. Everything falls into place, you can get a no-hitter. One thing didn't fall into place. You can't count on things like that. You can't get it back or cry over it. I'm just glad we won and I got the job done." Someone asked him if he compared himself to any great pitchers of the past. He snapped, "Don't go comparing me to anybody. Just think of me as the winningest pitcher on this team."

He stuck his head above the crowd of reporters suddenly and yelled to Tommy Davis, "Hey, I'm 18-and-3. I'm not going to eat any of those lousy hot dogs tonight. You better get me some steak."

Vida Blue sat in the living room of his apartment, listening to Steve Wonder's "Where I'm Coming From"—bam, bam. It was late in the morning and he was lounging in the blue and white room.

There are pictures of Reggie Jackson and Maury Wills on the walls, but none of Blue. Vida was saying, "I'm not all that impressed with myself. I don't like to think about it."

The phone rang. He shook his head sadly and trotted to it in his high-stepping gait. It was someone who wanted tickets. He said he'd see what he could do. He hung up, came back, sat down and said, "I got too many friends already. I don't know what they want from me. Just to touch me? Hell! Everywhere I go, people asking me when I'm gonna win twenty, if I'm gonna win thirty, why I lost a game? Hell! If I go anywhere, all they want to do is talk baseball. I get away from the ballpark, I get away from the writers, I want to think about something else."

The phone rang again. He swore at it and got up and answered it and said he'd see what he could do and hung up and came back and sat down again. He was wearing blue slacks, loafers, no shirt. He said, "Some people don't seem to realize we want to do some things besides sign autographs, that if we took the time to sign all they want there'd be no time left for anything else. Wherever I go, crowds gather around me. I'm the kind of guy likes to be alone a lot, but I can't seem to get away from people these days. And I get nervous and irritable and start snappin' at people before I realize it and I don't want to be that way."

The phone rang and he shook his head and got up and answered it and brightened because it turned out to be a girl and he sweet-talked awhile, then hung up and resumed his perch on the couch. He said, "I like the ladies, but I don't go head-over-heels. It relaxes me. It's not baseball, you know. Lots of 'em don't even know about baseball. That's a relief. But then they find out and they change and I start Bogartin'. On the other hand, if they don't know about baseball, they don't know about what I'm going through, so I can't turn to them for sympathy."

The phone rang again and he got up and answered it again and he said no, Vida Blue wasn't there, and he said yes, he'd tell him, and he hung up and sat down. He said, "It never used to bother me going to games, but now it bothers me. My stomach starts to feel upset as it comes time to go to the stadium. Sometimes I eat and it's OK and sometimes I can't eat and it's not OK. I think I'm scared. Knowing people expect so much of me all of a sudden. Not wanting to let them down. Lots of times now I just don't want to go. But I got to go. When I get there my stomach starts to tie up and I feel like I want to throw up. Just before I pitch, I feel like I want to. I haven't yet. I haven't gone that far yet," he said.

The phone rang and he said the hell with it, and let it ring and ring and ring until finally it stopped.

At the ballpark the writers were saying how they'd been expecting Vida to start getting up tight and snapping at them, and that maybe it was beginning to really happen now, and what a shame it was a guy couldn't take a thing like this better. Vida was riding up with Terry Brown, the elevator girl. "It's just something to do," he says. She says, "It takes his mind off the game, I guess. He funs me a lot. He never asked me for a date."

Some 21,353 saw him go eleven innings against Cleveland, leaving without a decision with the score 3–3. He had given up home runs to Graig Nettles and Ken Suarez. It was the first of the season for Suarez. The A's won, 4–3, in twelve with the victory going to Knowles, and by the time the writers got to the dressing room, Blue was dressed and leaving and didn't want to talk about it. "All I know is that I should have won, 1–0," he said before walking away.

The A's opened a road trip in Detroit. They won two of three and then went with Blue in the fourth. This was a Sunday afternoon and there was a tremendous turnout of 53,563. (The next game drew less than 20,000.) Vida was struck on the foot by a pitched ball while at bat in the fourth inning and, though he had a one-hitter and led, 5–1, after six innings, he was taken out for a pinch hitter. Fingers got his tenth save in the 6–1 victory, protecting Blue's nineteenth triumph.

Asked why he had been taken out, Vida said, "My foot hurt some, but I guess they want to save my arm some. It was hot and humid and the manager wanted to give me some rest." Asked why he had taken him out, Williams said, "I just didn't want to take any chances." There was some suspicion Finley had phoned in the instructions, but no one would say anything about it.

Outside the dressing room a large knot of fans waited, chanting, "We want Vida! We want Vida!" As he stood signing for them a Detroit writer asked him if it bothered him. He said, "The pressure off the field is getting worse than the pressure on the field. I don't mind this, though. I guess that's just a sign of me being a nice guy." Then he begged off with an aching foot and left. Later the foot was X-rayed and showed only bruises, no broken bones.

He was in Baltimore for his twenty-second birthday. A girl he knew brought a cupcake with a candle on it to the ballpark and came down by the dugout before the game and a photographer asked her to come on the field and pose with Vida but she said, "I don't think I better." And he said, "No way," and motioned for her to go back to her seat.

Blue was scheduled to go for his twentieth victory at Baltimore in a night game televised back to the San Francisco-Oakland Bay Area. There had been an advance sale of more than 27,000 and a crowd of 42,000 was expected, but a thunderstorm struck. Despite heavy rains, more than 26,000 fans passed through the gate and waited in the stands almost an hour before the scheduled starting time before greeting an announcement that the game was postponed with a chorus of boos.

Sitting before a TV set in a lounge at the San Francisco airport, Charles Finley turned away and said, "Our share would have been around $30,000."

Before he left the ballpark, Blue was asked if he was disappointed that he didn't get to go for his twentieth against the champion Orioles. He said, "No. I've got a job to do. I don't care if I do it against Little Leaguers." He was asked about the pressure. He said, "No pressure. I'm just having a little fun." Was there any truth his old contract had been torn up and replaced by a new one? He said, "It could be the truth, it could be a lie. You're not going to find out from me."

On the last Saturday night in July he went for that twentieth in Cleveland and didn't get it. Johnny Lipon took over as manager of the Indians for Alvin Dark that night and fired up his team and told them, "Swing at the first pitch. Blue is a control pitcher. He throws strikes and challenges most hitters. Swing when you get a good pitch because you're not going to get too many." The Indians came up swinging and Vida's curve came up flat and by the time he turned strictly to his fastball it was too late. An infield single scored two runs in the second and another single scored two more in the fourth and he was taken out for a pinch hitter after six, trailing 4–0, and his team lost, 4–1, and he lost his fourth game.

Baseball seems dead in Cleveland and there had been only 10,045 in the big stadium, even to see Blue. "Maybe I wasn't used to empty seats and so much quiet. Maybe I was just careless. Maybe I was just trying too hard," Blue said later.

The A's hadn't won in a week, but second-place Kansas City was losing, too, and remained 10½ back as the teams turned into August. The A's swiftly spun off seven wins in a row to straighten out.

He tried again before 35,623 fans, the largest crowd in Kansas City baseball history, and failed again. The Royals reached his fastball for pop-fly singles and his curve for home runs and Vida left after five trailing, 5–2, but the A's saved him from his fifth loss by rallying to win for reliever Fingers, 7–5. Newsmen found Blue sitting in front of his locker shaking his head and muttering, "Mercy, mercy, mercy me. It's beginning to get to me. I'm almost crazy from the pressure. You go to a town and the newspapers say sensational this and sensational that and record crowds come out screaming to see sensational you and, you know something, it's hard to be sensational when you have to be." He looked up at the writers and said, "Look, I know you got a job to do, and I appreciate that, and I've cooperated, but this time, this one time, why don't you go interview some of the other guys; they won the game, I didn't."

In the Kansas City dressing room, manager Bob Lemon said, "I feel for him. I remember when I was a pitcher and had a big year and it wasn't anything like the year he's had. You have a big year and suddenly everybody thinks you're one hell of a speechmaker."

In his dressing room, manager Dick Williams was asking the writers to take it easy on Blue. He had been talking it over with Finley and they agreed some restrictions would have to be imposed, such as no interviews in the dressing room before games or with Vida on days he was scheduled to pitch.

Williams was saying, "We want to cooperate. Vida wants to cooperate. He's tired. We don't like to put up bars. But you got to give him a break. You got a job to do, I know. Some of you get to talk to him only on the days he's in your town. But he's answering the same questions over and over. We've got a pennant to win. Sure we're far ahead, but big leads have been blown before. I'm taking no chances."

It was one of those seasons. Because of Blue there were distractions, but with Blue the team had won consistently and no other team was able to win consistently enough to press the A's. The Oakland team just kept going.

On the fifth of August at home against Milwaukee, Catfish Hunter won his fourteenth, 2–1. On the seventh of August, at home against Chicago, Vida Blue won his twentieth, 1–0.

In the first inning, with one out, he hit Mike Hershberger with a pitch. Walt Williams doubled the runner to third. Blue blazed pitches to league home-run champion Bill Melton and he popped up. But Blue walked Rich Reichardt to load the bases. However, he then got Mike Andrews on a looper to second to finish the inning.

With one out in the fourth, Reichardt and Andrews singled and reached second and third on a second-out ground-out, but Blue got Rich Morales to fly out for the last out. Between innings he was swallowing seltzer pills to settle his stomach. Others also seemed to feel the pressure. Rival pitcher Joel Horlen balked in a run in the fifth.

Williams was suffering, too. In the eighth, Luis Alvarado beat out a bunt off Blue. Vida pumped two swift strikes past Hershberger, then threw him a ball. He threw another ball but thought it a strike and glared at umpire Dave Phillips. He threw a third ball, then a fourth, which he didn't like at all. Neither did the manager, who came out to confer with him and exchange words with the umpire. After the manager went back to the dugout, Blue got Walt Williams to pop up for the second out, but the manager, feeling it should have been ruled immediately an automatic out on the "infield-fly rule" charged the umpire and challenged him so heavily, Phillips ordered the skipper into the dressing room. Cursing, Williams departed. There were two on with one out, but Blue got Melton to fly to right and then struck out Reichardt.

In the ninth, Andrews took a third strike, Tom Egan swung at and missed a third strike and Rich Morales flied to right. Blue heaved a sigh of relief and ran off as his teammates ran happily at him. He was a 1–0 winner, making him the first twenty-game winner for the A's in twenty years. He had eight shutouts, within one of the American League record set by one Babe Ruth when he was a pitcher more than fifty years earlier.

In the dressing room he seemed subdued, almost as though he had been a loser instead of a winner. He had given only three hits and no runs, yet he insisted, "It was one of my worst games." He said, "I hit some batters and threw some wild pitches. I wasn't sharp. I didn't feel good and didn't pitch good." He spoke so softly reporters on the fringe of the large crowd about him had to strain to hear him and several times asked him to repeat his words. He said, "I feel like a new man. I'm glad the strain of winning my twentieth is finally over with. I'm glad no one will be asking me when I'll be winning my twentieth anymore. I hope no one asks me about thirty." Someone did. He was bothered by it and said, "Man, I don't know anything about it. I'm just trying to take everything in stride. We won this one and let's let it go at that."

Watching, Reggie Jackson was shaking his head and saying, "I know what he's going through. I went through it. . . . I'm not sure it was worth it. They turn on you. He knows this is unreal. . . . From now on I just want to have good years, not great years, and be left to live my life in peace." Told this later, Vida said, "I'm sure he's right. . . . All I want to do right now is run, escape to some desert island to be left alone for a while." When it was pointed out to him that this wasn't the way it should be, that he was where boys dream of being, he sighed and said, "All I know is I waited all my young life for this and now that it's here I wish it would just go away."

The sweat was drying on his dark skin. He sat slouched, seeming to be terribly tired. He was half-undressed and it seemed to take a great effort for him to stand up and finish undressing and shower and dress in civvies and get through the crowd outside to his car and get home.

Here he played a song he had been playing and singing for weeks, "Smiling Faces Sometimes." He put it on and let it play again and again and again as he sprawled on the couch, his eyes closed, listening, humming a little to himself.

Smiling Faces Sometimes
pretend to be your friend.
Smiling faces show no traces
of the evil that lurks within.
Smiling faces, smiling faces,
Sometimes they don't tell the truth.

Smiling faces, smiling faces tell lies,
and I got proof.
The truth is in the eyes
'cause the eyes don't lie, amen.

Remember, a smile is just a frown
turned upside down, my friend.
So, hear me when I'm saying
beware of the handshake
that hides the snake.

I'm tellin' you,
beware of the pat on the back,
it just might hold you back.
Jealousy, jealousy,
misery, misery, envy.

I tell you, you can't see
behind smiling faces.
Smiling Faces, Sometimes,
they don't tell the truth.

Smiling faces, smiling faces tell lies,
and I got proof.

Your enemy won't do you no harm,
'cause you'll know where he's comin' from.

Don't let the handshake and the smile fool ya.
Take my advice, I'm only tryin' to school ya.
Smiling Faces, Sometimes.

CHAPTER THIRTEEN

In San Francisco, Glenn Dickey wrote in the *Chronicle* that Finley still held title to Blue's car, suggesting it was still the owner's, only on loan to the pitcher. This created some stir in Oakland and elsewhere and for ten days Vida had been denying it. Finally, Williams called Blue in and they talked to Finley on the phone about it and were instructed to call a press conference to straighten it out, which they did on the eleventh of August in Boston. Vida was to pitch that night. He stood against a wall and, without looking at anyone and speaking just loud enough for everyone to hear, said, "I've got the title to the car. It's mine. The story didn't bother me at all. It's my car." Then he walked out. Williams stood up and told the writers with a laugh, "The story is completely false." Then he ripped Dickey.

Later, Vida privately said, "Finley held the title to the car at first, I guess because he was paying for it. But then he had the title changed over to me. The gas company credit card he gave me was in his name because the bills were supposed to go to him. But he never attached any strings to the car. He gave it to me and said it was mine."

By then he was driving a Grand Prix, which fans did not spot so swiftly.

He was stopped for speeding by a motorcycle policeman once. He thought of telling the cop who he was, but he didn't want to

Bogart, so he didn't—but he didn't have to. The cop looked at him and said, "You don't play for Oakland, do you?"

Vida said, "I'm afraid I do."

The cop said, "You're not Vida Blue, are you?"

Vida said, "I'm afraid I am."

The cop smiled and shook his hand and said, "I wasn't going to give you a ticket anyway. Not just because you're Vida Blue."

Vida Blue said, "I understand."

The night game in Boston was the fourth in a row that had been televised back to the Bay Area. Finley had been making arrangements for these special telecasts, often switching the dates originally set for telecasts, but this one was delayed two hours by rain. Despite the bad weather, which included tornado alerts, there were 32,858 on hand and the Red Sox were not going to call it unless they had to. They did not have to.

With one out in the first, Blue gave up a single to Aparicio and a double to Reggie Smith. After striking out Yastrzemski, Vida walked Rico Petrocelli. With the bases loaded he struck out George Scott for the third out. Vida gave up a single in the second but struck out two. He did not give up anything for a long time after that. He had given up just three hits and was leading, 3–0, and had retired seventeen-straight batters when in the eighth he walked one and then gave up a two-run home run to Doug Griffin. Then, with one out in the ninth, he gave up a game-tying home run to Petrocelli.

A two-run homer by Davis and a one-run single by Tommy had given Blue his early lead and a two-run double by Jackson regained him the lead in the first half of the tenth. In the last of the tenth, Vida gave up two singles before Williams took him out and brought in Knowles, who got the last three outs to wrap up Blue's twenty-first victory, 5–3. Afterward, Vida was weary, nervous and impatient with the reporters and said, "I wish we could have started on time and gotten it over with. The long wait got to me. I admit I was shaking before the game. I'd walk out to the dugout, go back in the clubhouse, lie on the trainer's table, go out to the dugout again, then back to the table again. At the finish I was very tired."

After a while he said to one writer, "At the end of the season I'll let you count how many gray hairs I have. Oh, me, the pressure."

The victory completed his cycle of defeats of every foe in the league. At this point he had beaten Boston and Cleveland once each, Detroit three times, and the other eight teams twice each. The next night the A's completed a sweep of their series in Boston and raised their remarkable road record to 44–18. And it was on to New York, where headlines reported VIDA BLUE IS PITCHING SUNDAY and big ads proclaimed it "Blue Sunday" with, among other things, everyone with the last name of Blue admitted free. Blue sighed, "That's all I need, for them to find me some more relatives."

On the bus from LaGuardia Airport to the Hotel Americana, Tommy Davis played some tapes on his portable machine. Among these was one of a Martin Luther King speech. For a while there was silence. Reggie Jackson, sitting near the front of the bus, began to speak loudly as though trying to imitate King's voice, as though doing a documentary on Vida Blue's life. "In nineteen hundred and forty-nine," Reggie began dramatically, "in the town of Mansfield, Louisiana, lived a family named Blue. . . ."

Reggie went on and on: ". . . scouts came from miles around to see this wonder boy named Blue. Then Charles O. Finley came to Blue and said, 'Son, I'm going to make you a star! And in nineteen hundred and seventy, at the Oakland Coliseum, against the powerful Minnesota Twins, a man named Blue made baseball history. . . ." Referring frequently to "a man named Blue," Reggie wrapped up Vida's life in about ten minutes.

At the finish, everyone was smiling but no one said anything. Vida was smiling but he didn't say anything. Reggie just sat back, smiling, not saying any more.

The writers swarmed all over Vida in New York. Dick Young of the *Daily News* wanted an interview on short notice and was refused and complained publicly. Stories got out that Blue was on a high horse. Later, Vida met with Young and they talked it out. Vida says, "I saw his side and I think he saw my side.

"There's only so much of me I can give. I have only so much time. I think the writers overplayed me, but if I tried to get out from under some of it they got upset. I think they put a lot of the pressure on me by making me a superstar when I was really just a rookie having my first big year. They can't all get to know you well, but they can make you or break you with the public by what they say about you.

"Some players who are bad people are protected by the writers because they buddy up to the writers. I can't do that. If I like a man, I like him. If I don't know him, I don't know him. I can only be myself. I can't put up a front. If I'm not the same all the time it's because I'm not sure of myself. If I don't say the same thing all the time it's because I'm not yet sure what I think. I haven't lived long enough.

"The writers want scoops, something sensational, headlines. Most of 'em do a tremendous job, but when it's a kid like me under a lot of pressure who could live without a lot of public attention, they're a problem.

"I'm tired of seeing my name in big print. I don't like being a bumper sticker. You know, 'If You Drink, Don't Drive,' that kind of stuff: 'Vida Blue Is Beautiful!' "

He began drawing up a list of the ten questions he was asked the most which had came to bother him the most.

Williams agreed that Vida's telephone should be disconnected in every hotel. But when Williams himself wanted to speak to Vida he found he couldn't get through to him. He had to go to his room to see him.

Catcher Duncan said, "Vida is a different person than he was. Under the circumstances, 99 out of a hundred would be. Everyone expects so much out of him, and yet everyone is waiting for him to blow up. He doesn't get much privacy or much time to himself and he hasn't had a chance to think things through and look at them in perspective. Everything has exploded around him. At first he was a little cocky. Now he's very nervous about it all. He's not as cool or as thoughtful as he was. But he's handled it better than I would imagine anyone could.

"He's best among his teammates. Some of them may resent him. You know we have some outstanding players on this team who are being put in his shadow. Hitters like Reggie and Bando. A pitcher like Hunter, who's having a helluva year and is being moved around in the rotation to make room for Vida. Maybe they look at him and wonder sometimes what the hell this is. But, down deep, they understand. They see he needs them. He clowns around and cuts up behind closed doors and they see it's the only place he can relax.

"You know, you envy him sometimes, his fame and the money he's going to make, and then you look at what it is for him, and you can go home to the wife and kids and relax and you wonder if you're not just as well off after all."

There were 45,343 fans in Yankee Stadium on Sunday afternoon, including more than a hundred who were admitted free because their last name was Blue. There were blue scorecards and a Blue on the mound. There were less than 17,000 for the preceding game, less than 18,000 for the following game. "After the game," Blue smiled, "I'll just swing on up to the stands and say hello to all the Blues." And after the season? "I'm going to some isolated island and get away from you all, like they say in Mississippi," he said.

After hits by Mangual and Duncan, Blue squeezed in a run with a perfect bunt in the second. He retired ten straight batters before Gene Michael singled in the third. Mangual drove in a run in the top of the seventh and Blue had a three-hit 2–0 lead in the bottom half when he weakened. Roy White singled. Felipe Alou went out. Denny Cater singled. Ron Swoboda walked. Gene Michael doubled. Jerry Kenney doubled. Four runs were in. Blue got Clarke on a grounder and Munson on a strikeout.

In the eighth, Blue himself started a rally with another perfect bunt. With the bases loaded, Campaneris slashed a single for two runs to tie the score. Rudi walked to load the bases. Jackson fanned. But reliever Lindy McDaniel then uncorked a wild pitch and Vida raced home with the lead run. Another run followed. Vida gave up two singles in the ninth, but Williams stayed with him and a double-play wrapped it up for his twenty-second victory, 6–4.

Later, Curt Blefary said, "He not only did it with his arm but his legs. He handled the bat well. He has pitched better, but he is a remarkable all-around athlete who can help himself other ways when he needs it." Williams said, "This wasn't one of his best-pitched games, but it was one of his gutsiest games. I didn't want to take him out because he has so much courage he'll get the job done himself somehow if it can be done. He's a good, solid young man."

Vida was saying, "I feel I'm about to crack up. Physically I'm OK. Mentally I'm exhausted. Everything about today's game was exhausting—the crowd, the way it went, the whole atmosphere. I've reached the point where I just have to lock myself in my room, and I look forward to it." He kept pausing. A broadcaster pushed a microphone in his face and he pushed it away. Wearily he pleaded, "Why don't you fellows go write your stories?" After a while he began to just shrug in reply to most questions.

This month he is pictured in a painting on the cover of *Time* with the banner "New Zip in the Old Game." Profiled in *Sport* magazine the previous month, he is now the cover subject of another story in this publication. *Look* has a story on the reaction to him in his hometown titled "Where Vida Blue Grew."

Vida's list of the ten questions he was most often asked to answer:

1. Will you win thirty games?
2. Are you tired and do you think you can win the pennant, playoffs and World Series?
3. What goals have you set for yourself, how long do you think you can last in the big leagues and what would you like to accomplish?
4. Are you surprised by your success?
5. How much money are you making and how much money are you going to ask Finley for?
6. Do you really carry dimes in your pocket when you pitch and why?
7. Did Finley really ask you to change your name and did he really give you the car for yourself? What do you think of him?
8. Who was your hero, whose style have you copied and which pitchers do you compare yourself to?
9. Do you really like girls?
10. What kind of pitch did the batter hit?

When the team went on to Washington on August 17, Vida stayed on in New York to appear on the "Today" early-morning TV show with co-host and former major-league player Joe Garagiola. Vida kept smiling as he answered such questions as "Will you win thirty games?" and "Are you tired and do you think you can win the pennant, playoffs and World Series?" and "Do you really carry dimes in your pocket?" and so forth. That night he went on the Dick Cavett late-night TV show and kept smiling as he answered such questions as "Did Finley really ask you to change your name?" and "Do you really like girls?" and so forth. On both shows he wore sport shirts and slacks but no coats and ties.

He flies on to Washington to rejoin the team and go with an A's party to a reception at the White House, where Vida is the center of attention and asked to answer such questions as "How much money are you making?" and "How much are you going to ask Finley for?" Here he wears a coat and tie. A blue sport coat, red tie and red, white and yellow shirt. Nixon was asked if the wage-price freeze he had imposed on the nation applied to athletes, a very real problem to players with a limited time at the top, expecting big rewards for big years. He merely laughed. Finley, who was there, smiled and said, "I was hoping he would say it did." Instead the President said to Blue, "You are the most underpaid player in baseball." Vida said, "Yes, I am." Nixon added, "I'd like to be the lawyer who negotiates your contract next year." Blue smiled. Later Finley was not smiling when he said, "The President didn't have to say that. I already knew Vida was underpaid."

While walking toward the White House gate, gardeners come up to Vida and he shakes their hands and signs a few autographs. Finley invites Vida, manager Williams, some coaches and a few others of the group to lunch at a downtown fish restaurant. Vida helps hail a cab. In the back seat he keeps tapping the front seat of the cab, keeping time and humming. "I enjoyed that," he says. "I was happy to meet him. Yes, it was all right."

At the restaurant it takes perhaps ten minutes for him to be recognized. An autograph-seeker approaches and Vida signs for him. Soon others surround him. All the waiters want autographs, too. One gives Vida a stack of postcards and asks him to sign the whole stack while Vida is trying to finish his "Louisiana Fried Shrimp." All others, including the millionaire Finley, are ignored, and the commotion continues for the better part of an hour. Vida just keeps signing.

Back at the hotel, Vida has one of the Richard Nixon autographed golf balls the President has given his guests and is bouncing his as though it were a basketball. "I don't play golf," Vida grins, "I've got to use it for something."

Which persons does he admire the most? He says, "My favorite would be Muhammad Ali. To me he's cool. Also James Brown. And the late Robert Kennedy and John F. Kennedy. And the late Martin Luther King.

"And," adds Vida, "I like Mr. Nixon today. He's a real nice guy, I guess. He's a sports fan and I'm a sportsman. I respect the man in power. I think it's difficult to judge him. I think it's difficult to judge anyone's performance under pressure. And he's sure under pressure. Everyone goes around judging. And I doubt that many are qualified to judge. I'm not. I haven't lived long enough. I don't know enough about it.

"I've already been asked to speak in political things. I don't want to speak for anyone. I think that would be a bad way to use my popularity as a player. When the day comes I feel I can judge, when I feel qualified, maybe it'll be something else then. But to use popularity to exercise power can be a dangerous thing."

Politics pushed Blue off one major magazine cover. When word got out that *Time* was using Vida on its cover and when New York City Mayor John Lindsay jumped from the Republican to the Democratic Party to set the stage for a possible pitch for the presidency, *Newsweek* pulled Vida off its cover that week and replaced him with Lindsay.

In an emergency meeting of American League clubowners convened to discuss the Senators' financial problems in Washington and hear owner Bob Short's plea for permission to transfer the franchise to the Dallas-Fort Worth area, Short makes a pitch to A's owner Finley to pitch Blue in Washington.

"Even though we're almost conceding defeat, we like to fill the house," Short is quoted as saying.

But Blue is not scheduled to pitch in Washington and he is sent home ahead of the team to get some extra rest before his next start, though manager Williams asks the press not to publicize it. The writers do not.

Williams is a sharp, shrewd manager. He is tough, but the A's apparently needed driving. When they lose a game in Washington it ends a string of twelve-consecutive victories on the road and they fall four short of the 59-year-old league record in this department, but they remain within reach of the one-season road record for victories of 54 set by the New York Yankees in 1939. The A's are 35 games above .500 and 14½ games ahead of their divisional field.

Williams has to deal with a demanding owner and exercise authority on players who are used to all authority stemming only from the top. Williams has a special situation to deal with this season in which almost all the publicity being given his team is being given one young player, and he must be fair to the other players while helping that one player continue to produce under pressure.

Williams says, "From the first, Vida has worked to improve himself. He did his work when he wasn't pitching. He listened to advice and tried to improve. He never complained. I think two things have made him special. One, his natural ability. And, two, his poise. I guess he was born with poise and I think he got it polished in his upbringing. I was impressed meeting his mother. Nothing seemed to excite her. She was pleased but not overwhelmed as others might have been in her situation. Vida reflects this. He didn't go overboard with his first success. And the publicity hasn't padded his ego. The incredible amount of attention paid him has made him tense and unhappy, but he somehow still remains a nice, likable, well-mannered lad. We've protected him from some pressures, but it would be unfair for us to try to protect him from all. The publicity is money in the bank for the ballclub and money in the bank for him. If he is going to be as good as I think he is for as long as I think he will be he is just going to have to adjust to it and learn to live with it. Others have done it and he will, too, faster and better than most."

The manager sits in the dugout during pregame practices as darkness begins to fall and people begin to file into the vast stands surrounding us. His arms are folded across his chest, but his eyes dart about watching the actions of his players as he talks. He says, "This is a tough game. One thing that impresses me about Blue is when things go against him he takes it in stride. The other game when Petrocelli hit his homer off him he had struck out three straight times. He's good. So is Blue. Even the good ones can't beat the good ones all the time. Some players were upset. Vida was calm. He takes a reversal as a sign he has to get tougher. The players sense this and respect this. They relax when he's on the mound. This hurts him. It's almost like they think they're going to win without working as long as Blue is working. For example, we don't score as much when he's pitching. The guys aren't attacking as aggressively because subconsciously they figure they don't have to. Meanwhile, the other guys are taking every little thing they can get from Vida because they know he won't give them much. That's why I don't think he'll win thirty. I don't want you to write this now, but you can write it later. I hope I'm wrong, but he may not even come close. Partly because we're not going to take one single chance with him or his arm, we're not going to work him out of turn, in fact we're going to give him more and more rest. He's going to wind up with a helluva year, and for now that should be plenty good enough. He should win all the awards, and he deserves them. And he'll win more other years. Some year soon he very well may win thirty. He's going to be on top awhile."

We sat on the end of the dugout bench, apart from other players. Williams looked down at them and said, "A lot of guys have contributed to this pennant push and if we make it they'll all be responsible. No matter what Blue has done, it wouldn't have been nearly enough without what a lot of others have done. There's no way we'd be way in front without what Hunter has done or Dobson or Bando or Jackson or Campaneris or Green or Davis. It's been a little tough on these guys because they deserve more credit than they've gotten. We've figured out Vida's rotation the rest of the way and, barring rainouts and things like that, we hope to stick to it. Vida's going to start a lot at home. This town simply hasn't supported a league-leader the way it should have and the owner deserves the big gates a hot pitcher can bring him. This is a business, after all. Sometimes this may mean a Hunter gets pushed back a day. I've explained it to him and he understands. I don't say he doesn't resent it some. He's only human. Maybe some of the other players resent special attention paid Vida, but they understand. He puts money in their pockets. Since they invented this game, these guys have always had to live with some guys getting more attention than others. They pull for him and he pulls for them. The spirit is good."

He was asked about Finley and said, "Finley is a very smart man. He's also a very unconventional man. He has a lot of imagination and is not afraid to swim upstream, to go against tradition, to suggest something new and radical. He's a very strong man. He has the strength of his own convictions. He doesn't do things the way others do them. He does them his way. He's an individualist. I think this is to be admired. He's a very demanding man. He has his way he thinks things should be done and if you don't do them that way you're in trouble. He expects a lot of people. Those who don't want to give him what he wants don't last very long. But you can stand up to the man. You can argue with the man. He believes in having a say in how his organization is run and I believe he should have a say. It's his money and a man should control his own destiny. He's had his say to me. And I've had my say to him. If you do a good job for him, he appreciates it. You have to earn his respect, but if you do, you've got a lot. I'm my own man, too, but any manager who says he isn't accountable to a general manager or an owner is lying. We all are. Every man in every business is accountable to someone. Even most owners are responsible to shareholders. Finley has let me manage this team. That's all I asked and that's what I've gotten. I am the manager. And I'm a tough manager, too. In Boston they resented it, but it won for them. It'll win here, too. Like Mr. Finley, I expect people to do things the way I want them done, and if they don't produce I'll replace them. You see," he smiled, "none of us are all that different from each other."

Another time, another place, Vida said, "Williams is like all managers. If you're winning, fine. If not, not so fine. I was winning and we got along fine. I stop winning, I may see another side of him. I've seen another side of him with others. If you can't do a job for him, he can't use you. Well, this is true of all managers. And he's like all managers. They all have their individual ways of stressing a winning attitude to their athletes. When we got off to a losing start he cracked down fast. He asserted himself before things got out of hand. This was good. We gained respect for him. If we lose, maybe the players will turn on him. Managing's a tough racket and losing players often look to blame someone besides themselves. I'm sure he knows this. He's been hired and fired.

"In the long run, how he does here probably will depend on the foundation he builds. He has to respect his players as men first, then as athletes. He has to show them he cares about them as individuals. We'll see about this. This takes time to come out. We've been going good and it usually takes going bad to bring it out. I have no idea how much Finley runs him, but I think Williams is tough enough to quit any time he's not being allowed to run the show on the field. As long as Williams produces, I suspect he and Finley will get along fine. It's the same with the players. As long as they produce, they and Williams will get along fine. He's been just fine with me. We don't talk much. He puts my name on the lineup card and hands me the ball and I go out and do my job. He pats me on the rear when I do a good job. He doesn't cuss me out when I do a bad job. He wasn't a pitcher and he leaves a lot to his pitching coach. Posedel praises me more and criticizes me more. He gets more technical. He gets down to details. But Williams is his boss, too. And Finley is Williams' boss."

There are six weeks left in the season and the long-term mimeographed pitching rotation for Blue calls for ten more starts, so he would have to win eight of them to reach thirty. The writers keep reaching for this, though now it is nonsense. Vida Blue has just turned twenty-two, he is in his first full year in the majors, his team is far in front in the pennant race and no one is going to risk his arm and peace of mind in quest of such an impossible and unreasonable dream now.

He admits, "Privately, I am tired. I'm not throwing as hard as I was. When I reach back for what used to be there, it's not there anymore. I'm a little smarter than I was at the start of the season, so I can still pitch real good, but I've already pitched more innings by far than any season of my life before and I feel it in my arm and my legs and my whole body. And mentally I'm worn out, too. I just want to be sharp for the postseason play. That's what matters now."

It is a cruel thing to do, but it is pointed out to him that one day soon he will be standing on the mound in Baltimore to open the American League playoffs with the A's figuring he has to win for them to win the best-of-five series, and the Orioles figuring they may have to beat him to beat the A's and if they can beat him, it may make it easy to beat the A's, and no matter how much he has done all season it can all be washed down the drain with a poor performance under this sort of pressure. He closes his eyes and his face seems sad and he says very softly, "I know all about that and I just try not to think about it."

But it haunts him now and follows him around.

CHAPTER FOURTEEN

One off-day in August, Monte Moore, the A's broadcaster, invited Vida to his suburban home "to relax and get away from everything." Monte recalls, "He seemed to enjoy himself enormously. He stretched out. He played with the kids. He said he didn't know quiet places like this still existed. I felt for him. I've never seen the public go ape over a celebrity the way they have over this one. I think he's reacted marvelously. But it's been getting him down and I think he was glad to get away from it."

There was only one hitch. Moore invited Blue to take a swim in his pool. Vida accepted and jumped in. When Moore saw him splashing clumsily he realized the youngster couldn't swim, panicked and helped him out. "You're not going to drown in my pool," Monte shrieked, visions of Finley dancing in his head.

Vida says, "If I accepted all the invitations to go out with people I wouldn't have time to draw a deep breath. I know they mean well, but it's ridiculous."

Satchell Paige, the ageless black pitching immortal, says he has sent invitations to Vida Blue to go out with him so he can pass on some of his knowledge to his successor every time Blue passes through Kansas City, but he never has gotten an answer.

Vida sighs and insists, "I never got the message."

Someone tells Blue that John Brodie, the great San Francisco quarterback, is at a game, and Blue sends a message to Brodie he'd like one of John's football jerseys. John sends him one, but later is disappointed to find Vida still is wearing Namath's.

"When you win the Super Bowl, Vida will wear yours," some-one tells Brodie.

Namath is at a game and he says afterward, "That was the first or second baseball game I've enjoyed for quite a while. That guy Blue is a tremendous athlete. I was excited watching him pitch. You know, when you sit there and watch a guy, you can tell, being an athlete yourself, I mean, if he's special. You can see right away he has great natural ability, but you see other things, too. I admire him as much for his movements and the way he carries himself as for his performance. He's great to watch."

Someone says Vida keeps wearing Joe's jersey. Joe says, "He's got good taste."

Vida says, "He watched me pitch to the hitters. Next time I want to watch him pitch to the ladies."

Boston is in town and Vida drives to the ballpark, singing, "If you are looking for a hero, exciting and new, there's a boy in Oakland, name of Vida Blue . . . ." It is a Friday night and he will pitch. Rained out, Hunter missed his turn and should be going now, with Blue going in the next one, and Williams is asked about this at the ballpark. He says, "We sent Vida home early so he could pitch tonight, we advertised he'd pitch tonight, the fans expect him to pitch tonight, so he'll pitch tonight. Hunter understands."

In the dressing room, Hunter says, "I understand. I don't like it, but I understand. I'm having my best season, too. I pitched a perfect game a few seasons back and got a lot of publicity then, but I've never won twenty and I have a chance to win twenty this year. I know I'm helping this club win the pennant. I like to pitch in turn and I think in the long run it's best for all concerned. So sometimes I cuss Vida under my breath. But that's nonsense. You can't stay mad at Vida. He's too nice. And he doesn't have any say over it any more than I do. He's a working man like me and he does what they tell him to do. His situation this year is very sensational and very special and they have to accommodate it. I can see that. I can see how much more crowded the stands are when he pitches than when I pitch. And I can read the stats, too, and I know he's earned some of this. It's not easy to take, though. I can't say it is."

Vida says, "I'm sure some of my teammates are happy for me and some are jealous of me. It's human nature. They were all working hard and most of them were producing pretty good. Most of them had waited for this a long time and they weren't getting out of it what they thought they would. I come along and in one quick move I scoop off all the gravy. They have a reason to gripe. But they haven't said anything to me. We haven't discussed it. We let it lay. I try to treat them nice and they've sure treated me nice.

"The problem is I haven't been able to lead a normal life with the guys. While they're out chumming, I'm talking to some writer or doing some TV show. The crowd is always around my locker, not theirs. There's so many people around me, I can't even see them. I forget about them sometimes. I get to thinking of myself, not the team, and I don't want to do that.

"We've been a happy family. I like most of the guys real well. There's a few I don't care about. There's some bad apples in every barrel. But that's an opinion. Some don't like me, I'm sure. But we get along. Only I haven't been as free to cut up with them as I'd like. The ones I run some with, like Tommy and Reggie, they know me. The others don't yet. But I think they know I don't ask for any special favors or attention. I just do what I'm asked to do. I have no choice.

"Sometimes I wish guys like Reggie and Sal were having bigger years. They're having great years, but not their greatest. If Reggie was going for fifty, sixty home runs, it would draw some attention to him and take some pressure off me. I'd like to divide this up. But what can I do, go out and deliberately lose to Boston?"

The headline across the top of the sports page of the *Oakland Tribune*, all in blue, read IT'S BLUE FRIDAY, and there was a two-column story on the game noting that seven of his last ten scheduled starts would be at home and another two on television, and there was a picture of him, seven inches wide and ten inches deep, smack in the middle of the page, and there were 31,494 on hand, twice as many as would turn out the next day. There was a festive air. A lot of the fans wore Vida Blue buttons, Charlie O., the mule, pranced around, and a Dixieland Band played before the game.

Gary Peters, the good pitcher facing Vida, said, "I'm more anxious to hit against him than I am to pitch against him. I take a lot of pride in my hitting and I want to test his pitching for myself." The first two times he hit against Vida, he struck out. He admitted later, "I was impressed, man, was I impressed. He throws as hard with control as anybody I've seen. If he gets one more pitch he'll be almost unbeatable."

But the third time Peters got to hit against Vida it was something else. This was in the eighth inning. Billy Conigliaro had hit a ground ball through the infield. Then Duane Josephson bunted between the mound and first trying to sacrifice and Blue slipped going for it and Davis fumbled it when he got to it and two were on. Then Peters got his bat on the ball to put down a sacrifice bunt, moving the runners to second and third. Doug Griffin lined a letter-high fastball to left for a single scoring a run. That was the fourth and last hit off Blue and the only run, but it was enough to beat him.

At one point in the contest, Blue fanned five-straight batters. He got Aparicio on a high fastball. Behind 3-and-1, Vida got Yastrzemski swinging on two curves. He got Smith swinging on a fastball. He got Petrocelli swinging on a fastball. He got Scott on a curve. Later, Yastrzemski, a three-time batting champion, said, "He's just super. I didn't think a man could throw that hard that long. And he really showed me something when he came in with breaking pitches from 3-and-1."

But, as had been happening, opposing pitchers were fired up to beat Blue and Peters was pitching superbly, too. He scattered six hits. He got out of a jam in the sixth when Campaneris led off with an infield hit. Rudi then struck out. Campy stole second. Jackson also struck out. Davis beat out an infield hit as Campy sped to third. But then Bando bounced into a force-out. Peters retired the last ten men he faced. In the ninth, Jackson fouled out, Davis grounded out and Bando fouled out, and Blue had lost, 1–0; his fifth loss.

He was sitting with his arm in ice when the writers got to him, and he looked at their long faces and said, "Hell, I ain't done nothing but lose a ballgame." He finished off a beer and flipped it into a trash can. He said, "I felt fine. My curve was behaving better than it ever has. When I get beat like that, when I've got good stuff, there's nothing I can do about it. It's just one of those things."

But they kept pressing him and the fingers of his right hand began to beat a tattoo on the tabletop. Someone asked, "Do you feel less pressure now than before you got your 20th?" And he said, "Yup." Tap-tap-tap. Someone asked, "Did you slip trying to field the bunt?" And he said, "Yup." Tap-tap-tap. And someone asked him what sort of pitch he threw Griffin and he made a face and said, "Man, it was just a pitch, it was a baseball, and I threw it and he hit it, and that's all there was to it." And then there was silence for a while, except for that tap-tap-tap. Someone said Griffin hit a home run off him in Boston. Vida said, "Yup." Tap-tap-tap.

Someone came up and asked what sort of pitch Griffin hit. Blue looked around at the other guys and shook his head and rolled his eyes. "Where you from?" he asked the writer. The writer said, "The Palo Alto *Times*." Blue smiled and said, "Oh, the big leagues." The writer said, "I'm just doing a job." Vida said, "All right, I know that. I'm sorry. That's all I'm trying to do, too. But what do you want me to tell you, how I hold the ball across the seams, how I twist my wrist! I just pick it up and throw it. He hit it. They scored. We didn't. That's it. It's over. It's history. OK?"

Someone pointed out that Boston was the first team to have beaten him twice this season, and that weak hitters had hurt him, and he was asked if he thought they were especially tough. He said, "They're all tough. Maybe a hitter doesn't get a hit all year, but he can get one that beats you. Maybe you beat a team all year, but they can turn around and beat you. I suppose some are tougher than others, but I don't want to rate 'em. They beat me. In Boston people talked about that close left-field fence. Here it's supposed to be an airport out there and they beat me again. They just beat me. No reasons. No excuses."

After the writers left he sat in front of his locker, his pants at half-mast, soaked from drippings from the ice-pan, and he said,

"You win some 1–0—and I won a couple—and you got to lose some 1–0."

He was asked about a story in *The Hollywood Reporter,* a show-business publication, that a producer wanted Blue to play in a movie based on the life of a black liberation leader by the name of "Fanon" to be scripted by James Baldwin, and Vida said he'd said he knew nothing about it but had gotten a telegram offering him the role but would just pass it on to his manager. He also had a telegram that read "You are good on TV, but better in person." It was signed "Vicki." He said, "I don't know any Vicki. And he smiled. There was a picture of a pretty girl taped on his locker. He said, "It's just a girl." There were also pictures of his brother Michael and sister Sandra taped to the locker.

He showered and dressed in his jeans and Joe Namath jersey and Tommy Davis said, "Man, when you going to learn to dress?" and Vida laughed and needled him. "Man, when you're as good as me, you don't have to dress."

There were some packages in his locker and he filled his arms with them and left. Outside, fans waited for autographs. This time, he felt he was prepared. He said, "I'm sorry, I'd love to, but as you can see my arms are full." He kept trying to work his way through the mob but it was persistent. A lady dragging a lad along behind her shoved him in front of Blue and said, "Sign his pennant." She grabbed it from the boy's hand and waved it in Vida's face, almost poking it in his eye. He said, "Ma'm, I'm sorry but my hands are full." She said, "He's a child and he loves you and he wants your autograph." Vida said, "Oh, lady, I love children and I hope they love me, but please . . ." She said, "I'll hold your packages for you." He said, "You'll hurt yourself." She said, "No, I won't." He said, "Oh, you make it so hard. Lordy, lordy." And he kept moving, and they kept pressing their scraps of paper and programs and pennants at him. Finally, he got to his car and put his packages down to open the door and that was his mistake, at that moment his arms were empty and they poured all over him, kicking some of his packages under the car and stepping on others, and they said, "Vida, please, just for me, just me, please, Vida," and someone said, "Your arms are free now, Vida," and Vida leaned his head back and looked at the heavens and said, "Mercy, mercy, mercy." And he began to sign.

Finally in his car, he had trouble driving it out of the lot without injuring someone because the fans swarmed all over it. It was now two hours after the game. He had lost, and yet hundreds remained around him. Finally, in the dark night, on the open freeway, he sighed and was silent for a long time. After a while he was singing, "Smiling faces sometimes . . . pretend to be your friend . . . ."

The schedule calls for him to pitch again four nights later, on Tuesday night, rest, at Oakland against the Yankees. Finley, who is an absentee owner and commutes from Chicago to some games in Oakland, is in town on this day and has awakened Vida early to ask him and Reggie to attend a businessman's luncheon at noontime, and Vida has agreed and says, "I'm not supposed to do anything on the days I'm to pitch, but he's the boss. He asked me as a favor and I wasn't going to say no."

Awakened early, he is prowling around his apartment and is upset because he can't find his record by "The Temptations" of "Smiling Faces Sometimes." He looks through the stacks of many records once, twice, three times. He looks on the floor, under some newspapers and magazines, behind the couch. He is growing desperate. "Hey, Davis, you seen my record?" he calls upstairs.

"No, Blue, I ain't seen your record."

Asking this visitor to look through the records again, he goes upstairs to ransack the house. The record is not found. Blue returns empty-handed and full of frustration. "Someone stole it, or borrowed it," he mutters. "Record doesn't just disappear."

"Maybe Doug Griffin took it," someone says.

Vida says something obscene, then laughs and goes to get a big glass of milk. He downs it practically in one swallow, refills his glass, sits down and ponders the situation.

Enter Reggie Jackson, the savior, bearing a record in one hand. "That my record?" Vida asks suspiciously.

"Naw, that's my record," Reggie says.

But it is the right record, or at least right enough. It is the hit record of the tune as recorded by "The Grateful Dead," and Reggie puts it on the player and it begins to play and peace returns to this place.

After hearing it through twice, Blue is temporarily satisfied and he gets up and goes upstairs, muttering, "Someone got *my* record."

"You can have this one," Reggie says.

"Yeah, but it ain't mine," Blue says as he disappears.

Reggie gets up and takes off his jacket and tie and shirt and slacks and sits down in his shorts. He feels at home here. Now he is relaxed and listens to the record and talks about baseball and Blue and his own bid for a home-run crown, then he stops talking about baseball and talks about music and life. He is a very tough person and does not trust many people, but if he finds he can trust you he is a good friend, and he has befriended Blue. He is intelligent and has had some experiences which Vida has been experiencing and he can counsel him some. I had heard it said that he was jealous of Blue, but it is people saying such things that have turned him off people, and it is hard to detect a trace of envy in him for his friend. Of Blue, Jackson says, "He is the greatest natural athlete I've ever known."

Blue returns and they sit around rapping awhile. Some kids come in and they con them some. The phone begins to ring, but Reggie just takes it off the hook and leaves it lay. After a while it is time to go. Reggie puts his clothes on and Blue puts his clothes on and in fancy duds they are powerful-looking and good-looking young men. We get in Reggie's powerful, good-looking new car and head off for the Berkeley area, where the luncheon is. On the way, Jackson is saying, "It's good you got you a manager. I didn't get one in time when I had my big year and I blew a lot of loot. Take the bread while they're dishing it out. Later on they won't give you no charity." Blue said he was worried about all the dinners he might have to attend after the season. Reggie smiles and says, "Set a fee. That'll scare most of 'em off."

The place is found, Spenger's Fish Grotto, and Finley, suffering from a toothache, wanting to take some of the speaking chores off his shoulders, is waiting for them out front. He has had serious salary and holdout troubles with Reggie in the past and faces such problems in the near future, but he greets them warmly. It turns out to be the monthly meeting of Emeryville industry leaders, influential suburbanites Finley is courting in an effort to spread the appeal of his franchise throughout the area. He has a couple of young publicists placing A's yearbooks and tickets to a forthcoming game at each place in the small banquet hall. All eyes are on Vida and Reggie and Finley. Before long, members of a local Rotary, lunching in an adjoining room, move into the back of this room to sit in on the special sports show.

The session opens with the Pledge of Allegiance to the flag. The toastmaster then talks business briefly, but lightly, cracking jokes and imposing fines on members who have been remiss in one way or another. The two ballplayers sit with Finley and the officers on the dais. The ballplayers have the only black faces in the room. They seem restless as they pick at something called "shrimp-steaks."

As most of the food disappears, the toastmaster stands up and introduces Finley. He looks out over the crowd of a couple of hundred and compares the size of the crowd favorably to attendance at his games in Kansas City. He points out he is doing better in Oakland but not what he would hope to be doing. He says, "You get what you pay for. Well, gentlemen, we're not getting what a championship contender should get." He asks their support. He speaks of the money and time and energy he has invested in building his team and the ridicule he has endured from "jerky sportswriters," which gets a laugh.

He speaks of the managers he has hired and fired. He says, "You gentlemen are all businessmen. When you hire a man to do a job and he doesn't do a job, what do you do? You replace him with another man. That's what I have done." He makes a joke that if in his insurance business he had promoted a plan to insure the jobs of his own managers, he'd be broke today, and everyone laughs. He praises his present manager, promises a pennant and a victory in the playoffs, predicts a World Series for the Bay Area between San Francisco and Oakland. In such an event, he suggests, the A's would win. With players like the two he has brought with him today, how can he lose, he says.

He introduces Reggie first as one of the greatest outfielders, one of the all-time sluggers and a player he would say a lot more about if he did not have to negotiate a new contract with him after the first of the year. He sits down, the crowd applauds, Reggie gets up, the crowd cheers. Reggie says very nice things

about Finley. He says they'd had their differences, but he knew
that when he needed a friend, Finley was always there. Asked
privately later if he'd been sincere, Jackson shrugged and smiled,
"What else could I say?" He makes a sharp, polished speech, with
some slightly shady stories included, which brought the house
down, and several of the businessmen were observed turning to
one another and remarking on how surprisingly able at this the
ballplayer was.

Then Reggie sits down to cheers and Finley stands up and
introduces Blue as "The most underpaid player in baseball" and
sits down and Vida stands up to a great ovation and there is a
lot of talk in the seats about how good-looking he is. Blue thanks
Finley and the group for having him, says he isn't a speaker and
says he feels the best way for him to do his thing is through a
question-and-answer session, but he might just as well answer a
couple of questions before they are asked, and he says, "No, I am
not going to win thirty games" and "Yes, I am the most underpaid
player." Everyone laughs and the questioning begins. He gets the
usual ones and answers them in the usual ways.

It goes smoothly except when someone asked him why with the
pennant clinched were the A's continuing to pitch him at the
risk of ruining his arm. Vida purses his lips, shakes his head a
little and says, "In the first place the pennant isn't clinched. In
the second place a pitcher is supposed to pitch and the risk of
ruining your arm is one every pitcher runs every time he pitches.
I'm paid to pitch and as long as the other guys go out and pitch
ahead of me and the other players go out to the field, I have to go
out in my turn, too." Everyone applauds and that is it.

He gets a big hand and the meeting is adjourned and everyone
crowds around the podium to get autographs. Almost all the
businessmen go up. The waiters go up, and even the waitresses,
some of them coming from other parts of the large restaurant.
"I didn't know who was here. When I found out, wow!" says an
elderly waitress. "Will my grandson be thrilled. My, isn't he
good-looking."

Eventually they escape, shake hands with Finley and flee in
their car, breathing deeply with relief.

Vida said, "Now I'm worn out." Reggie said, "Now we got to

play a game tonight." They did not seem happy at the prospect. Reggie said, "There comes a time every year when you either are way ahead or way behind, when you have played a long season and still have a long month or so to play, when it becomes an ordeal. You don't get many nights off and you become tired, mentally as well as physically. If we were still in a tight fight for the pennant we wouldn't be thinking tired, we'd be fired up, but we're not. We got to be careful to clinch this thing. We don't win one of these things every year." Vida said, "Oh, don't you? I thought you did. I just got here and I thought this was the way it always was." Reggie laughed and said, "Vida, my man, you will find out another year it may be another thing. I promise you, you will see the other side of the coin." Vida said, "I can't wait," and buried himself in his seat.

At the apartment, Reggie peeled down to his shorts again while Vida changed into his Joe Namath outfit and asked Mudcat if there'd been any business. Mudcat said Davis had handled the calls. Davis said some people had called but he didn't remember who. Mudcat said, "Man, you don't write nothing down." Blue said, "Mud, Davis can't write." Davis said, "Man, I been answering phones and taking messages all day for you. I can't do all that and write things down or remember things, too. Anyway, I'm not your social secretary. I'll tell you what you should do. . . ." Smiling broadly he made a suggestion. Giggling, Vida declined. Reggie said, "I'll tell you, Mud, I think that was a helluva good idea." Mud said, "These cats don't know about good ideas. They only have bad thoughts." The music played, the kids came, the phone rang, Blue napped, Reggie left, the afternoon passed.

Vida came down to leave early because he had to go to Alameda to pick up Mangual, who was without his car for the day. We got into his Grand Prix and he drove it like a man in a hurry. He said, "I don't really drive fast, I just get places quick." He revealed that lately he had been going to the mound with about $2 in change in his pockets. "I don't just got dimes now," he giggled. "Finley gave me a quarter when I won my thirteenth. Cronin gave me a quarter. Little kids send me nickels. I don't know if that means I'll win 200 games. I do know I do a lot of jingling and jangling out there. I got to cut it out. I got enough burden on my back without carrying all that silver on my hip. It's

heavy. And when you lose 1–0 it don't seem to do you no good,"
he concluded as the neighborhoods flew by.

He was asked what would happen if his arm really did go bad.
He shrugged and said, "I'd try to get into pro football."

We picked up Mangual. Blue displayed a silver medal hung on
a chain around his neck that Mangual had given him. Mangual
said it represented St. Martin, "a black saint . . . everything for
the poor people." "That's me," Blue said. "The most underpaid
superstar in baseball." As we drove he sang, "Vida's still a youngster, he's just a boy, but let me tell you, he's the real McCoy . . . ."
It was four hours before gametime and we stopped in a coffee-
shop to get something to eat. Blue ordered a patty-melt hamburger, french fries, a Coke *and* a chocolate milkshake, and got it
down fast. It was suggested that this might not be the wisest
pregame meal. He smiled and said, "It's easy to throw up."
Mangual looked sick at this.
When no one recognized Vida, he called over the waitress and
said, "I just thought you might like to know who is honoring you
with his presence eating here today." Pointing to Mangual he
said, "This is Vida Blue." Mangual nodded modestly. The waitress
said, "That's very nice. Who's Vida Blue?" Vida Blue seemed
shocked. Smiling broadly he said, "Why, he is just about the best
football player there is." She said, "Oh. And are you a football
player, too?" And Vida said, "No, I'm a baseball player." Turning around so she could see the name on the back of his green
and white jersey, he said, "See, Namath. I'm Joe Namath, just
another ballplayer." And she said, "That's very nice" and left.
And Vida said "Some days are too good to be true." He paid the
bill, bought some Sucrets and went away passing them out as
though they were candy.
We drove up to the nearly deserted parking lot a bit before
five in the afternoon and he had smiles and handshakes for the
guards and other workers as he passed through the hole in the
underside of the concrete bowl, through the A's offices, teasing
secretary Mary Brubaker, who wanted him to take some mail he
didn't want to be bothered with down the elevator and into the
dressing room. In the offices, Mike Haggerty was busy answering

calls concerning Blue and worrying what Finley might want from him.

Finley sat in the press lounge having a drink and talking about Blue. He was distressed at the continued attention paid to the story that he wanted Vida to adopt the name "True." He said, "It's most unfortunate because there's not a word of truth in it. It makes him look bad, like a wise guy. When he signed, I negotiated with him over the telephone. Shortly afterward I asked if he had the nickname 'True.' He said no. I asked him if he'd like to adopt it as a middle name. I said he could go to the courthouse and it would only cost a couple of dollars. He said he didn't think he would. I didn't know his was his father's name or his father was dead. Anyway, his decision was fine by me.

"I have five boys of my own. I appreciate boys. This is a very humble boy. Somewhere along the way we all meet Mr. Humility. This boy has humility. Since I met his mother, I appreciate him even more. I know he has had a good upbringing. I do not believe he is the type of boy to permit all of the attention he's getting to go to his head. Considering that he is a boy of his age with only a high school education, I think he has done a helluva great job in coping with all the attention paid him. I have found him to be very understanding of everyone's problems and very appreciative of everything done for him.

"My father taught me the formula I live by—the three S's, S plus S equals S, sweat plus sacrifice equals success. If you're willing to do more than your competitor you will come out on top. I have found Vida Blue willing and eager to pay the price. He has qualities you seldom find in an athlete. When before the season I offered him $13,000, if he had asked for more I would have given it to him, I was aware of the no-hitter he had pitched, but he just accepted it and I was so pleased it led to my giving him the Cadillac, and it was given him with no strings attached. As were the fringe benefits that went with it.

"If he had held me up for more money, I wouldn't feel as kindly toward him and as inclined to give him things. Where increases in salary are concerned, you must remember that while there is no limit—other than the problem created by the price-wage freeze at the moment—to the amount a player can be raised, you can only cut a player 20 percent in one year and 30 percent in two. This creates an inequity. If a player does better than expected, he merits an increase, but if he does worse than expected he deserves a decrease, and the increase must be kept in line with the permissible decrease. A lot of other things enter into it—including seniority. A player who has produced over many years deserves more than one who has produced for one year. But we will take care of Vida. I understand he has a manager now. I don't think that's necessary. I could deal with Vida directly. I only hope his manager is as humble and appreciative as Vida."

We went to his private box on the second level. Here he was hosting some friends. A young man was employed as a runner to fetch hard drinks and other refreshments and was kept busy. Vida was warming up. Williams had said, "I'd like to lock him up in a glass jar between games." Now Finley said, "I'd like to lock him up in a safe between starts. I worry about him and about his arm, of course. We are dealing with a most fragile and precious property. I worry as much for him as for myself and for my team. I have nightmares about it. But I do not like to associate this good young man with bad dreams. All we can do is exercise the proper precautions and let him pitch. We will not overwork him, and if there was the slightest suspicion of any physical problem we would not work him at all. We want the gate his appearances bring, but we will not risk his future for these. He is our future. Or, rather, he is a major part of our future. Our other players are a vital part of this, too. I have worked hard and spent a great deal to assemble this fine team and I will not rest until we are world champions."

The crowd roared as Vida threw his first pitch. As Horace Clarke flied out, Finley applauded lustily and turned to his friends for approval. When the next batter, Thurman Munson, singled, Finley made fists, shook them and said, "Well, no no-hitter tonight." When the next batter, Roy White, doubled, driving home Munson, Finley tilted his head in despair and said, "I must say he lost his shutout early." When Felipe Alou grounded out, Finley nodded. "Let's get going, now, Vida." As John Ellis struck out, Finley clapped once and ordered another drink.

The Yankees were pitching their ace, Mel Stottlemyre, and as he set the A's down in their half without incident, Finley was silent. As the A's took the field for the second inning the owner pointed to each player in turn around the field and many of those in the dugout and bullpen and recited the price he had paid for each. After Ron Hansen grounded out and Ron Swoboda and Gene Michael struck out, Finley became animated. As the A's batted he rooted for each batter in turn, but to no avail.

He looked around him at the gathering of 18,288 and spoke of his disappointment that his team had not been rewarded with greater attendance here, but said, "I believe this is the greatest potential area for baseball in the country as we will begin to be rewarded for our sweat and our sacrifices here in the end." When Blue opened the third inning by recording his third-straight strikeout, Finley clapped hard. And as Blue finished the inning by setting down two more, the owner beamed, ordered another drink and ordered his team to get that run back.

The A's did not even get a hit. As they went down again, Finley spoke of the innovations and promotions he has proposed for the game, those accepted and those not accepted, and the dark-age stupidity of others in the game who were so resistant to change, even for the better, who could not see what was best for them and their sport. The innings passed, and as Blue struck out two in a row to reach twelve rivals in a row retired, Finley cheered. When the string ended on a double down the line by Swoboda, he groaned. But as Vida got the next two on a foul-out and strikeout, he was out of the fifth.

We were past the halfway point now, however, and a horrible thought occurred to Finley. "We can't possibly let him lose 1–0 again, can we?" he asked. As the sixth inning passed, another horrible thought occurred to him. "We can't be victimized by a no-hitter, can we?" he asked.

A negative answer to this was provided in the home half of the seventh when Rick Monday opened with a safe bunt for the first hit off Stottlemyre. Finley clapped. "All right, let's get something going for our young man," he said. When Dave Duncan also bunted safely, Finley stood up, smiling. "This is it," he said. It was not. Mike Hegan tried to bunt, too, but Stottlemyre got to it in time to throw out the runner at third. Brown then bounced back to the pitcher, who wheeled to start a double-play that suddenly ended the threat. Finley sagged down in his seat in disappointment. "We must get this young man some support," he said.

It was a crisp, cool night and the owner sat shivering. He pointed out with pleasure that Jim Grant now had "Mudcat" and Jim Hunter now had "Catfish" on the backs of their uniforms instead of their last names. "All of these things add to the appeal of the game to the fans," he said. He pointed out how his attractive young miniskirted ball-girls had served lemonade to the umpires at midgame, and how he even had attractive young miniskirted ball girls. He pointed to the Dixieland band. He said, "We do what we can to make this a fun thing for the family."

His tooth was aching now, and so was his spirit. Blue got through the eighth, but so did Stottlemyre. Finley said, "This fine young man simply can't lose 1–0 again." Blue retired three in a row in the ninth, finishing with a flourish with his tenth strikeout, of Bobby Murcer, one of the league's heaviest hitters. He had allowed only four hits, just as he had in his previous 1–0 loss, and walked none. In the A's ninth, Jackson fouled out and broke his bat in a swift, fierce rage of disgust. Monday flied out deep to center. Duncan popped to second. Blue had lost, 1–0, again. And Finley shook his head sadly and walked off.

When the first writers got to Blue he was soaking his pitching arm and holding a beer in his other hand and looked at them and said, "Hold on, wait 'til everyone gets here. What I have to say I only want to say once." The writers nodded and waited, standing over him, watching him, and, after a while, some drifted off. As others came up they observed the silence curiously. Finally one asked, "Are you getting tired?" And Blue said, "Hold it, is everyone here now?" Asking about one writer whom he did not see, he asked, "Where is that front-runner?" At this precise moment the writer came rushing in. Jackson, sitting in front of his locker with his head hanging, looked up, saw him and said, "Get the hell out of here." The writer said brightly, "Hi'ya Reggie." Reggie cursed and lowered his head.

Blue said, "All right, lets get started." The writer who had asked the question "Are you getting tired?" repeated it. Vida said, "No, I'm not getting tired. Did I pitch like I was tired? I feel as good as I ever did. I'm throwing as good. I'm satisfied with the game I pitched. I'm not happy I lost, but when you lose 1–0 you can't kick yourself around the room over it." A writer pointed out that this was two-straight now by this score. Vida said, "So the guys didn't get me any runs. So all season they got me runs. Stottlemyre is a helluva pitcher. Other guys are good, too. This guy pitched a helluva game. He can stop anyone."

There was a long period of silence as though defeat was an embarrassment. Blue laughed and said, "What's the matter with you guys? If I'd won 1–0 you'd have a million questions." He poked his head above the crowd and called to his teammates, "Extra, extra, Vida Blue loses two-straight." It was the first time he had done so this season. The room was quiet.

Someone asked Vida if this ended his chances for thirty. Vida slammed his fist on the table with great force. "Forget that stuff," he said. "Forget thirty. I don't want to hear that silly question again." Someone asked him what he had thrown White. Vida stood up, his left arm dripping, made a face and said, "Mercy, mercy, me," he said. "I just picked up the ball like this, see, and I just threw it like this, see, and he hit it, like this, see. It was a pitch and he hit it. It was a baseball I threw him."

A writer rushed up and asked, "Are you getting tired?" Vida wheeled on him and asked, "Where you been? I already answered that question. I said I only wanted to say things once tonight." And the writer said, "I'm sorry, Vida, but you were the one who asked us to wait. I was talking to some of your teammates. When I noticed you were talking I came back." Vida said, "All right, all right, I'm sorry. What was the question?" And the writer asked, "Are you getting tired?" And Vida said, "Of course I'm getting tired. I know how many innings I've pitched. I don't feel like I did at the start of the season. I'm not throwing as hard. It's got to take something out of you." And he went off to shower.

Jackson still sat with his head hung. I asked him about breaking his bat when he went out in the ninth. Reggie said, "I was frustrated. I wanted a homer to tie it for that man in the worst way. We owe that man some runs. It is a shame that he should pitch two games like he's pitched and lose two games like that." It was pointed out to him that he was just one of nine players and could not hold himself responsible. He said, "I have to hold myself responsible. I have responsibilities. It is my job. I am paid to do the job. If the others do it, I don't feel bad. If they don't, I feel bad. I know you can't hit all the time, but this is two in a row like this and it is tough to take. That man is having one of those years you don't have very often and I want him to get the kind of record he should out of it."

He was half-undressed, his strong body moist with sweat, his muscles still bunched. He did not move until the room had almost cleared and Vida returned, then he went to his friend and took his hand and talked to him softly for a few minutes, then he went off to his shower.

As Vida dressed he said softly, "It's OK. What they don't seem to understand is you probably pitched better losing 1–0 then you did winning 3–2 or 4–2 or 4–3. They just look at the W and the L. After the bunt failed I said to myself, 'Well, it looks like 1–0 again.' But I didn't really accept it until Reggie went out. As long as he had a swing, I had a chance. When he went out, I figured that was it. All right, it's OK, I can accept it. So it's two in a row like this. That's the game. I'd feel worse if I pitched bad and won. Except that the team would've won."

He had treated the writers and broadcasters well all season. He didn't try to figure out who might be important and who might not be, and he took time for most of them, even those who did not ask him for time at reasonable times and he answered all the same questions he got so tired of answering, and he even tried to answer those he had no answers for. He didn't think technically, so he didn't answer technically. He didn't want to pretend that the only way a hitter could get a hit off him was if he made a "mistake"—if he got a fastball too high or hung a curve or something like that. He tried to say that they were good, too, and no matter how good he was, no matter what he threw, they were going to hit it sometimes. Some of the writers could not accept this. It was too easy.

There were ten to twenty members of the press around him

after every game, within minutes after every game, before he'd
even had a chance to consider what had happened in the game,
pressing right in on top of him until he must have felt trapped,
mikes stuck in his face to inhibit his language, and others around
him or coming at him at other times, and he wasn't used to this,
he just didn't have any experience with it, and he handled it fine,
all things considered, although it was beginning to wear him
down some as the season wore on. He'd been misquoted some—
which will happen—and had some simple things treated sensa-
tionalistically—which will happen—and it scared him some and
was making him a little shy.

Even the writers themselves, most of them, anyway, could see
how they had to begin to bother him sooner or later, but it wasn't
the writers or the broadcasters who were troubling him. They
were just the representatives of the whole world, which seemed
to want to devour him. They were the ones he had to deal with.
He came back from his shower and sat down and said, "I don't
mean to put the guys on. It's just a way out for me. I can see
they're stuck with this, too. I can see that they got a job to do.
But their bosses want them to write something outstanding and
it bothers me what they write sometimes."

I said, "I've been told by athletes who've been around awhile
that the best thing to do is to just answer all their questions as
honestly as you can and then just forget about it, don't even read
what they write, or if you do read it, don't let it bother you,
because you have no control over it, and they control what the
public thinks of you."

And he said, "I can see that. I'm trying to do that. I'll try
harder. But it's hard. The thing is, my answers don't always
satisfy them. They want me to say I'll do this or that and I really
don't know if I can. The writers aren't the heavies. Not being able
to do what I'm suddenly supposed to do is the heavy. Living up
to myself is the heavy thing. Losing 1–0 is the heavy. I can't
pitch much better than that. It'd be easy to say I could win
thirty, but it's hard to do. Not when you lose 1–0. And that's
what this game is, losing sometimes 1–0. The writers are just
there to try to find out for the fans what happened. But I don't
always know what happened. Or at least why it happened. And

it happens the way I don't want it to happen sometimes, which is heavy."

He went outside, where a pretty girl waited to console him, and he touched her cheek, and he smiled at her and she smiled at him and said something sympathetic, and she went with him and then stood off to a side and waited as he worked his way through the waiting fans, signing autographs before he could go.

CHAPTER FIFTEEN

On the last Friday in April, when he'd won his sixth, he came steaming into the dressing room whistling "whoooowheeee" through his lips, wearing a grin as wide as his face, and his whole body seemed animated as he replayed the game, almost batter by batter, and he radiated power and pleasure and could not sit still for the excitement that coursed through him. He was like a child who has gotten the present he wanted.

On the last Sunday in August he got his 23rd victory, and he walked wearily to his locker later without a sound, almost expressionless, and he did not even want to talk about the game, and you sensed he felt some depression over it as he sat quietly resting, a man who had done a hard job and gotten through it somehow.

He stopped Washington, 4–3, on six hits, striking out ten, in the first game of a doubleheader before 24,971 fans. He gave up a bases-empty home run to Del Unser in the fifth inning and a two-run home run to Tim Cullen with two out in the ninth, but Jackson's 25th homer had helped him to just enough of a lead to last.

Afterward he said, "I didn't pitch well, but I got the win, so everybody's happy. No, I wasn't satisfied. Were those tough hitters who hit me? Everyone's tough for me. I'm just a pitcher. The press exaggerates too much. They write that certain players are superstars this or super that. They always want to compare players. Well, I just want to be a good pitcher on a winning team.

I'm tired of being a superstar and I'm tired of the whole season. All I want now is to get away on an island with a mermaid and forget the rest of the season." Catfish Hunter coasted to his seventeenth victory with a 9–0 shutout in the second game and the A's took to the road 16 games to the front, turning into the final month.

In Los Angeles, Vida appeared with other prominent athletes on the "Sports Challenge" syndicated television quiz show. He was asked to sign so many autographs he was almost late getting in front of the cameras. An executive tried to call off the last two boys who were hanging onto Vida's coat, requesting his signature. A voice boomed, "Please let them finish or I won't be able to go home. Those are my sons. Vida Blue is the biggest name around our house." The voice belonged to Bill Russell, the retired basketball great, who was grinning broadly, who refused to sign autographs during his career.

In Minnesota, the A's lost the first game of a twinight Friday night doubleheader, 9–4. In the second game, Steve Brye hit his first major-league home run in the second inning, off Blue. Jackson singled in a run off Corbin to tie it in the third. It remained 1–1 until there were two out in the last half of the ninth inning, when George Mitterwald hit a home run off Blue to beat him, 2–1. He had given seven hits and one walk, struck out twelve and was charged with his seventh loss. Afterward he had little to say. "He hit a good pitch. He just hit it. It seems like the guys who aren't supposed to hit much hit me the most. I was not letting down. I'd lost three out of four 1–0 and 1–0 and 2–1, and I don't call that letting down."

Detroit's 31-year-old Mickey Lolich was coming fast in the pitching statistics. He was working hard, pitching well and was catching Blue in victories, innings and strikeouts. Detroit manager Billy Martin was talking to writers right and left, campaigning for Lolich. He was saying, "If my man passes him in the stats, my man should get the Cy Young Award and maybe the MVP, too. You can't start out a season saying someone is the best pitcher and then not pay any attention to what happens the rest of the season. I think my man is the best man."

Someone said Vida had pitched Oakland to the pennant when

the pennant was still at stake and Lolich was coming on now when the pressure was off, but Martin just shrugged.

Lolich himself said flatly, "I think I should get it but I think he will. He's the pheenom who's been getting all the press, and is on the first-place team, not me. It's always that way with me. First I was overshadowed by Denny McLain on my own team. Now I'm having my greatest year and this kid gets all the credit. The writers are on his side. I have two chances, slim and none." In the Los Angeles *Times*, John Hall wrote:

> *I have been handed the responsibility of casting the American League Cy Young vote in this territory, so it figured it would wind up in a mess. Most of the summer, Vida Blue appeared to be the biggest look this side of San Quentin. But what do you do now about Detroit's Mickey Lolich, who has done just as much and maybe a little more with a lesser club? It's nervous time.*

On the same day in the same newspaper, Jim Murray wrote:

> *Is it a bird? Is it a plane? Is it a man? It is faster than a speeding bullet. Stronger than a locomotive. Can it talk? Where did they find it, in the bullrushes? Was it once a ride at Disneyland? Why, no, it's SUPER BLUE!*
>
> *Surely it's one of the great put-ons in the history of sport. Now, look here, Charley Finley, enough is enough! This is a made-up character like Captain Video or Little Orphan Annie or Jack Armstrong, the all-American boy. How can anyone believe in a Vida Blue? Shucks, do you believe a guy comes down the chimney on Christmas Eve? Think John Wayne won the Burma Road? Get outta here, Virginia, there's no Vida Blue. . . .*
>
> *. . . I thought I would go down to the clubhouse the other night and nail this Big Lie once and for all. I figured I'd have no trouble recognizing Vida Blue. He'd be the one with the halo, flying around the ceiling. I would inspect him for wires and mirrors, but most especially for any signs of mortality. . . .*
>
> *I must say they did it up nicely. Vida Blue is as handsome as a movie actor. He has legs on him like a Greek*

statue, the chest of a shot-putter, and, while he doesn't fly around the room, he does flit from end to end so abruptly you get the sensation you're interviewing him running alongside a moving train. . . .

Restlessly, wearily, Vida Blue said, "I didn't say I was a superstar, you did."

Vida said, "I don't care about Mickey Lolich. He's a fine pitcher. I hope he wins fifty games. If he pitches better than me, he deserves the awards. They can give him all the awards for all I care. All I want to do right now is wrap up a pennant. You're not going to get me into an argument over who's a better pitcher. That's for others to decide, not me."

Back home the A's seem up tight. They have been so far in front for so long they seem to have passed their peak and the manager and some of the veterans are worried about the way they are playing. In a Monday night game, Dobson gives up back-to-back home runs in the ninth inning as the A's lose to the Angels, 4–2. During the game, Williams and Campaneris are ejected by the umpires for arguing over decisions. After the game, in the dressing room, Dobson is sitting in front of his locker with his head in his hands for a long time, and when he looks up he sees a writer walking through with a smile on his face. "Get the hell out of here if you want to smile. We don't need you," snaps the depressed pitcher.

A few minutes later, while the writers are waiting in the hall for Williams to emerge from the coaches' room, Charles Tonelli, a slender, bespectacled, mild-mannered reporter for the suburban *Hayward Daily Review* walks up to Blue and remarks that Lolich has won another game that day. Loudly, Vida says, "I hope he wins four more." As the writer retreats rapidly, some players ask Blue what that was all about. Vida says, "Don't worry about it."

But word of the incident soon spreads. By now, Tonelli is with the other writers, smiling now, perhaps in embarrassment. Equipment manager Frank Ciensczyk sees his smile and snaps at him. The writer snaps back. Williams storms out to see what the fuss is about and when he finds out, ejects Tonelli, saying, "We're dead serious about what we're doing." Hunter makes a move at Tonelli, but the clubhouse door is closed between them. Bewildered, Tonelli says, "I just passed an innocent remark." But it was passed under pressure.

The next night, only 6,878 turn out to see Vida face the Angels. The bubble seemed to have burst. With one out in the first inning, Ken Berry singled. Jim Fregosi grounded out. Ken McMullen then hit a pitch into the bullpen. Billy Cowan walked. Jim Spencer singled. Tommy Reynolds singled in a third run. Blue got out of the inning. And he got through the next two innings without giving up another run. But then he was taken out for a pinch hitter. The A's lost, 6–1, and he took his eighth loss. Williams said later, "For the first time all season, Vida just didn't have it. He asked to be taken out." Vida later admitted, "I didn't have anything. My elbow felt a little tight. I couldn't get loose. Let's not say anything about it, except I was bad and I got beat." But he had dressed and gone by the time the writers got to his locker.

He got away from it.

His next start came on a Sunday at home against Minnesota. That day he was ripped for seven hits, including a home run by Mitterwald, surrendered a season-high six walks and left after pitching the eighth trailing 5–1. With the help of Jackson's two homers the A's tied it at 5–5 to take Vida off the hook before the Twins won it in the tenth, 7–5. Later Vida said, "I shut them out for five innings, then fell apart. I'm tired. I can't go the distance anymore. And I'm doing what I said I wouldn't, trying to pitch cute."

Privately he confided, "I'd like some time off. The pennant is about clinched. There's no way we can lose it now. If I could just get away and hide from everything for about a week I think it would do me a lot of good and make me a new man for the playoffs. But I can't ask Williams for that. I haven't asked any favors all season and I can't ask now. If the other pitchers don't ask for a break, how can I?"

He sat, sweaty, tired, depressed, in front of his locker, his long arms hanging at his sides, his head down.

Others were told, and Williams was told. The manager later

said, "I heard that, but I don't believe everything I hear. If he asks me, I might go for it."

Before Vida left a writer asked him for an interview. Vida asked him to put it off for another time but the writer said he couldn't. Vida said OK and sat down. When he was done and the man had left, Vida said, "I want to answer all their questions. I guess I just got to hope they don't twist my answers. But it's like giving little pieces of me away each time. If I keep giving pieces of myself away, after a while what will I have left?"

The A's, who were not drawing well now as they coasted toward the pennant, had scheduled a Fan Appreciation Day at season's end with special prizes to be distributed, but now it was announced that it had been canceled because the club was so busy with playoff and possible World Series plans. There was a lot of bad talk about this. Later, however, it was reinstated and held. But just before the season ended, publicist Haggerty quit.

Hunter won his twentieth in Kansas City as the A's closed in on the flag. The A's clinched the pennant in Finley's backyard, Chicago, on the fifteenth, beating the White Sox, 3–2, in the first game of a doubleheader with the help of a double by Jackson and a two-run homer by Bando, handing twenty-game winner Wilbur Wood his twelfth loss. Mudcat Grant got the victory in relief of Chuck Dobson. Champagne flowed and Finley patted Bando on the back and said, "Nice little hit there, bud." There was some wildness. Jackson threw manager Williams into a shower, but when he went after Finley the owner said, "Let's wait'll we win everything, then you can do what you want."

A few days later, Blue was sent back to work in his regular turn in Milwaukee and failed for the fourth-straight time to win his 24th. He gave up five hits and five runs in five innings, although Jackson and Bando helped bail him out with homers as the A's rallied to win, 6–5. Reggie's tied him for the league lead. On the nineteenth the A's won in Milwaukee for their 55th victory on the road to set a new American League record. Reaching for a few records were all that remained to be accomplished in the last week or so of the season. "It has been," said Vida Blue, "a very long season."

Tempers flew in a twinight twin-bill loss at home to Chicago.

White Sox pitcher Bart Johnson almost hit Jackson with a pitch, then did hit Epstein with one. Later the A's Fingers hit Ed Hermann with a pitch and threw one high and tight to Johnson, which he bunted toward Epstein, who charged from first. As Epstein reached the ball, Johnson stopped running toward him and began to backpedal. Epstein caught up to him, tagged him hard with the ball, shoved him down and swung. Soon players on both sides were swarming on the field scuffling around. In time, order was restored. Later, Blue pointed out he'd had no part in it. He said, "As the man said, I make love, not war."

The next night he faced the Sox with the understanding he would only go five innings to tune up for the playoffs. He tossed two-hit shutout ball over that stretch but the A's did not score, and after he left the White Sox came on to win, 3–0. On the last Sunday of the season he was given his last start of the season and was told he only had to go seven as a final tuneup for the playoff opener the following Saturday. He tossed three-hit shutout balls over this stretch and since the A's got him runs and went on to win, 7–0, he, on his sixth try, got credit for this 24th victory. "I learned one thing the last couple of weeks," he said. "I learned I'm not yet ready to pitch cute. I have to throw hard all the way."

He wound up with one less victory than Lolich. And his 301 strikeouts were three less than Lolich's total. He wound up with 24 complete games, five less than Lolich had. He pitched 312 innings, 63 less than Lolich. He also wound up with just eight losses, six less than Lolich. And 88 walks, four less than Lolich. And eight shutouts, twice as many as Lolich. And a 1.82 earned-run average, by far the best in the majors and much better than Lolich's 2.92, which was only tenth best in this league alone. And Blue had been at his best when it counted the most, pitching his team to a pennant when the pressure was on.

He sat on a stool at game's end and he said, "What do the statistics mean to me? I don't want to know them. They're just numbers. I don't want to know what Lolich did. I know I won 24. OK, that's fine. That's a lot. A lot more than I expected. Maybe some year I'll win more. And probably a lot of years a lot less. I'm just starting. I got a lot of years to go. I'm just glad this one's about done. I'm glad the team won." Someone smiled and said, "You're not tired, are you?" And he said, "You answer for me. You started working this season in February, too. This is the end of September. Aren't you tired?"

Then he showered and dressed and wearily worked his way out through the remnants of the crowd of 10,687, which waited for him outside.

Jackson had hit his 31st home run in that one to take the league lead, but Bill Melton of the White Sox hit three in the last two games to win by one. The A's won their 100th game of the season and Hunter won his 21st, 2–1, over Kansas City in the next-to-last game of the season before only 769 fans, the smallest in the A's history in Oakland, and then they won their 101st, 8–7, over K.C. before 1,415 on the final night. They lost 60, finished with a .627 percentage, 16 games in front of Kansas City in second place.

Davis finished as the team's only .300 hitter at .324. Mangual was .286, Jackson .277, Tenace .274, Bando .271, Rudi .267, Duncan .253, Campaneris .251, Monday .245, Green .244, Epstein .237. Campaneris had 34 steals and Jackson 16. Jackson led with 157 hits and 32 homers. Bando had 24 homers. Bando had 94 runs-batted-in, Reggie 80. With a 7–5 record the second half, Blue finished atop the pitchers at 24–8 with a 1.82 ERA. Hunter wound up 21–11 and 2.96. Dobson was 15–5 and 3.81. Segui was 10–8 and 3.14. Reliever Locker had 6 wins and 7 saves.

There were no parades in downtown Oakland.

The playoffs poised over his head like the point of a sharp blade, Vida lay in the dark in his room listening to records. "Smiling Faces Sometimes." And waited.

CHAPTER SIXTEEN

On the flight from Oakland Thursday, the last day of September, for Baltimore and the first game of the American League pennant playoffs Saturday, the second day of October, the A's and their ace, Vida Blue, had seemed relaxed. Vida listened to music on a headset, teased the stewardesses and was teased by his teammates.

But when a writer asked him how he felt about what he faced, Vida seemed to tense up tight. He talked to the writer, but he sat up straight in his seat while doing so and he stared straight ahead and did not look at the writer and expressions of worry seemed to pass across his face.

"No matter what I do, I'm thinking about the game," he said. "I want to win. I want it bad. I pitched two real good games against them, but that was back in May. We haven't seen each other for a long time. I don't know how I'll feel. I guess if I can win the first one it might give the team the lift it needs to go all the way. Well, I guess it's too late now to worry about things like that. I can't change anything at this point."

He was quiet then.

In Baltimore, he went into hiding.

Baltimore was bedecked with a festive air for the playoffs. It called itself "Flagtown, U.S.A.," and bunting and banners blew in the breeze along the downtown streets of this old city. Hotel clerks at establishments hosting baseball visitors wore yellow plastic straw hats and yellow plastic buttons instructing others,

"Smile, You're In Baltimore." The strains of "Take Me Out to the Ballgame" mingled in the air with "Maryland, My Maryland," and the sounds of revelry drifted from packed cocktail lounges.

The A's were staying at the Hilton and Charles O. Finley mingled with the crowds there, glowing in a double-knit sport coat of a color he called "Vida-blue." Normally, Charlie O. wore his team's green and gold on these occasions, but this was not a normal time. Most of the crowd seemed to be made up of hundreds of reporters and broadcasters all seeking to speak with the 22-year-old youngster who had been the sensation of the season and now faced the pressure of the playoffs.

In Las Vegas, the oddsmakers had installed Baltimore as the favorite to win the playoffs, but many rated Blue the pick for the opener. Jimmy "The Greek" Snyder called Vida "a 60-cent pitcher," which by his terms was a compliment of the highest order. He explained that it meant bettors had to risk at least 60 cents and sometimes as much as 80 cents to back Blue in what otherwise would be an even-money bet, that they had to put down $1.60 to $1.80 on Blue to win back an extra $1.00 if Blue won. At the peak of his career, Koufax consistently was an 80-cent pitcher, which was, by The Greek's terms, the best ever.

Baltimore figured to be favored. They had won 100 or more games in the regular season for the third-straight season, had won three-straight Eastern Division titles and were going for their third-straight American League pennant and second-straight World Series championship. They had swept their two previous best-of-five pennant playoffs in three-straight games and entered the playoffs with a streak of eleven-straight victories through the end of the regular season for the second season in a row.

Manager Earl Weaver's Orioles were a veteran group, smart and tough, blessed with powerful hitting from Frank and Brooks Robinson and big Boog Powell, an outstanding defense and superlative pitching from a quartet of twenty-game winners, Dave McNally, Mike Cuellar, Jim Palmer and Pat Dobson. And they entered the playoffs with the psychological edge of having won their last five in a row from the A's.

Manager Dick Williams' A's were in postseason play for the

first time. And, although they were not yet ready to reveal it, their pitching was in poor shape from sore arms suffered by Chuck Dobson and Blue Moon Odom, which would put them on the sidelines.

Their chances seemed to hang on the strong left arm of the near-rookie Blue. No one on the A's was admitting it, but it was a good guess most felt that way.

Baltimore's Boog Powell confided, "They're counting on getting off to a winning start with him. They're really counting on getting two wins from him and picking up the third along the way somehow. And we know he's capable of giving that to them. But we also figure we're capable of taking it away from him. We figure if we can get to him in the first game somehow, it'll break their spirit and set them up for a sweep." Frank Robinson said, "He's great, but so are we. He's just a kid and we're men. We got a chance. He's only one person and he's the key and that's a hell of a load to lift."

Through Thursday night, Vida remained in his room with his roommate Mangual and a friend or two and the telephone cut off and the television on and he admitted he was trying not to think about the game. He says, "I don't want to get up tight. I don't want to overdo it. I just want to relax." But he can't relax. He is restless. He wanders restlessly around the room, the forces of his fate bearing down on him. He admits later he does not sleep well.

On Friday, Hurricane Hazel has brought rain with her to town, but the A's adjourned to Memorial Stadium in hopes of loosening up with a workout. Reporters went along on the team bus, but Blue and Mangual did not. They drove to the ballpark later in a rented car and slipped in a side door. The weather prevented any workout, and the A's remained cooped-up in their clubhouse until the session was cancelled.

There were reporters in the clubhouse when Vida entered to retrieve some personal belongings he had placed in his locker. They immediately swarmed all over him and began to ask how he felt. He stood up very straight and said, "Now don't go asking me any questions. I'll just go out and pitch. I'll throw the ball and if they hit it, they do, and if they don't, they don't. But I'm not going to answer any questions. All I'm going to do is go back to the hotel to get me some rest."

A writer asked, "Why won't you answer questions?"

And Vida said. "I have my reasons. Vida Blue's reasons." And starts to walk out.

And someone called to him, "Are you up tight?"

And Vida looked back and asked, "What's up tight?" Then he shrugged and went on his way.

The writers were annoyed and many condemned him among themselves and some cursed him for his lack of cooperation and some sympathized with his situation. They asked the A's captain Sal Bando about him and Bando said, "Fame has changed him. He's more of a loner now. He's not as carefree as he was. He may have lost a little confidence. I guess he's just trying to pull himself together for a big effort. After all, it's a big game."

Mudcat Grant said, "The field's awful from football played on it and the rain. The weather's awful. Maybe he feels awful. This is the biggest ballgame of his life. He's honest and he doesn't want to say anything wrong which might hurt him or his chances." Dick Williams hustled the writers out to the soggy, rutty field, where the rain had let up a little, and said, "Please, he just wants a little peace and quiet. He's twenty-two years old. Maybe he's afraid to talk. He's done his best for you guys all season. He rates a break."

On the Orioles' side, the veteran McNally, who would face young Blue in the opener, showed a great deal of understanding. He asked, "Can you imagine what he's gone through this season? Can you imagine what he's going through now? In his first year and at his age?" He shook his head sympathetically.

Blue admitted later he did not sleep well again that night.

On Saturday morning, he was up early to have breakfast in the hotel coffee shop with Mangual. A writer, Glenn Schwarz of the San Francisco *Examiner,* sat down at a nearby table and waved at him. Later, he recalled, "He seemed to be looking straight at me without seeing me. It was a long time before he acknowledged my wave, and when he did, it was with a sort of slow, circular motion. His actions didn't seem to have any malice in them. It was as though he was in a trance."

The rain was so heavy that Williams took his team to a meeting in a ballroom instead of to the ballpark. While they were in the meeting, they were given word that the game had been called off for that day. Vida says he cursed at first, because it meant more waiting. His nerves by now were stretched taut. When he came out of the meeting, writers crowded around him. He simply stood there with his hands over his ears, refusing to hear their questions or give answers. He got away from them as soon as he could.

His attorney, Bob Gerst, had been talking to Sandy Koufax, who was in to broadcast the game, and they talked to Vida awhile and Vida posed for some pictures with Sandy, then retreated to the privacy of Gerst's room. Here, he watched the Notre Dame-Michigan State football game, rooting enthusiastically in what probably was the first real relaxation he had found, and the San Francisco-Pittsburgh playoff for the National League pennant, apparently taken especially by Willie Stargell's batting mannerisms. "Whooee, some slugger," he smiled, sympathizing with the slumping Pirate.

He rooted for Notre Dame in the football game. Why? "Because I figured they'd win," he smiles. "I'm always for a winner."

Lunch was brought up to the room and Blue began to appear relaxed, finally, as though the reprieve really had done him some good, after all, and the chance to watch others compete on the television screen had taken him away from his own concerns.

That night, he went to dinner with Angel and Gerst, at the Chesapeake Restaurant and the conversation was relaxed and agreeable. Even the rich crowd in this expensive restaurant went for autographs. Even the maitre'd and the wine steward asked for autographs. A doctor asked Vida for his signature on a prescription pad. Vida smiled and signed and signed.

When he began to eat, he pleaded with the people to let him finish his food first, and with the help of the attendants there he finally was permitted to put fork to mouth without interruption. He sipped a Tom Collins first, but it didn't seem to excite him much, and he didn't finish it. He ordered a big lobster cocktail, but ate only half of it. He did eat a big slab of prime rib and a baked potato and drank a couple of glasses of milk with it, and he topped it with a hunk of cheese cake.

Later, he led the party on a walk. As kids came up, he kidded with them and seemed to enjoy it. He signed autographs for them and teased them, telling them he was Johnny Unitas—"Don't you recognize me? Here, I'll call an audible for you." He went back to his hotel room in good spirits and up to his room before reporters could reach him. Then he sat in front of the television set, his eyes fixed on the flickering images, but not seeing them, his mind somewhere else, his mind on the mound.

He slept on and off through the long night and got through the long morning and got out to the ballpark where the weather had cleared so the game could be played and he dressed slowly and lay down awhile and then went out and warmed up slowly. Flags hung from the railings and a band played as the great arena filled up with 42,621 fans and the bright eyes of the television cameras focused in on the scene for those across the country in the San Francisco-Oakland area.

Before the game, Baltimore manager Weaver pleaded with his players, "He's tough, so you got to play him tough. Lay off the high fast ball. You can't hit it, so why go for it? If he starts getting too high with it, it'll be called against him and he'll get behind and he'll have to come down with something better. Just lay off it."

But, at first, they couldn't. Paul Blair and Dave Johnson popped it up and Merv Rettenmund struck out on one in the first inning. And Frank Robinson and Boog Powell fanned on high fast ones to start the second to make it three-straight strikeouts, before Brooks Robinson grounded out to finish off another 1-2-3 inning.

Blair said later, "He was throwing so hard those first few innings, we never had a chance. He'd throw that high fastball and it'd tail off a foot or so just as you'd start to swing and you just weren't going to hit it. It was entirely too hard to hit. We started then to say on the bench, 'Lay off that high hard one.' That's what Weaver had been telling us, but I guess we had to learn for ourselves."

Meanwhile, McNally was struggling. Rudi got to him for two bases in the first inning, but the veteran pitcher got out of that. Bando got to him for a double to start the second. Then Mangual reached him for a triple, bringing Bando home with the first run.

Then Duncan ripped a double to right, scoring Mangual with the second run.

With a man on second and no one out, Williams then surprised almost everyone by ordering his eighth-place hitter, Dick Green, to sacrifice. Ordinarily, with a man on second and the pitcher next up, the batter would not sacrifice. Green did, moving Duncan to third, while being thrown out for the first out. Williams then ordered Blue to bunt in an effort to squeeze the run home. But Weaver had warned the Orioles to beware of this and when Duncan broke from third a split-second too soon, several Orioles hollered, "There he goes," and McNally delivered his pitch very wide, where Vida couldn't reach it, and Duncan was caught off base and run down for the second out. Blue then struck out for the third out and McNally was out of a jam.

Two runs had scored, but Williams later would be criticized for conservative strategy which may or may not have enabled the pitcher to avoid a knockout blow. McNally seemed stronger in the third and got through it without trouble, striking out two.

The crowd was roaring and Blue was bearing down, throwing every pitch very hard, and the Orioles were trying to hold back, hang in there, hoping eventually to pick him apart if he went wild or tired. After Etchebarren flied out to open the home half Mark Belanger walked, but McNally popped to third and Blair struck out to end the inning.

Tommy Davis singled to open the fourth and, after Bando flied out, Mangual doubled to right to drive in Davis with the third run. McNally got through the inning without further scoring, but Blue had a 3–0 lead now and seemed to have everything in hand, his good left hand.

The first sign that he was weakening in the humidity came in the last half of this inning, however. Dave Johnson went fishing for a low curve and golfed it into the left-field corner for two bases. Rettenmund took Blue to 2-and-2, fouled one off, then hit the next pitch into the right-field corner and the run came across. Blue stood expressionless, except that he seemed to be squinting in the sunshine. He drew a deep breath and went to work on Frank Robinson, firing hard and fanning him on three fast ones.

This brought up Boog Powell. A swarm of yellowjackets converged on the big blond at one point and he stepped out of the batter's box just as Blue pitched. The umpire ruled it "no pitch" and ran the flying creatures away before the game continued. Blue may have been more unsettled than Powell, who, playing with a bad hand, promptly ripped a pitch to right for a single, but the runner stopped at third. There was only one out. However, Blue bore down and got Brooks Robinson to hit down on the ball to Campaneris and the shortstop started a swift double-play, ending the inning.

McNally got three in a row in the fifth. And so did Blue. McNally got through the sixth without trouble. So did Blue. After Campaneris opened the seventh with a double, McNally set down three-straight.

Blue had thrown more than a hundred pitches going into his half of the seventh and, while he was sailing along on a three-hitter with a 3–1 lead, they were waiting him out now and he was getting a little wild.

Working carefully on Frank Robinson, he went to 3-and-2 on him—missing close with a couple of pitches both he and catcher Duncan and manager Williams thought had cut corners—and then walked him with a close pitch home plate umpire Hank Soar called against him. Blue's back stiffened and he struck out Powell. This brought up Brooks Robinson. Blue got a strike past him, then Brooks got his bat on the next pitch and hit a grounder past Bando's desperate dive at third for a single and the Baltimore crowd began to make a lot of noise.

Blue got Etchebarren swinging high and he flied to right for the second out, the lead runner taking third. This brought up light-hitting shortshop Mark Belanger. Blue said later, "I didn't take him light. I only needed one out. I got him to hit the ball on the ground. It was just hit where no one was and went through the infield." Belanger bounced Blue's 122nd pitch over second into center, F. Robinson scoring to slice Vida's lead to 3–2.

From the dugout steps, Williams was watching Vida closely, but when the manager turned to Duncan, the catcher signaled that the pitcher was still strong. Williams didn't want to take his ace out. He hadn't had to take him out very often all season, and to do so now could be psychologically disastrous. He looked at Blue, but Blue looked away.

Vida says, "I still felt strong, I still felt I was throwing hard. I wasn't thinking about how many pitches I'd thrown and I guess I wasn't as aware as I should have been how often I was going to 3-and-2 on the batters, getting behind them, having to come in with better pitches.

"I knew they were not going for the high hard one so much, and I was getting wild high in spots. But it was unpredictable. I didn't want to get cute. I wanted to blow them down. For the first time I began to hear the noise of the crowd. I felt very alone out there. I felt as though I had to do it."

Curt Motton came up to pinch-hit for the pitcher. He said later, "As soon as the inning started the skipper told me and Don Buford to loosen up in case he wanted us to hit and we went back to the clubhouse and swung bats and waited and I was very nervous and very anxious. When the call came that I'd hit for the pitcher I went into the on-deck circle while Belanger hit and watched Blue to try to see if he still was throwing hard and it seemed to me he was. It's not normally my style, but I decided I'd choke up on the bat and just swing and try to get a piece of the ball. I kept telling myself to lay off the high fastball, to make sure I got something I had a chance of hitting. I was sweating pretty good."

Blue says, "I saw him standing there, choking up, and I wanted to blow him down. I didn't care who he was, I knew he could hurt me. I wasn't going to be scared. I was ready to throw the curve first, and I did, but I got it a little high. I went back to the fastball and threw the next pitch right by him. I threw another and he got just a little tick of it. I was ahead of him one ball and two strikes and had him set up for a strikeout. I went inside and high, curve and fastball, on the next two and thought I cut it on both, but both calls went against me." Duncan says, "I thought he got both of them across the inside edge." Williams, raging in the dugout, said later, "Motton should have been called out on strikes. There were some debatable calls. It was a typical Hank Soar game."

But Motton insists, "Both pitches were too far inside or I wouldn't have run the risk of taking them. I told myself, 'Fastball. Be ready. Be quick.' The fastball came. I was ready. I swung quick. I think it was inside, but you can't always tell with him, his ball moves so much. All I know is I hit it. I saw it going through. It was the greatest thrill of my life, getting this hit off that man."

The ball went into the left-field corner and Motton sped to second as Brooks Robinson came home with the tying run. Blue says, "He didn't crush it or anything, but he hit it to the right place. It was a bad pitch because it wasn't high enough. When I saw where he pulled it, right down the line, I knew the lead was gone and it was like a lot had gone out of me."

He seemed to sag on the mound, scuffing his toe on the rubber as the crowd roared at him. The fans were hollering on every pitch now. Williams stood almost defiantly on the dugout steps, refusing to remove his star pitcher, who was still strong, who was still throwing hard, who had given up two runs on a walk and three hits in this inning. Blue moved around on the mound, adjusting his uniform as though pulling himself together.

Blair came up. He had been put out by Blue three-straight times in this game and eleven-straight times in his career. He says, "I thought of bunting, but I saw Bando playing in tight from third, so I figured that wouldn't work. I never choke up on the bat, but this time I decided I would and just try to take a quick, short swing and hope I hit the ball and hope I hit it where no one was. I tried to wait him out, but he got ahead of me at one ball and two strikes and I had to swing at the next two and fouled both off and Duncan almost held one of them. He finally threw me a ball. I figured he was throwing too hard not to throw me the fastball, so I was looking for that and when it came, I went for it and I hit it on the ground, but down the line, over third, and it was a hell of a feeling."

Blue says, "It was a good pitch. I don't know how he hit it but he hit it. This one was hit to the right place, too. That's the game." Two runs raced across and suddenly Blue was behind, 5–3. Williams did not remove him and Vida got Johnson to hit on the ground to the shortstop to end the inning, but as he ran off the mound the Baltimore fans were cheering against him.

"Running off I knew it was all over for me. It was a funny feeling. I'd been within one out. One lousy out. All that pitching all season and then one out whips me and takes so much away from me. You get seems like a million outs and then you can't get one and it takes away so much from everything you've done and it takes away so much from your team. All right, I still had hope we could get 'em. If I couldn't, *we* could. Inside, I guess I knew better. It's as though it wasn't meant to be."

It wasn't. McNally was ahead now, setting the A's down. When Williams sent Fingers out to pitch the eighth, the fans chanted, "We want Blue, we want Blue," as though to humble him, but it did not bother Blue. He knew all too well what's behind the smiling faces and he was not going to let them cut him with the sharp edges of their emotional triumph.

He waited while the A's went after McNally without luck, and when it was over he waited for the writers, ready to atone for what they regarded as his sins, determined to perform as he felt a true pro would.

Slumped on a chair in the locker room when the press arrived, dejected, he said simply, "I had the lead and I let it get away. I blew it. I didn't make many mistakes, but against that club you've got to be perfect. I had good speed. I had good stuff. I had good rhythm. My control was on and off, though. I would get it and then lose it. I wasn't too tense. They're just a tough team. They waited me out a lot and some calls went against me but I don't say they were bad calls. I couldn't get them to hit the pitches I wanted them to hit and I had to come in with a little better pitches, which they were able to hit. They didn't hit me hard, but they hit me hard enough. I was never overconfident. I knew I had the lead, of course, but I kept working hard. I guess I threw a lot of pitches, but I wasn't too tired."

For almost an hour he sat there and answered all their questions, patiently and completely. It probably was the hardest hour of his life, but he handled it with grace. Writing in *The Sporting News*, assistant managing editor Ralph Ray said, "Vida took his medicine like a man. He drew more attention from the press in defeat than did any of the Orioles in victory. Blue answered all the questions and offered no excuses." Glen Schwarz of the San Francisco *Examiner* wrote, "It must have been tough, but he could not have behaved better." Ron Bergman of the *Oakland Tribune* wrote, "It's strange, but he always was better after defeats than victory. And he was beautiful after the playoff defeat, which must have been a terrible time for him."

Blue told the writers he hadn't talked to them for two days before the game because he didn't want to say anything that might stir up controversy and he wanted to concentrate on the game, but he was sorry if he had made their jobs harder and hoped he could help them now. He was asked for criticism of umpire Soar, but he would only say, "He's human and I'm human, and it's enough for me to pitch the game without trying to call it, too." He was asked if the humidity had worn him out and if perhaps Williams should have removed him, but Blue said, "No, I didn't feel tired and when Williams asked me I told him I wasn't tired." Vida even took the blame for missing the suicide squeeze bunt, although the pitch had been far outside. "I should have thrown my bat at the ball, anything to help the runner, that was my job," Blue said.

He sat there, sweating heavily, trapped by the group but making no effort to escape. He said, "It's far from over. We're only down one. We got as good a chance to win tomorrow with Hunter as we did today with me. If they need me I'll be ready to go again. I hope they don't need me, but this thing may go all five games. I could start in the fourth game with two days rest. I could go to the bullpen and pitch relief in the third game with one day's rest. I don't know how good I'd be, but maybe I could get something done. It's up to Williams. He's the boss. If he wants me I'll be ready. I'd kind of like to think I'll get another chance."

Williams was saying, "I'm not going to risk his arm for anything. The rainout hurt because it removed the off-day. We're going to go every day from now on. I think Hunter can take them tomorrow. Then we can go home even. I'll admit if we were down two games to one I'd be tempted to use Blue in the fourth game. That'd be an awfully big game for this team then. If we were ahead two games to one I'd probably wait to see if we went to a fifth and final game to use him.

"He pitched good. We played good. We just got beat. They're a good club. I don't think I played too conservatively. I was at the bottom of the batting order going for every run I could get. I didn't take him out because he's my best and he was going good. Their hits weren't that hard. We got some calls that were hard to take. It was a big game, but it wasn't the last game."

Bando said, "It was a game we should have put away early. We had McNally hurt and should have finished him off. It's like we figured three would be enough for Blue. Usually it would be. This time it wasn't. But that's no excuse for us not getting him more. They were there for us to get."

Weaver said, "They had us in trouble and they lost us. We got them in trouble and we got them. That's the difference. The killer instinct. Experience. It's not over yet, but this was a big one to win. Beating that Blue was a big thing for us and for them." Frank Robinson said, "It was a nice one to win. I'll tell you, you're not going to make much of a living hitting off that guy very often."

Blue was saying, "It's not a question of wanting to pitch again, it's a question of wanting to win. I want another chance, but, hell, I'd rather we'd wrap this up in the next three-straight and never need me again."

That night, unable to sleep, he picked up the phone and started to talk to the telephone operators and wound up talking to most of the operators for a couple of hours until around three in the morning. Thrilled, the gals called a writer to tell him and they wound up talking to the writer for hours about what a great guy Blue was.

Hunter did not have it. Two home runs by Powell and one each by Brooks Robinson and Elrod Hendricks beat the A's in the second game of the series. Bando doubled and Duncan singled him home in the fourth when it was still close. Jackson doubled to open the sixth, but Davis bunted out and the rally died. The Orioles wrapped it up with the last of their round-trippers and Cuellar coasted home, 5–1.

On the plane back to Oakland the A's tried hard to remain relaxed. Vida clowned around with the stewardesses and posed for snapshots with them. At dinnertime he took his silverware and beat time to tape-recorded soul music and several players joined him. After dinner he grabbed a basket of fresh fruit from one of the stews and walked up and down the aisles passing out the goodies.

But back home he admitted it was a tough time to get through. He said, "We all felt it. We had played well almost all season and won our division big and now it was going down the drain in a couple of days. It doesn't seem fair somehow that what you do all the long season means so little and what you do in a few games after the season means so much. We fooled around, trying to take our minds off our situation, but we had our backs to the wall and we knew it."

They had no one to pitch the third game except part-timer Diego Segui. If they could get through it somehow, they could turn back to Blue, then back to Hunter with short rest and hope for the best, but there was no way they could go with either with less than two days off and hope to survive.

They did not survive, though they came close and tried desperately.

Two walks and a single loaded the bases for Baltimore in the top of the first inning of the third game, played before a disappointing turnout of 33,170 in Oakland's concrete shell, and a fly ball fetched the Orioles' first run. Reggie Jackson, who had singled with a man on in the first, homered to tie the game in the third. Brooks Robinson's two-run single broke the tie in the fifth. Frank Robinson doubled in a run and later scored the final Oriole run in the eighth. Reggie ripped his second home run of the game for the A's last run in the eighth, and Jim Palmer choked them off after that. It ended 5–3, a sweep for Baltimore.

Blue and other A's walked slowly from the dugout back to the dressing room in despair. Jackson did not at first join them. For five minutes he sat alone, slumped on the dugout steps, his head hidden in his arms. Finally he rose and slowly went the way of the rest.

In the dressing room, Charlie Finley walked up to Dick Williams and patted him on the back. Williams said, "I'm awfully sorry we didn't finish strong." Finley said, "What are you sorry about? We'll be back next year. And then we'll win it all."

Williams told his players he was pleased by their performance all season and proud of them now. He told the writers, "The A's are a great club which lost to a great club. We'll be back, better than ever. The experience will be good for us. I'm disappointed, but I'm not depressed."

Jackson said, "I don't want to hear anything about next year. This was this year and this was our chance and we blew it. You don't always get other chances. Maybe we will, but this one is gone and there's no way we can get it back."

Vida said, "It's gone. That's all, it's just gone. We played and we lost. We gave it our best and it's history." He was asked if he was glad the season was over. He said, "Yes, for me, I am. For the team, I wish it had gone right on through the World Series to the championship. It would have been a thrill to pitch in a World Series. It would have been if we could have won it. But it's been quite a year for me, a great year, I guess, and I have no complaints, and I'm sure glad it's finally over."

In the celebrating Baltimore dressing room the Orioles, who were talking of taking on Pittsburgh in the World Series, were saying, "Beating Blue was the big thing."

Boog Powell said, "We felt when we got by that guy in the opener we'd get our sweep. He's just a baby, but he's their big man and he's some kind of man."

In the Oakland dressing room, Vida sighed and said, "I had a job to do and I didn't do it." He shrugged as if to shake bad thoughts, to be rid of them. He was asked if he was going home to Mansfield. Affecting his best southern style he laid his head on its side on his shoulder and rolled his eyes and said, "Ize a-goin'." And he gave some soul handshakes to teammates and reporters and strolled out of the clubhouse.

CHAPTER SEVENTEEN

A month after the season had ended, Vida Blue seemed a new man. He had relaxed with a respite from pressure and seemed refreshed. Writers still wanted to interview him. *Gentleman's Quarterly* did a major layout on him. (Good-bye, Joe Namath jersey?) He remained in demand for appearances and business. Fans still followed him wherever he went. But the playing of the season was over, the pace had slowed some and he seemed able to stand back and see things better than he had. "I guess I survived," he grins.

He had gotten home and he kept going back home in between monthly trips back to Oakland for reserve service and regular trips elsewhere for other bits of business. He walked in the door and his mom said, "How'you, Bud?" and he said, "Jus' fine, m'dear," and went up to throw his things in his room, which she had painted gold for him in his honor.

On the unpaved streets of his hometown he was a hero. A writer asking a dozen young boys if they know Vida Blue is suddenly overwhelmed by kids creating a cloud of dust as they scramble to get in close to point out they are close, personal friends of the pitcher. "Vida Blue, yes, sir, he's my main man," declares eight-year-old Curley Biggins.

The boys, including Vida's eleven-year-old brother, Michael, play ball all the time, hoping they will be the next Vida. They lose their baseball in the collard green, corn and okra patch of 72-year-old Mrs. Geneva Johnson, and if she can see it she will pick it out for them, but if she sees them trampling her beloved garden she will chase them and they must crawl back later by moonlight to retrieve the precious horsehide.

Vida coaches them in football, outfitting them in jerseys bearing not his major-league number, 35, but the 14 he made famous in Mansfield High. Not many famous athletes came out of this area. Bill Russell was born nearby, and Grambling College isn't far away. Still, Blue is a rare one.

He pays special attention to his brother Mike. Vida says, "I'm going to make him into that quarterback I might have been."

He goes to visit Johnson Elementary School and a writer tags along. Blue booms down the bumpy road in his Grand Prix until he arrives at the almost-all-black school. Inside, he enters a second-grade classroom. He is a frequent visitor and not unexpected. The teacher smiles as he enters, puts down her book and asks the class if they know who the visitor is. "Vida Blue," they say quietly. It seems that they are welcoming a friend rather than hailing a hero.

The teacher gives up her spot at the head of the class and Blue begins to play counting games with the students. They help him spell his name in yellow chalk on the blackboard. Before leaving he gives them some batting tips. That's right, batting, not pitching. Leaving, the teacher thanks him. He says it is nothing. To him it is not. He enjoys it. He says, "I usually try to get there at recess so I don't disrupt things too much. But I think and the teachers seem to think it helps the kids to have a friend from their hometown, their own school, who's making good. It encourages them to do good."

He says he would like to do more for the people of his neighborhood. He says, "I don't know what I can do, exactly, but there must be things I can do. These people don't want charity, but they could use some help. There are some underprivileged people. There are not enough parks and playgrounds and recreational programs for the kids.

His mother, still young at forty-two, sits rocking in a room decorated with some of his trophies and awards and pictures and says, "In places like this, no one starves. We all share what we have with one another. We all help one another. In places like this, neighbors are neighborly." Vida walks down Mary Street, shaking hands with neighbors he has not see for a while, accepting gracefully their congratulations for the year he has had.

He is in and out, keeping busy. The phone keeps ringing. His mother giggles and says, "Mostly, it be girls. I heard him tell them so many different stories already, I know what to say to them when they call when he's out. Oooh, my, he sure likes the ladies. I wouldn't want him any other way, though, nice-looking boy like that.

"But I'm just as glad he doesn't want to get married yet. I know a mother's supposed to want her children to get married to give her grandchildren, and I know Vida, he likes children, sure enough, but a mother wants her son to make a good marriage, and Vida, he isn't settled down enough yet.

"I don't worry about him, except for his driving, and I already told him, 'I give you up, when you kill yourself with those fancy cars of yours, don't you come crying to me. I'll bury you with one of those big cars in there besides you,' that's what I told him. Except for when he's behind the wheel of a car, he does all right.

"He can handle himself. He got maybe a little fussed with all the publicity and attention he got, but he come out of it OK. He's just a growing boy, learning all the time. I guess he will make a lot of money. I don't think he cares about money. He always fusses at me for fussing at him about money. But I'm more worried that he's happy than that he's rich. Rich won't make him happy. But happy will make him rich."

Visiting his cousin Freddie Henderson in Atlanta, he goes with Fred's wife, a social worker, to visit a school for emotionally disturbed youngsters. Here, too, he is recognized and welcomed warmly. He speaks to the children in their classrooms and in their residence rooms, plays with them, encourages them. Later, Fred says, "The way he has with youngsters is wonderful. Maybe it wouldn't mean much if he wasn't who he was, but when he gets there what counts is how he is, and he is beautiful. He takes to them and they take to him naturally. It doesn't matter if they are handicapped. He makes them feel whole. These are troubled kids and he eases their troubles, and when he leaves they feel they have found a friend."

At the Los Angeles home of his attorney, Bob Gerst, Vida watches the Notre Dame-USC football game, starting out rooting for Notre Dame. "Forget it, Jimmy Jones," he snorts when the USC quarterback pulls a poor play. But when Jones begins to pull off better plays and USC begins to pull far ahead, Vida begins to get disgusted. He starts to call the plays for the Notre Dame quarterback and makes calls that seem better than the player makes and suggests he could do better and you are moved to wonder if, indeed, he could not. As the game gets out of hand, he surrenders to USC graduate Gerst and goes out to the backyard to shoot baskets.

After wolfing down some delicatessen spread out by Mrs. Gerst and slipping into some sweats provided by Mr. Gerst, Vida adjourns with the two Gerst sons, Danny and Dave, and neighborhood kids to the nearby Webster Junior High School playground to play some football. Soon it seems a hundred kids are swarming all over the place and Vida is coaching and officiating in full-scale scrimmages. Back again later, he is treated to a taped song sung to the tune of "Lida Rose" and sent him by J. W. Sindall, a fan:

> *Vida Blue, oh sweet Vida Blue,*
> *You lift the A's right to the top,*
> *Vida Blue, oh neat Vida Blue,*
> *You got the fastball with the hop*
> *One, two, three,*
> *See the strikes go whistling by,*
> *One, two, three,*
> *Let the batter step up,*
> *You'll not let up,*
> *Vida Blue, we're pulling for you.*
> *To help the A's go all the way.*

As the song goes on, Vida grins, rolls his eyes, says "Yeh, man," and begins to tap his foot in appreciation.

> *Vida Blue, the guys back of you, we know,*
> *Will join us when we say,*
> *All credit to Catfish*
> *And others who threw,*

But Vida Blue,
We really love you.

When it ends, Vida says, "Play it again." This time he sings along. He leaves later, singing, "Vida Blue, oh sweet Vida Blue . . ."

He sits in a room high atop the Beverly Hilton Hotel, speaking of the last part of his season. He says, "I got tired of people wondering what happened to me. I don't know what happened. I don't even think very much happened. A man can win fifty in a row and lose the 51st. No matter how many you win, you're gonna lose sooner or later, you're gonna lose some, too. The funny thing is people don't seem to recognize that you usually pitch better losing 1–0 or 2–1 than you do winning 4–3 or 5–3.

"Things began to happen that weren't happening the first half of the year. Also I got tired and wasn't throwing quite as hard, and I tried to get too cute. Also, we were so far ahead the incentive wasn't there and I wasn't as eager. I guess a lot of things entered into it. But I still pitched good all but three or four games all year. And I came back to throw hard and pitch good in the playoff. It just didn't work for me there. I feel bad about it. I let the team down. I have to live with that. But I'm not going to let it get me down. I had a good first year, maybe a great one, and I'm going to come back with another one, and I'm going to have better ones."

He leaned forward and said, "I'm going to be more of a team man from now on. For one thing, I'm more established and maybe I can work with the young pitchers some and learn something myself while trying to teach them something. For another, I am going to be with my teammates more. It wasn't all my fault that I wasn't this past season. People were paying me a lot of attention and I had a lot of demands on my time. I doubt that it ever again will be as bad because I'll never again be new. It may stay bad if I stay good, but at least I'll know what to expect from it. I'll be able to deal with it better. I just wasn't prepared for it this first time and it overwhelmed me.

"I been told that the most important word for me has to be 'no.' Well, I've learned how to say no. I'm going to be gracious and cooperative, but I'm going to draw lines and I'm not going to be afraid to say no, nicely, when it's necessary. The last part of this season I was selfish. I was thinking Vida Blue, not the Oakland A's. That was bad. It's not me. There were two team parties —one thrown by Bando, one by a fan. I went to Bando's but should have gone to both. If the team went I should have gone. I'm part of the team.

"I didn't go out of my way for teammates who were having troubles. I didn't go out of my way to be pleased for teammates who were doing well, to congratulate them. I was too wrapped up in myself. Well, that's not like me and I won't be like that again.

"The problem is I didn't even see it until after the season was over. But I see it now and I'm going to do something about it. I began to get back down to earth in the playoffs and I'm going to be a man of the earth from now on. I didn't do or say any harmful things, but I also didn't do or say any helpful things. I did my part for my team, but I should have done more."

He was asked how he felt about his own record, and how he felt about the American League Cy Young Award, which was to be announced shortly. He said, "I think I had a great record. If I have as good a record every year the rest of my life I'll not only be satisfied, I'll probably wind up in the Hall of Fame. Now, wouldn't that be something!

"It turned out it wasn't as good as it could've been, but it also was better than it might've been. I think it probably was the best record of any pitcher in baseball last season. In the stats, there's not much to choose between me and Mickey Lolich. He was better in some things, I was better in some.

"When writers ask me, I say I'd vote for Mickey if I had a vote. I would, too. I'd never vote for myself. But if you ask me, I have to say in all honesty, I think I deserve it. And I'd love to get it because I may never get a chance to get it again. I may and I may not. You never know."

When it was pointed out to him that he also should be figured as the favorite for the American League Most Valuable Player award, he seemed surprised, but when it was pointed out to him that few regular players had outstanding seasons this particular season, he could see he had a chance. He said, "Well, that would be something, almost too good to be true. I can see if I beat out Lolich for the Cy Young, I may get the MVP.

"Some say pitchers shouldn't be eligible for the one, because other players aren't eligible for the other. And we go out there only every four or five days. But if we account for more victories one way or another than the next guy and if we win big games, I don't see why we shouldn't be eligible.

"Most years I'm sure Bando or Reggie are MVP for the A's. Maybe this year I was. And we won our division. Brooks Robinson, Frank Robinson and those pitchers for Baltimore figure, too. They won their division. Minnesota's Tony Oliva won the batting title. I can't believe I'll win the award. But if they give it to me, I'll take it."

He went shopping for fancy boots, singing, "Vida Blue, sweet Vida Blue . . ."

He won both awards. First he was announced as his league's Cy Young Award winner. From the votes of two writers in each league city, he polled 98 points to 85 for Lolich, 23 for Chicago's Wilbur Wood and 8 for McNally. In first-place votes, Blue got 14, Lolich 9, Wood 1. Told by telephone, Vida enthused, "You're kidding! Vida Blue? Cy Young Award? I'm just in shock. I'll be damned. I'm very happy for me. Whoopee and hip, hip, hooray!"

Calming down he commented, "I really wanted to win the award. Why? Because I like winning. It makes me someone special. I think I'll go out and have a big, fancy dinner. This means I'm going to have to wear a necktie and everything. And if I can find a young lady, she can go, too."

Told he was the youngest-ever winner of the award, Blue laughed and said, "It's about time the old fogeys gave us young cats some credit."

Sighing he said, "It means a great deal to me, though I can't say it wipes out the disappointment of losing the playoffs."

There was little criticism of the voting, as the majority clearly preferred Blue over Lolich. Not only had Blue produced more under pennant pressure, but it was noted that Lolich actually finished little stronger, since both were 5–5 over the final five weeks. Also, Blue came the closest of all pitchers to being overpowering. He not only had eight shutouts, but nine one-run games.

It was pointed out that with just nine more runs spread over six games his record easily could've been 30–4. He pitched a one-hitter, a two-hitter, a three-hitter and six four-hitters. His ratio of 209 hits in 312 innings was easily the best in baseball.

The record of the National League Cy Young Award winner, the incomparably consistent Ferguson Jenkins, 24–13, did not compare with Vida's. Only two first-year pitchers had ever worked as many innings as Vida, none in nearly sixty years, and none ever compiled a similar record of excellence.

So it was not surprising when, shortly, the American League Most Valuable Player award was announced for Blue, too. From the votes of two other writers in each league city, Vida polled 268 points to 182 for runnerup Bando and 170 for Frank Robinson. Again, he had 14 first-place votes, with Bando drawing 4, Brooks Robinson 3, Frank Robinson 2 and Lolich 1.

Blue followed Lefty Grove in 1931, Spud Chandler in 1943, Hal Newhouser in 1944 and 1945, Bobby Shantz in 1952 and Denny McLain in 1968 as the sixth pitcher to win this league's MVP laurel since the writers took it over forty years earlier, and he followed the National League's Don Newcombe in 1956, Sandy Koufax in 1963 and Bob Gibson in 1968 and the American League's McLain in 1968 as the fifth major-leaguer to sweep the Cy Young and MVP honors.

Johnny Bench, a few weeks shy of twenty-three when he was named National League MVP in 1970, had been the youngest ever to win an MVP award until Blue, four months past the age of twenty-two.

"Now I am truly honored," he said when told. "I am overwhelmed, really. It's hard to believe. I'm just starting. This was my first full year. I thought I might win the other award. I thought about winning this one, but I never really thought I would. I don't know if I deserved it. I hope I did. That's for others to decide. I thank them for deciding in my favor. I will take it. And I will try to live up to it and honor it."

Invited to numerous postseason banquets, he gave a speech in a sincere but casual manner that began:

*I want to thank you for inviting me here tonight. I know
I was not your first choice. I know you originally planned
to have Mickey Lolich. (Pause for laughter.) (Pauses, looking at audience. Takes off coat, begins to loosen tie, pauses
again.) I better tell you what I'm doing. My manager knew
I was not used to giving speeches. And he knew I'd have
to give some this winter. He said when you're not used to
giving speeches you feel naked in front of an audience and
the best way to get used to it is to practice your speeches
standing naked in front of a mirror. So that's what I did.
And felt like a damn fool. But I did it. And now that I'm
standing up in front of you with my clothes on, I can't
remember a darn word of my speech. So I thought it might
help if . . . (pause for laughter).*

*(Fixes tie, puts coat back on.) Well, I guess I just better
carry on as best I can. I won the Cy Young and Most
Valuable Player awards. I don't want to win an Academy
Award. . . .*

From here, he discusses his brief career, gives credit to his
teammates for their help, speaks lightly of being a bachelor, making commercials and seeking a raise from Finley. He concludes:

*But money isn't the big thing, really. It's getting the
chance at life. I did a "This is Your Life" TV show recently.
They didn't do my life, they did Satchel Paige's life. Now,
there was maybe the greatest pitcher who ever lived and
he pitched twenty years before he ever got a chance in
the major leagues because he was black. I am black and
at twenty-two, in my fourth year as a professional, I have
won baseball's two biggest awards. I couldn't help but be
moved by the differences between us. If I am never half
the pitcher he was, I still will have ten times the oppor-
tunities. And I think this is what this year has meant to
me. Realizing the chance is there to do almost anything I
want to do and am able to do. And am willing to work.
And I am willing to work. A lot of people like you out
there have treated me very well. I am grateful. And I will
try to repay you with my performances in the future—on
and off the field.*

In the television studio where he met Paige, family and friends came from all over the country and many years back in Satchel's life to greet the aging immortal, but Paige's greatest reaction came when Vida walked in. Satchel leaped up, stuck out his great right hand and exclaimed enthusiastically, "You're one man I *wanted* to see!" Blue was there as a representative of today's young major-leaguers. He rehearsed his few lines with a stand-in before a surprised Satchel was brought in to take part in the show, which is "taped live," then forgot his lines during the taping but bluffed his way through. "Pitching is easier" he laughed.

He did another Dick Cavett ABC-TV show, this one with Willie Mays acting as guest host. Willie, calling Vida "the biggest thing to happen to baseball in years," gave Vida a Willie Mays watch and Vida gave Willie a Vida Blue glove. At one point, Vida commented that with all the public attention paid him, his social life sure had changed. Mays smiled and said, "I'm proud you're doing all you can."

Blue's biggest off-season entertainment role came when he accepted the opportunity to tour U.S. service installations in Vietnam, Thailand, Spain, Okinawa, Wake Island, Hawaii and Cuba, entertaining G.I.'s as the sports celebrity of the year with the Bob Hope troupe on his annual Christmastime trek. It is a rugged trip the veteran entertainer leads, with short plane hops to many shows given in many locales in all kinds of weather in a short time.

Vida admits it was more rugged than he expected it to be, though his part of the performance was not too tough. There were plenty of prominent personalities, beauty queens, singers and dancers to back up the star comedian, and Blue had only to swap a few carefully polished lines with the leader, talk to the troops informally and sign a lot of autographs. He admits he was moved by the climax of each show when the cast joined the audience in singing "Silent Night."

He says, "There was something about that moment, far from home, all those young boys, many of them in great danger, all of them far from home, many of them with heads bowed, all those voices raised in that religious song, that reached a man. Mostly, it was just an experience. There were things there, hurt men, that I guess I'll remember forever. And then there was that singing of 'Silent Night.' There was a lot of fun, but I was glad to get home."

Annually, the show is taped, cut and released as a television special. In Vida's portion he is introduced by Hope as "That amazing young man from Mansfield." Here are some of the lines:

> *Hope: How come you weren't paid more money for pitch-ing?*
> *Blue: Mr. Finley pointed out I only used one arm.*
> *Hope: If you don't get a big raise, will you keep pitching?*
> *Blue: Sure—with my right arm.*
> *Hope: I used to be a pretty good ballplayer when I was your age.*
> *Blue: I didn't know that.*
> *Hope: What, that I was a pretty good ballplayer?*
> *Blue: No, that you were ever my age.*
> *Hope: What's the most important thing for a ballplayer?*
> *Blue: What is it? I forgot.*
> *Hope: You gotta have heart. C'mon, sing.*
> *Blue: I only do two things. I pitch baseball. And I chase girls. I don't sing.*
> *Hope: I'm the manager here. Sing.*
> *(They sing, not too badly, complete with patter.)*
> *Hope: We took Johnny Bench with us last year. You know, he took out eight different girls one night.*
> *Blue: Records were made to be broken.*
> *Hope and Blue: You gotta have hearrrrttt . . .*

Blue was offered two movie parts. One film was to be called "Nigger Charlie." He was not to play the title role but a hired killer in the western epic. In the end he would get killed. By the end, so would almost everyone else in the film. Blood dripped from every page of the script.

The other was called "Tigers in the Sky" and he had his choice of three different parts in this Vietnamese war film.

In one part he would portray a Private Haley and would get to speak less than ten words. In another part he could portray a

Corporal O'Brien and get to speak more words, including such as (under fire) "I do believe these obscenities are trying to tell us something" and "C'mon, you obscenities."

In the third part, as Lieutenant Elblein, his first scene would find him ejecting from his crippled jet, his second scene would find him parachuting down, landing and "striking his head on some sharp rocks on the side of a hill," and his last scene would find him being carried off on a stretcher, covered with blood, half-conscious, moaning, "Oh, God, I can't see."

Blue truly would seem to have some potential, especially for light-comedy roles in films, but Gerst decided the above two weren't the right ones. Vida has the looks, smile, personality and speaking ability to carry a Poitier styled role with tight direction and might in time make something of it, but he chose to delay his dramatic debut for the time being.

Gerst himself had some heavy scenes to play with Oakland owner Finley. Blue had made $14,750 in salary for 1971, plus $6,365.58 as his share of the playoff money, plus the Cadillac and the free gasoline and gift of clothes money. His manager felt he was entitled to something more substantial for 1972 and was armed with some powerful statistics to support his case.

Aside from the contribution Vida's victories made to the A's pennant push, he made a heavy financial contribution to the team bank account. His starts drew more than a million fans. The entire American League drew less than 12 million fans. Only six teams drew as many as a million. The per-game average was 12,200.

These starts did include opening-day, the All-Star game and the playoff opener. However, in 39 regular-season starts, Blue drew 909,422 fans for an average of 23,318 per game. In twenty starts at home, Vida drew, in round figures, 370,000 fans, for an average of 18,600. In nineteen starts on the road he lured 530,000 fans, an average of 28,300.

The A's drew 914,993 fans in 74 dates in Oakland for an average of 12,362. Without Vida, the A's drew only 540,000 or so for an average of only 10,000 or so per date. Blue was worth between 8,000 and 9,000 customers per game at home. He was also worth between 11,000 and 12,000 customers per game on the road.

The A's get the large share of the receipts at home, the small cut away from home. It can be estimated that Vida was worth close to $1 million in extra gate receipts to the A's.

Oakland attendance was up 136,638 from 778,355 in 1970. Possibly the pennant push—there was no pennant race—should be credited with this. But Blue was the key figure, and he drew almost exactly twice the amount of the increase. In a hotter sports town his draw might have been incredible. As it was, counting even the special games, Blue's starts pulled in 1,005,602 fans, an average of 32,438 per game.

Finley was kept busy insisting he would not move his franchise to Washington or anywhere else. Meanwhile, he was kept busy avoiding exact figures where Blue was concerned.

He said, "Blue will receive a substantial raise. This will not include any bonus clauses based on attendance. I don't want my players counting people in the stands when they should be thinking of the game."

He was asked what he would do if Blue asked for $100,000.

Finley said, "I don't know. I've never had a player ask me for $100,000."

Before Gerst entered the first bargaining session with Blue and Finley in the owner's offices in Chicago, a writer who knows Finley predicted to Gerst that Finley would open with an offer of $45,000, close with an offer of $50,000, refuse to pay a penny more and make a point of refusing to trade or sell the pitcher to a team that might pay him more.

Gerst asked for $115,000 for his client and said he would settle for the average of the ten highest-paid pitchers in the game, whatever that might be, whether it turned out to be more or less, pointing out that, inexperienced or not, Blue had to be considered one of the ten most valuable pitchers in the game.

Of "known salaries" he mentioned Bob Gibson at $150,000, Ferguson Jenkins at $125,000, Tom Seaver at $120,000 and Jim and Gaylord Perry at around $90,000 each. He said other top pitcher salaries might bring this down and he figured out an average of around $92,500. Later he came down to $85,000.

Finley was not taken by these suggestions. He asked what floor they were on and, when it was confirmed that it was the twenty-seventh, he said they had as much chance of getting that kind of money from him as there was of him jumping from that height. He opened with an offer of $45,000 and closed with one of $50,000. He said he would not pay one penny more. Gerst asked if he would consider selling or trading the pitcher and Finley said flatly he would not. Gerst said the pitcher would not pitch for $50,000 and Finley said that then he wouldn't pitch.

Blue was silent, though present, for most of the negotiations. The session lasted seven long hours, at the close of which the opposing parties felt they were in an absolute stalemate.

This was early in January and they parted with Blue feeling the player's position in such sessions unfair, since he had no alternative to playing for whatever the owner offered in the town in which his contract was held other than giving up his career, and the owner no doubt feeling he had been as fair as circumstances warranted, pending a review by the wage-freeze board.

Blue went home to Mansfield determined to rest awhile and then begin running and preparing himself for the new season, while fulfilling only the few engagements he had agreed to accept after the first of the year and refusing all new commitments. He politely declined a return visit to the White House. Turning the pages of a calendar, he got to July and August and September of 1972 and said, "I want the people to think as much of me then as they do now. I don't want to be a one-season sensation, a flash-in-the-pan. I know all seasons can't be like the last one, and I know second seasons often are the toughest of all, but I intend to do what has to be done to have as many good seasons as possible."

He left the negotiations on contract to Gerst, sure it would work out somehow. Gerst wasn't so sure, torn between wanting to get what he felt was right for his client and not wanting him to hold out for it to the point where it might handicap his season. The attorney had been led by Finley to believe that the negotiations were a private matter, which Gerst respected by refusing public comment on them until, to his surprise, details began leaking out to the press and finally Finley began to negotiate openly with the public at a press conference presumably called to introduce new and fancier uniforms for his team.

At first there were hints from Chicago writers that other owners were watching the Finley-Blue battle closely and wanted Finley to "hold the line" to fight inflation for them. Then at the luncheon, Finley told the press about his offer of $50,000 and Gerst's request for $115,000 and said Blue approached him privately later, asking him not to mention the meeting to the attorney, and said he'd settle for $85,000. Finley said he told him he "would not pay him one penny more than $50,000" and repeated that to the press.

Finley did not mention several letters from Gerst repeating requests to be traded or sold if not paid his price and threats to not pitch, and he said he would not sell or trade him, even if he sat out the season. The owner said, "It's unfortunate, in my opinion, that Vida saw fit to use an attorney in his negotiations. I'm fearful that he's receiving the wrong advice at this time and I honestly don't know what the end result will be."

He added, "There's no doubt we need Vida Blue. I'm not trying to take any credit away from Vida. He did one helluva job and I feel my offer is satisfactory to both parties concerned." He concluded Vida just might sit out the season and conceded his ace was not his only holdout. He pointed proudly to the uniforms and changed the subject to the special days he planned for the coming season, which he said he hoped would boost his team attendance well over the one-million mark.

Gerst turned to the press and suggested that Finley was trying to "blackmail" Vida by threatening to let his career end rather than pay him a reasonable salary. "He said," Gerst said, "that when the day comes he has to mortgage the franchise to pay the players, he'd get out of baseball. Maybe that day has come. My firm might be interested in buying the club. Mr. Finley said he'd have to raise ticket prices to meet the players' outrageous demands, but when we asked for financial information on the A's so we could determine if our demands were legitimate we were refused.

"I asked him to give me one reason our concept of averaging out the top pitchers' salaries didn't make sense and he said, 'I don't have a reason. I don't blame you. I'd ask the same myself. He's worth it. But he's not going to get it.' "

The attorney sighed and shrugged and held up his open hands

to the heavens as if to say there was no way to argue with that. He complained that he was being made into the heavy in this whole affair when he merely was trying to do a reasonable job respectably.

As Finley began to give interviews to all reporters who sought them and made statements to the press almost daily, Gerst began to reply in kind. The statements became charges and counter-charges. Soon it seemed each was calling out his side of the case to strangers who strolled by. What had begun in private became public. The sports pages of the nation's newspapers carried bold headlines and long stories and columns of analysis of the Blue-Finley-Gerst affair and it was featured in television and radio sportscasts for months. Ron Bergman's weekly roundup reports on the Oakland A's in *The Sporting News* were almost always devoted to The Holdout. Before the season even was scheduled to begin, Blue was the cover subject of a major story in *Sports Illustrated*. He was pictured in uniform, but he was not yet back in uniform.

Wherever this writer went—through a gambling casino in Las Vegas, by a swimming pool in Palm Springs, to a movie in Los Angeles—he heard washroom attendants, retired bankers, sales-men and even salesladies, taxi-drivers, barbers, TV actors, movie actresses, almost every type imaginable discussing the case. Their sentiments seemed mixed. Some thought Gerst and Blue right, some thought Finley right. Most felt Blue would give in and play, and all seemed to want him very much to play. Blue, himself, was not saying much for public consumption. The in-fighting was out in the open between Gerst and Finley.

Finley said, "We gave him a Cadillac worth $10,000, a gas-and-oil credit card worth $1,500, and $1,000 for new clothes. He was paid $25,000 for that after-shave commercial and $10,000 by the state milk industry for another commercial. There's no way I'm going to be forced to raise ticket prices or mortgage my ball club to pay the astronomical salaries players are demanding. We didn't draw a million fans. We didn't win the World Series. We didn't even win the American League pennant. All we did was win our division. His attorney has brainwashed and browbeaten him. Vida is receiving bad advice. Vida is squandering his money.

He wouldn't be asking so much if he didn't have to pay an attorney to negotiate for him. It won't help him one cent. And he'll have to pay the man ten to fifteen percent. Vida will play for $50,000 or he won't play. I will not raise my offer, and I repeat that I will not trade or sell him. I have made him a fair offer, and that is it as far as I am concerned."

Gerst said, "Finley is trying to blackmail Vida by holding the end of his career over his head as a threat. He is trying to end his career by making me look bad. He is trying to make me the fall guy in the negotiations. He lied about the negotiations. He said Vida is working for an agent who gets fifteen or twenty percent of his salary. This is not true. I receive a flat fee based on the number of hours I work. It's a standard legal fee to a great extent. If Vida wants to give me a bonus at the end of negotiations, that's fine, but we don't have that in a contract because we don't have a contract. Finley failed to mention he had his own attorney at the negotiating sessions. Who pays him? Mr. Finley just dealt for Denny McLain, who lost 22 games last season, but has a $75,000 contract. Is this going to force him to raise ticket prices or go bankrupt? If he can pay a 22-game loser $75,000, why won't he offer a 24-game winner that much? What Vida makes on the side doesn't take Finley off the hook. Salary is what counts."

Gerst said that in an attempt to break the impasse, he suggested to Finley an arbitration panel of three owners, one of his choosing, one of Finley's, one chosen by the other two owners, but this was refused. He said he asked for permission to have Vida play in Japan, but was refused. He said he offered to have Vida sign the $50,000 contract, provided the reserve clause was not included so Vida could bargain for himself with another club or be assigned to another club by an impartial panel the following season, but was refused. He said Vida might have an invalid original contract on two counts: One, that he was a minor when he signed it. And, two, that it stated that if he was retained on the roster of a team at the double-A level for ninety days he was to receive an additional $1,000, if retained on the triple-A level for ninety days $1,500 more and if in the major leagues for ninety days $5,000 more, but to the best of his knowledge he had been paid only the $2,500 on the first two points.

The attorney indicated he had spoken with Marvin Miller, the counsel for the Players' Association; with Arthur Goldberg, Curt Flood's attorney, and expected to testify before Sen. Sam Ervin's Judiciary Committee hearing on possible monopoly and anti-trust violations in sport, and suggested he hoped his client's case would benefit by rulings expected from the Supreme Court and Congress. Miller said, "What Finley is doing is threatening to retire Blue. I trust the Supreme Court justices read the papers." Miller's assistant, Dick Moss, added, "In the reserve system, the player has no power. What Finley is saying is, 'I won't trade him and I won't sell him. Either he accepts what we've offered or he's through with baseball.'"

Gerst said, "Michael Burke, the president of the New York Yankees, was reported to have said that Vida would be paid $75,000 if he were playing for the Yankees, and he would pay anything to get Vida for the Yankees, even a million dollars. Burke was courageous for suggesting a figure and it would be satisfactory at this point, but the only figure that seems satisfactory to Finley is the one he has named. At this point, I think it should be clear that it is not only a matter of which of us is right, but a matter of a man flatly refusing even to negotiate. I want the public to see just how unfair and dictatorial this man is. He demands perfection, which is why he hires and fires managers almost every year; but when a player produces, he will not pay him for it. I want to show just how much of a prisoner a player like Vida is in the system.

"I don't think the other owners can run the risk of conspiracy to support Finley's restrictive attitude because of increased congressional and judicial interest in such a situation. I believe, in fact, that the commissioner will make sure Vida gets what he wants or is traded. [Gerst's prediction proved to be accurate.] The public outcry will be enormous if he doesn't play. Here's a franchise fighting for survival. I told Finley that if Vida doesn't pitch, he might as well throw a million dollars out the window."

Finley said, "I guess I'm a lousy businessman. Here we are talking about $20,000, when there is the possibility of Vida sitting out the entire season. I stand to lose $500,000 at the gate. But I'll lose that before I go any further. It's a matter of principle. No outsider is going to tell me how I must conduct my business. I've been disappointed for quite some time over how this has been handled by Vida's agent. I feel that Mr. Gerst has temporarily hurt Vida's wonderful image. I know for a fact that many of the statements attributed to Vida have no foundation at all. Vida is one of the finest young athletes I've ever had the pleasure of meeting in any sport."

Rumors spread that Blue was breaking with Gerst and was about to sign with Finley on his own. Gerst said, "I know of no such intention on Vida's part. Finley expects Vida to cave in. He seems to think that I'm forcing Vida into this. He's trying to make me the fall guy. I talk to Vida every day. He's hopeful the situation will be resolved. But he's a tremendous young man with a great deal of pride and Finley underestimates him if he thinks he'll give in. He has too much pride to compromise and he won't pitch while carrying a grudge. He understands the consequences and he's prepared to go all the way. Vida told me, 'I couldn't live with myself if I didn't stick up for my principles.' And I told him, 'I wouldn't be much of an attorney if I didn't advise you to stick up for them.'"

In March, Finley said he was going to go to Blue's home to negotiate with him personally. Gerst said Vida had told him he wouldn't be home to Finley, and added, "Blue has specific instructions he will not be available at any time to see Finley. All calls are referred to me. Mr. Finley knows there is a written agreement between the Players Association and owners which guarantees any player the right to be represented by an attorney at all times during negotiations for his contract and the owners to not have a right to attempt to negotiate outside the presence of a player's attorney."

Bitterly, Gerst added, "When Finley lets a guy like Blue just rot, he may not be the best person to be associated with or to work for."

The dispute took a turn when Gerst and Blue called a televised press conference in Oakland on March 16th to announce that he had agreed to work for Dura Steel Products Company in the Los Angeles suburb of Santa Fe Springs, and was withdrawing from baseball. Reading a prepared statement, Vida said, "I have received an offer from Earl Epstein, President of Dura Steel Products Company, to start a new career in private business as vice-president in charge of . . . public relations. . . ." As he read, he started to smile, and then started to giggle. The reporters on hand started to smile and laugh. Vida said, "Scratch that. C'mon guys, this is supposed to be serious." He then read on:

"This is a wonderful opportunity and one that I feel I should take. It is with deep regret and sadness I announce my leaving baseball. I had hoped my career could have been longer. While it was short, it was packed with excitement."

At the conclusion of this statement, he refused to answer any questions and left.

However, since he clearly had not been able to take the announcement seriously, it was hard for the reporters and all who viewed the TV tapes later to do so either. But Gerst insisted it really was a serious matter. He said, "Sure, if you saw the way it went you might have been skeptical, but if you know Vida, you would know it was just embarrassing for him to use the title 'vice-president.' He's a 22-year-old black kid who's just a high-school graduate and the company he's joining did $173 million in sales last year. I realize some people are skeptical. But I negotiated this deal for a long time. Vida is being paid more than Finley is offering, and in making public appearances for the company and representing it, Vida will be more than worth it. He has no business experience, but he has a name. He starts out using a name. He is capable of learning something about business, too." Epstein said, "Vida will be actively involved in our sales and marketing effort. He will work with dealers, call on customers and so forth."

"What if Vida settles with Finley?"

"We'd talk," Epstein said. "We don't hire people here for one day. But if Finley offered Vida a hell of a lot more money, Vida and I would have to talk about his situation here. I wouldn't be pleased, but I'd talk."

Gerst said, "Vida has taken this job because he feels there is no future for him in baseball. If that future opens up again, he is not prohibited from pursuing it."

Blue said, "Frankly, I still hope I'll be playing baseball. But I'm prepared to do other things instead."

When he heard about it, Finley said, "I'm sorry to learn that Vida has decided to retire from baseball. He had a great year and had a great future ahead of him. Should Vida have a change of heart any time in the near future and decide to return to baseball we would be extremely happy to have him with us. As long as he is retiring, I'm happy that he has selected the steel industry and is starting out as a vice-president. I personally spent five years with U.S. Steel in Gary, Indiana, the first four years serving my apprenticeship in a machine shop."

Dressed in navy blue flared slacks, a gray, mod sports coat, a white shirt open at the collar and brown boots, Vida sat down at his new desk, sighed, shuffled some papers, and said, "Man, what a job I've got. Look at this—bills, bills, bills."

After Vida announced his withdrawal from baseball, Finley persuaded some of Vida's friends on the team to arrange a meeting without Gerst in hopes of a possible settlement.

Blue and Finley met in Finley's apartment in Oakland. "We talked for three hours." Finley reported later. "I thought we were making some progress. He was supposed to be coming over Sunday, but he called to say he couldn't make it. I'm disappointed."

Gerst later confirmed that Vida had met alone with Finley and had talked to him for the first time in more than two months. "Finley kept saying he wanted to meet with Vida alone," Gerst said. "Well, he did and it hasn't changed anything."

Later, Vida went to Arizona on his own during the pre-season training camp, to meet with Finley again.

After this meeting, Finley announced to the press that Vida had first agreed to terms but then backed out. He said that Vida had authorized Finley to have a press conference and to quote Blue as saying that he was "a crazy mixed-up kid."

When asked about this, Blue stated that he had never agreed to Finley's terms at their meeting in Arizona, had never agreed to a press conference and had never agreed to the statement that he was "a crazy mixed-up kid."

No further meetings were set, but Finley continued to send emissaries to Blue to try to persuade him to sign.

But Blue resisted and went to Los Angeles to start working for the Public Relations Department of Dura Steel and made a number of appearances for the firm on the west coast.

Shortly thereafter the steel industry executive and his attorney called another news conference to announce another venture. This was in New York on a sound stage where they were shooting a sequel to the successful movie *Shaft*, which concerned a black detective and had almost an all-black cast. It was announced that Vida had signed an MGM contract to play a part in a third film in what now was a "series." The movie had not yet been written or titled and Blue's part was not specified. Asked if he had ever done a part in a movie or TV show, Blue responded by saying, "Vida Blue can do anything he wants to. That's what you call cocky confidence."

Gerst said, "We're not trying to fool anybody. Vida would rather be playing baseball than doing these other things. But if he can't play, we have these alternatives. Even if he plays, he'll make the movie—next winter. But unless the other owners enter into it, it does not now look like he will be playing this season." Writer Charles Maher of the Los Angeles *Times* called it, "The Latest Installment of the Charlie and Vida Road Show."

Things became a little more amusing when it came out that among Dura Steel's products was a line of medicine cabinets, including something called an "over-john" that hung over toilets. The product became a national news item and *Sports Illustrated* called the whole affair a "bathroom farce."

As the scheduled opener drew nearer, however, many no longer laughed at the situation. Some accused Gerst of seeking personal publicity and many clearly were concerned that even if Finley was wrong, at this point Blue had waited too long to get started to have a good season. Since athletes who sit out a while often never regain their original form, now Vida was really endangering his entire career for money he could have made up later.

Almost everyone had his say. The veteran Frank Lane, currently general manager in Milwaukee, said, "When Charlie asked me, I told him I thought that $40,000 would be a fair salary. He told me he was going to give him $50,000. Now the sentiment among baseball people is that $50,000 is fair." Angels' general manager Harry Dalton said, "Finley was more than fair. I think it's an absolute shame for a young man to give up $50,000." Other Angels also spoke out. Clyde Wright said, "What he's doing is stacking up a whole lot of pride into a career of one year." Eddie Fisher said, "If Blue stays retired, he'll regret it the rest of his life. I can tell him about the pride I've had over 12 years and it's taken me my whole career to reach $50,000. He is either getting bad advice or doesn't realize what baseball can mean to him. He could have had his whole future secured within five years." Ken McMullen said, "He can't consider himself a superstar after one year and he shouldn't be paid like one. He's attempting to stage a holdup and it's not fair to baseball. I don't think there's any player sentiment on his side."

Even some of the A's and his friends on the team seemed to have turned on him. Manager Dick Williams said, "We would miss him badly, but we have added a couple of top pitchers and could win without him." Sal Bando, the captain, said, "While Vida may be worth more than $50,000, I think it's a fair first raise." Curt Blefray said, "He's foolish for giving up $50,000. He could have made it $100,000 with endorsements." Even Reggie Jackson said, "What Vida's being offered isn't that bad. I believe in getting all you can, but if Finley gives him $92,500, what's he going to have to pay him five years from now? I've been in the big leagues for four years and I've hit 132 home runs and I don't make $92,500 and there's no way a second-year pitcher should make more than I do."

But the comments were not all one sided. Red Smith, *The New York Times*, Melvin Durslag, Los Angeles *Times*, Milt Gross, Shirley Povich, Washington *Post*, Ben Dickey, San Francisco *Chronicle* all wrote columns that were sympathetic to Vida's cause. Everywhere arguments raged about L'affair Blue.

Glenn Dickey, writing in the San Francisco *Chronicle*, was highly critical of Finley.

"He [Finley] simply looks on the negotiations as a game. He likes to drag them out for maximum publicity, but baseball players tend to have very tender egos and they do not understand that it is all an ego-trip for Charlie. Reggie Jackson was enraged by Finley's negotiations two years ago and Blue apparently had the same reaction this year. It affected Jackson's play, and it may affect Blue the same way. But Charlie doesn't seem to care."

In the Chicago *Tribune*, Robert Markos wrote "Negotiations apparently are not Finley's business. He prefers to deal in ultimatums. His ultimatum to Vida Blue is self-defeating."

Also in Chicago, Rick Talley of *Chicago Today*, wrote "Finley is wrong. Blue is worth every penny he asks . . . and what he made last year shouldn't matter.

"Finley, however, holds the aces. He knows it and his true self usually shows when he holds the best hand. Other baseball owners have been equally tough on superstars by invoking the reserve clause . . . but few have done more damage to baseball's precarious position than Finley."

Mel Durslag, writing in the Los Angeles *Herald-Examiner*, wrote "Reflecting on his [Blue's] functions of 1971 and the notoriety he brought Oakland and baseball, you can't see him as only a $50,000 man in today's market.

"Vida is being penalized for lack of seniority. For what he delivered last year for $14,750, plus a car, Finley should be embarrassed.

"Blue may be relatively new to the majors, but he offers a dimension that pitchers with years of experience aren't able to match.

"And even if he falls on his face, which isn't likely, he will have earned his money for the excitement he has interjected into the game."

And Red Smith, writing in *The New York Times*, said "Charlie Finley is perfectly capable of cutting off his nose to spite his face . . . but what he is saying this time is that sooner than pay what he admits Blue is worth, he would freeze out a 22-year-old who pitched a no-hitter breaking into the majors, led the team to a divisional championship with a personal one-loss record of 24 and 8 and in his first big-league season won the Most Valuable Player Award in the American League and the Cy Young Award as the best pitcher in baseball.

"If Charlie Finley can do that, then he has a death wish bigger than his Napoleon complex."

The mail piled up in sacks awaiting Vida's return. Finley sent one of his players Gene Tenace, who had caught Vida in the minors as well as the majors, to visit with Blue in hopes of talking the pitcher into signing, but Tenace returned empty-handed. Finley then sent Blefray to visit with Vida, but Curt, too, returned without his prey. Mike Epstein said, "I'm sorry for Vida. He's obviously hooked up with the wrong guy in Gerst." Tommy Davis said, "When I introduced Vida to Gerst I had no idea it would come to this. I've talked to him, but I haven't tried to influence him." There was a rumor among the A's that Finley would fire Davis, despite the value of the veteran who'd had a good season, in reprisal for having brought his star pitcher to the attorney. Asked about this, Davis smiled and said, "We'll find out." He did. He was released.

As the cut-down date came and went, the A's cut to the 25-man opening day limit by placing Blue on the restricted list, which meant he could not play for the first 30 days of the season even if he signed. But, then, all the players in the major leagues went on strike for more money and other benefits in their pension plan and the season did not start when it was supposed to begin, the first week in April. Vida was not in uniform, but then, neither was anyone else. And the players stopped criticizing Vida and began to criticize the club owners who would not give *them* what *they* wanted. And since no one else was playing, for a while, it was not noticed that Vida Blue was not playing.

Hunched over, his hands fussing uneasily with the crease of his slacks, his handsome face somber, some of his youth seeming to have gone from him, Vida Blue said, "If I said I didn't miss it, I'd be telling a damn lie. I've been in baseball my whole life and I love the game. You don't just up and say you won't think about it no more. The more you're away from it, the more you realize you really will miss it. I never wanted these contract negotiations to get to the place where there wouldn't be a stopping point. I never wanted it to get to be something laughable, like a man's life and future was a joke. But I'm man enough to feel I'm justified in my feelings. I had to stand up for what I felt was right and reach for what I felt I deserved."

He looked down at his hands and they were empty.

The season finally started, without Blue. The players strike had ended in its second week and the teams, scheduled to open play

April 5, opened ten days late on April 15, but Vida's holdout held. The strike, which had actually lasted 13 days, had over shadowed him. Once others began to perform, he slipped further into the shadows and his stories drifted from the sports pages.

As the players put on their uniforms, Vida made a morning appearance at the grand opening of a hardware store run by one of Dura Steel's customers. Company president Epstein noted, "There were thousands of people there. Also Miss Burbank." That night, he appeared to sign autographs at a store in Woodland Hills. He was not working out, except with his signing hand. Without Blue, the A's averaged less than 6,000 fans for their first five-game home stand.

Late in April, Gerst wrote a letter to major league baseball commissioner Bowie Kuhn requesting that he advise the other American League owners they could deal with Vida and that if they came up with an agreement they could make appropriate payment to Finley. In response, Kuhn, intervening officially, called Gerst and Blue and asked if they would attend a meeting with Finley in Chicago. They began the meeting in separate rooms at the Drake Hotel at 2 P.M. on the last Thursday in April and went almost straight through the night until the following noon.

"First," Gerst reported, "we tried to make a settlement based on a two year contract for the 1972–1973 seasons. But we were unable to come to an agreement.

"One of the proposals Finley offered was a $15,000 fee to be paid by a third party. Blue refused on the grounds that he had already turned down an offer of $25,000 from Aqua-Velva and Dura Steel and besides, Blue felt that he actually worked for Mr. Finley and that Finley should pay his salary and not someone else."

As the conference dragged on, Vida went to bed in the early morning hours as Gerst, Finley and Kuhn continued negotiating.

"Finally," Gerst continued, "it was agreed that an extra $13,000 cash would be paid to Vida for playing in the 1972 season." "Our agreement," Gerst added, "was of course subject to Vida's approval, since he was still in bed and not at the meeting."

However, a dispute developed as to how the information about the additional $13,000 would be released to the public.

"Finley wanted it stated that $5,000 was to be paid to Mrs.

Blue, Vida's mother, and $8,000 to be classified as pre-payment of his previously agreed-upon college tuition bonus that had been in his original contract with Oakland," Gerst explained.

"That college tuition bonus really didn't exist anymore since the option period had already lapsed.

"But in any event, I would not agree to Finley's proposal of how the public statement would be worded. Finley wanted it to sound as though Blue had backed down completely and Finley hadn't conceded anything.

"At one point Finley stormed out of the meeting declaring that he was not coming back but returned an hour later with coffee, doughnuts and some newspapers."

"When Vida returned to the bargaining session, he insisted that the public release of the details of the additional moneys be accurate or he would not sign the contract.

"Finley refused to agree to the public disclosures of the facts behind the additional payments to Blue, and we left.

"However, Commissioner Kuhn insisted that the offer remain open for three more days. Despite Vida's request that he not release the details of the meeting, Finley released a story to the papers that Blue had agreed to terms and then had reneged.

"The following day, however, Commissioner Kuhn held a press conference refuting Finley's statement to the press, stating emphatically that Blue had not agreed to the terms. Kuhn ordered that the offer remain open.

"Finley objected strongly to what he felt was interference on the part of the Commissioner."

Meanwhile, President Nixon, interviewed at a barbecue in Texas, commented on the situation, suggesting "Blue has so much talent, maybe Finley ought to pay. It would be a great tragedy if a young player with all of that talent stayed out so long."

Finley reacted more cautiously to the President's intervention than he had to the Commissioner's. He said, "I want the President to know that every effort has been made and is continuously being made to sign Vida. I have always been a great admirer of President Nixon. He is extremely well-versed in athletic talent and knows a great athlete when he sees one."

"Howard Cosell of ABC News approached us," Gerst stated.

"He gave us an opportunity to tell our side of the story to the public and to say whether or not we were going to sign with Oakland.

"We felt that the wrong impression had been given by Finley about Vida's reneging on the agreement and we wanted the facts clearly stated to the American public. Howard Cosell gave us that opportunity and we took advantage of it. Vida and I taped our appearances for Howard's show on Monday morning.

"We were very careful to word our statements so that we accurately reported the offer and how the special payments were to be made. Vida also admitted that he would go to Boston the following day and accept the offer and officially sign with Oakland.

"Vida was still worried about his confrontation with Finley in Boston, however."

Blue flew to Boston to meet with the Commissioner and Finley, and on the first Tuesday in May, the second day of the month, Vida signed for the $63,000 "package." This was nearly four months after January 8th, when Finley stated he would not pay one penny more than $50,000 and that if Blue did not accept he would not play baseball anymore.

Blue signed nearly three months after the teams went to preseason spring training, nearly one month after the season was scheduled to begin, and nearly three weeks after the season actually began.

He missed only 18 playing days, but was in no shape to pitch for several weeks. At a press conference, wearing a wild Hawaiian-style sports shirt under a bright checkered sports coat, but seeming subdued, he admitted, "I haven't had myself on any real conditioning program. I've been making appearances for Dura Steel." Asked then the first question of the new season which seemed to concern him, "Will you continue to work for the company during the season?" Vida fixed the reporter with a long, unsmiling look and simply asked, "How could I?"

And he went away to get some sleep before beginning one of the earliest comebacks in any athlete's career. Some suspected he would never be now what he might have been. However, though not as much would be expected of him under the circumstances, everyone would be watching him and that fearful pressure figured to be more forceful than ever. He had set a high standard for himself.

Whether for money alone or for dignity, he had stood his ground a long time at great risk. Seeming disillusioned and no longer so young, he now returned to his baseball future.

It had been a remarkable first season, perhaps the most unusual in the history of the game. It certainly had moments of extraordinary success, joy, excitement, frustration, despair and finally even recriminations.

Flying back to Oakland with his team, Blue betrayed some of the bitterness that had developed. He told a writer, "I'm not happy, but I signed. Charlie Finley has soured my stomach for baseball. He treated me like a damn colored boy."

Later he explained, "I just had to get that off my chest. I had wanted to be treated like a man, with dignity and respect. But Finley has always talked down to me. I just won't take that.

"Hell, nobody can spoil baseball for me. I can't hold a grudge anyway. I just want to play baseball, to pitch again. I want to have an even better season this year."

And so, in the spring of a new baseball season, the extraordinary and bizarre first season of Vida Blue really came to a close.